THE GRAVEYARD SCHOOL

THE
GRAVEYARD SCHOOL

An Anthology

Edited with an introduction and notes by
JACK G. VOLLER

VALANCOURT BOOKS

CONTENTS

INTRODUCTION

It is common for literary critics to claim, often off-handedly, as though the conclusion has long been foregone, that there is "little usefulness" in the idea of a "Graveyard School," that the label is simply "a generic term that lumps together such very different poems as Parnell's 'A Night-Piece on Death,' [Blair's] *The Grave*, Young's *Night Thoughts*, and Gray's *Elegy*".[1] And indeed while it is self-evident those poems have distinct identities and that the cultural and conceptual distance between them is considerable, I hope this anthology will show they have meaningful points of connection and commonality as well. The fact so many works sharing those same points—imagery, tropology, sentiment, setting, didactic purpose—were produced in so short a span of time suggests quite strongly that the issue at hand is not that there was no "Graveyard School," but that scholarship has been insisting on too narrow, too "academic," a definition of such a school for us to see that there was something happening that does indeed merit recognition as a recognizable cultural movement—keeping in mind that "cultural movement" is a concept for which sharply delineated boundaries are, experience and history have repeatedly shown us, not a strict requirement, or even necessarily desirable.

Many "school" designations, whatever the nature of their origin, often bring together artists with conflicting (and evolving) philosophies and practices, thus inevitably grouping, or at least associating, works that may have relatively little in common. But if we consider a "school"—and where is the term used as anything other than a convenient shorthand?—a marker of general tendencies and predilections as perceived by contemporary or subsequent readers, the term, however much critics may mistrust it now, acquires some historical and cultural value, and it is precisely for this reason that "Graveyard School" may be regarded a legitimate

---

1 James Means, "Introduction." Robert Blair. *The Grave.* Augustan Reprint Society, 1973.

9

cultural construct and even, within limits, a useful scholarly tool. As with other "school" designations, it may not have the precision necessary to provide a finely nuanced understanding or delimiting of different poets and their canons—can "Lake School" alone sufficiently distinguish between Wordsworth and Southey? or even between Wordsworth and Wordsworth?—but "Graveyard School" does provide a helpful shorthand for recognizing and understanding a general poetic mode, and sense of public taste, in the 18th century—and no one is arguing that it be considered a genre—and how that general trend may have been influential for subsequent poets and writers, particularly though far from exclusively those working in the Gothic tradition.

The objection of critics to the validity of "The Graveyard School" label is based in large part on the evangelical connection found among some of the earliest writers identified with the Graveyard School, particularly Robert Blair, James Hervey, and Edward Young. There is certainly no questioning the sincerity of evangelical purpose among those writers, but their intentions may hardly be regarded as definitive and prescriptive of the nature and limits of their works and their considerable influence. As James Means has noted, Blair used his "gothic machinery . . . to make his argument palatable to an irreligious age" (i), but that machinery, in true Frankenstein form, escaped his control and his precisely defined purpose once it entered the realm of public discourse. However much they may have deplored the Gothic tradition—had they lived to see it—that was shaped in part by their works, these early Graveyard School writers produced works that influenced subsequent writers and subsequent cultural tradition, and it is in that influence and shared vocabulary of imagery—and in the evolving nature and purpose of that imagery, not in any authorial intent—that "the Graveyard School" may indeed be said to exist.

What, then, characterizes a "Graveyard School" work? An aggressively literal definition might require the immediate presence of a graveyard of some sort, the meditation-ground for a poet whose reflections on death are prompted or conditioned by the presence of funereal artifacts and the atmospheric influence of gloomy yews, hooting owls, and cawing rooks. To a significant degree this obtains for Augustan-era Graveyard literature, with its high degree of intertextuality and relatively homogeneous cohort of authors, and even in modern manifestations of the form the presence or at least recollection of a physical burying space, however bereft of yew and rook, is a noteworthy element that comes close to being a necessary, if not sufficient, condition.

Melancholic musing is another requisite part of the psychological atmosphere in Graveyard School works until the rise of the Gothic, at which point simple horror may be the dominant emotion. But in earlier works, melancholy may be present in sufficient potency to minimize the required accompaniment of the obvious visual scene-setters. Of course Milton's "Il Penseroso" establishes the emotional paradigm for early poets in the Graveyard tradition, from Parnell and Blair onward; the paradigm perhaps becomes cliché, but the Graveyard School helps prepare the ground for Romanticism by becoming a poetry of the (often willingly) isolated Self; indeed, so closely associated became the poetry of such a Self and the mood popularized by Augustan Graveyard School verse that Coleridge deliberately blurred the distinction between the lyric and the elegiac mode. Whether the mild melancholic of Milton's poet wandering his grove or the uneasy midnight seekers of Parnell, Thomas Warton, Elizabeth Carter, and so many others, Graveyard poetry is a poetry of isolation, self-scrutiny, and solipsistic exploration of the farther corners—and, at times, darker registers—of human thought and feeling.

Yet while the poetry of melancholy certainly overlaps with any "Graveyard School" definition, the two are not synonymous even in the 18th century, let alone in post-Romantic expressions of the School (expressions which are not included in this anthology due to considerations of space). Nor is the Graveyard School identical to the elegy, though here the relationship is indeed quite close and again, at times, overlapping, for some elegies may be considered Graveyard School, and indeed many works in the Graveyard tradition, including its most famous, are "Elegy" by title. Yet traditional elegies—works reflecting on the passing of a particular individual —are typically poems of praise and remembrance tinged with grief, and while they often have a didactic dimension they do not find their motive force in unsettling, powerful emotion. They focus on life lost, on mourning, on the spiritual and worldly implications

of death, to be sure, but until the eighteenth century elegies typi-
cally eschew flirtations with metaphysical dread in the heightened
emotional registers that are created by invocations of fear or horror.
Graveyard School poems are increasingly concerned with the latter,
and when the tradition begins to leave off its Christian didacticism
for the sake of a "purer" emotional thrill or for solipsistic introspec-
tion, the distance between the traditional elegy and the Graveyard
School poem increases. (Yet the elegy has never completely lost
sight of the Graveyard School in that both, in the modern era, have
become introspective and reflective while retaining an interest in
what may loosely be called the metaphysical; the lyrics of Jackson
Browne's "For a Dancer," which reference spiritual longing as well
as lowering a body into the grave, come to mind here).

Despite this elusive and protean quality, however, there is some-
thing about funereal contemplation that remains close to the heart
of humanity's artistic explorations of death and its implications
for life; from our beginnings we have invested burial sites and the
artifacts associated with the funereal with a special power that
included not only the spiritual but the cultural and the emotional,
and in its fascination with these places and their meaning for us
the literature of the Graveyard School keeps alive one of the most
long-standing concerns of the species.

Given all this, it is inevitable that we must understand "The
Graveyard School" in a loose—yet, I contend, nonetheless help-
ful—sense of the word, a sense loose enough to allow for the
changes that occur from the *memento mori* of Classical culture (not
"Graveyard School" but a contributing influence) to the age of
Parnell to that of, say, Edgar Lee Masters's *Spoon River Anthology* or
Robert Wrigley's "Cemetery Moles." Even attempts at definition
by scholars friendly to the concept of the "Graveyard School" must
fall short when subjected to this sort of chronological and cultural
stretch. Peter Thorpe's eight-point definition of "graveyard poem"
works reasonably well for the pre-Gothic tradition of graveyard
school poetry, but leaves every cemetery poem since the 1790s,
if not earlier, unaccounted for.[1] Indeed, for Thorpe the School

---

1 Thorpe is himself cautious in offering his definition, preceding even his limited
delineation with the disclaimer that the graveyard school "does not constitute a
sharply-defined genre" (54), although "some useful generalizations" are possible:

effectively disappears with the Augustan period.

I believe the Graveyard School is very much with us yet. Like the Gothic (another "mode" of nefariously slippery boundaries) to which it helped give shape, the Graveyard School has done what so many other cultural expressions of the human spirit have: it mutated, and it continues to do so. It adapts, alters, morphs; it is fluid and adaptable; it is, if one may be forgiven the pun, a living form because its concern is not with ghosts in a melancholy cemetery but with life, with wondering and doubt and a reaching after any truths that may be shrouded in the darkness and mystery that marks the end of life. The grandest and most daunting of those mysteries is death, and while cultural treatments and understandings of death vary with a host of factors, its power to compel our interest, absorption, and dread does not change and most certainly does not disappear. That is why we still write of death today, and though our language and imagery and conceptualizations do not align with those of Parnell or Hervey or Gray or Wordsworth, we still think of cemeteries and what they mean, and in that lies the heart and enduring power and relevance of the Graveyard School.

About this Volume

As the foregoing makes clear, the "Graveyard School" is a concept without sharply demarcated boundaries, so most, but not all, of the works presented here feature a graveyard setting, or ghosts, or even a *memento mori* sensibility. The purpose of this anthology is to both present key Graveyard School works from its originary period, the Augustan age, and to show some of the influence of the Graveyard School, to begin to map its penetration into larger literary culture. To this end I have included works that reflect some aspects of Graveyard sensibility without necessarily having

---

such works, Thorpe claims, (1) must serve a *memento mori* function; (2) thematically engage the "transitoriness of life"; (3) be set at night in a churchyard; (4) depict the physical decay of a corpse, as in Blair; (5) acknowledge the "Death as leveler" trope; (6) "adopt and maintain an exceedingly gloomy and funereal tone" . . . "established by a certain stock imagery or diction"; (7) move toward "some sort of reconciliation, usually Christian, with the fact of death"; (8) and feature a speaker in solitude (*Eighteenth Century English Poetry* [Chicago: Nelson-Hall, 1975], 54-56).

both feet planted in the cemetery, as it were. This anthology also hopes to demonstrate that Graveyard School influence extended well into the Romantic period, spreading out like a river reaching an estuary. Thus it is there are "graveyard" works by Wordsworth, the Southeys, and other Romantic-era writers who, while repudiating many of the practices and didactic assumptions of Augustan poetics (and of the Gothic) nonetheless register the power and appeal of some elements of "Graveyard" verse. There is a great distance from "Elegy Written in a Country Churchyard" to "We Are Seven," but there is also a direct, if faint, line of connection as well.

That connection is along various cultural axes, as well. The Christian moralizing—indeed, sermonizing—that characterizes early Graveyard School works gives way (even as Blair, Hervey, and Young continue to hold a place of note in late-18th and early-19th century cultural consciousness) to works that articulate a less strident morality, that evince political sensibility, or that seek to do nothing more than provide Gothic thrills as the School undergoes its first great evolution into the Gothic and Romantic modes of horror or reflection.

As noted, this anthology closes with the Romantic Period due to considerations of space, but certainly not for lack of material. The Victorians do not lose interest in the Graveyard, by any means, continuing to write of cemeteries but also transferring their interest, spectacularly, from the literary to the actual: the "rural cemetery" movement of the 19th century, however motivated by practical considerations, turns the graveyard itself into a readily accessible text, its esoteric allusiveness distilled into the imagery of the ordinary—angels and urns—and its lessons evident in the simpler text of the epitaph and the iconography of the memorial and the physical space itself.

Textual Note

For the texts of the works presented here I have followed early editions wherever possible, typically those last edited or approved by the author; source texts are noted for each work. While spelling and punctuation are generally kept close to the original in order to present something of the original feel of the works, I have taken the liberty of regularizing (for which read "reducing") capitalization and some punctuation issues (heavy use of the semicolon and the em dash, particularly), modernizing orthography, making minor formatting adjustments, and have also all but eliminated the heavy italicizing so characteristic of much eighteenth century verse and prose, largely in deference to ease of readability for modern readers but also because some of these elements could and often did vary substantially from one edition of a work to another.

JACK G. VOLLER

JACK G. VOLLER is Professor Emeritus of English Language and Literature at Southern Illinois University Edwardsville, where he taught classes in and published works on Gothic and late-Eighteenth Century Literature and British and American Romanticism.

Alexander Pope, "Elegy to the Memory of an Unfortunate Lady"

Pope (1688-1744) is of course one of the representative figures of Augustan literature, and as such may seem an unlikely presence in this anthology. But his "Elegy," while not a Graveyard School poem in the strictest sense of the term, is a contribution to the nascent poetic and aesthetic currents that surrounded the Graveyard School in its earlier moments. A heroic elegy that imitates Roman models, Pope's poem is so direct in its statement of grief and outrage that the work is often understood to be a foray by Pope into the realm of sensibility. It clearly is a work that seeks to achieve its primary effect by emotion, not by reason or appeals to morality. The poem commemorates a suicide, and does so in terms so strong that the poem has been condemned by some, including John Wesley, as a commendation not only of the unfortunate Lady, but of suicide itself. While that could hardly have been Pope's purpose, it remains that this poem is emphatic in its supernaturally precipitated compassion for the dead woman and its curse of the lady's guardian and his descendants, presumably because he refused to let the lady marry for love. The fact that Pope is vague regarding the circumstances of the lady's death—a fact that for many critics means the work is of a lesser order than most of Pope's other productions—may mean only that Pope wishes to direct our attention not to a moral or religious judgment of the lady and her act, but to an emotional response to the pathos of her situation. The poem, then, is neither about the suicide (itself only indirectly referenced, after all) nor about the ghost, although it is with a dramatic supernaturalist gesture that this poem begins; as one critic has noted, "Pope . . . capitalizes upon the momentary reaction of horror . . . to intensify the pathos of the lady's fate; the ghost provides a pretext for his further reflections, rather than true imaginative center for the poem."[1] Pope is far from the world of Gothic or Graveyard horrors, to be sure, but this early work helps point the way to sensibility's darker register.

The text of this poem, first published in 1717, is taken from *The Works of Alexander Pope*, 9 vols., London: Millar et al., 1760.

---

1 Patricia Meyer Spacks, *The Insistence of Horror: Aspects of the Supernatural in Eighteenth-Century Poetry* (Cambridge, Mass.: Harvard University Press, 1962): 54.

What beck'ning ghost, along the moonlight shade
Invites my steps, and points to yonder glade?
'Tis she!—but why that bleeding bosom gor'd,
Why dimly gleams the visionary sword?
Oh ever beauteous, ever friendly! tell,   5
Is it, in heav'n, a crime to love too well?
To bear too tender, or too firm a heart,
To act a lover's or a Roman's part?
Is there no bright reversion in the sky,
For those who greatly think, or bravely die?   10

Why bade ye else, ye Pow'rs! her soul aspire
Above the vulgar flight of low desire?
Ambition first sprung from your blest abodes;
The glorious fault of angels and of gods;
Thence to their images on earth it flows,   15
And in the breasts of kings and heroes glows.
Most souls, 'tis true, but peep out once an age,
Dull sullen pris'ners in the body's cage:
Dim lights of life, that burn a length of years,
Useless, unseen, as lamps in sepulchres;   20
Like Eastern kings a lazy state they keep,
And, close confin'd to their own palace, sleep.

From these perhaps (ere nature bade her die)
Fate snatch'd her early to the pitying sky.
As into air the purer spirits flow,   25
And sep'rate from their kindred dregs below;
So flew the soul to its congenial place,
Nor left one virtue to redeem her race.

But thou, false guardian of a charge too good,
Thou, mean deserter of thy brother's blood!   30
See on these ruby lips the trembling breath,
These cheeks now fading at the blast of death;
Cold is that breast which warm'd the world before,
And those love-darting eyes must roll no more.

Thus, if eternal justice rules the ball,[1]   35
Thus shall your wives, and thus your children fall;
On all the line a sudden vengeance waits,
And frequent hearses shall besiege your gates;
There passengers shall stand, and pointing say,
(While the long fun'rals blacken all the way),   40
Lo! these were they whose souls the Furies steel'd
And curs'd with hearts unknowing how to yield.
Thus unlamented pass the proud away,
The gaze of fools, and pageant of a day!
So perish all whose breast ne'er learn'd to glow   45
For others' good, or melt at others' woe!

What can atone (oh ever-injur'd shade!)
Thy fate unpity'd, and thy rites unpaid?
No friend's complaint, no kind domestic tear
Pleas'd thy pale ghost, or grac'd thy mournful bier.   50
By foreign hands thy dying eyes were clos'd,
By foreign hands thy decent limbs compos'd,
By foreign hands thy humble grave adorn'd,
By strangers honour'd, and by strangers mourn'd!
What tho' no friends in sable weeds appear,   55
Grieve for an hour, perhaps, then mourn a year,
And bear about the mockery of woe
To midnight dances, and the public show?
What tho' no weeping Loves thy ashes grace,[2]
Nor polish'd marble emulate thy face?   60
What tho' no sacred earth allow thee room,
Nor hallow'd dirge be mutter'd o'er thy tomb?[3]
Yet shall thy grave with rising flow'rs be drest,
And the green turf lie lightly on thy breast:
There shall the morn her earliest tears bestow,   65
There the first roses of the year shall blow;
While angels with their silver wings o'ershade

---

1 *ball*: the earth.
2 *no weeping Loves thy ashes grace*: carvings of Cupid on her tomb.
3 As a suicide, the Lady would not have been buried in hallowed ground and
would not have received customary funeral rites.

The ground, now sacred by thy reliques made.

So peaceful rests, without a stone, a name,
What once had beauty, titles, wealth, and fame.   70
How lov'd, how honour'd once, avails thee not,
To whom related, or by whom begot;
A heap of dust alone remains of thee,
'Tis all thou art, and all the proud shall be!

Poets themselves must fall, like those they sung,   75
Deaf the prais'd ear, and mute the tuneful tongue.
Ev'n he, whose soul now melts in mournful lays,
Shall shortly want the gen'rous tear he pays;
Then from his closing eyes thy form shall part,
And the last pang shall tear thee from his heart;   80
Life's idle business at one gasp be o'er,
The Muse forgot, and thou belov'd no more!

Thomas Parnell, "A Night-Piece on Death"

Parnell (1679-1718) was an Irish cleric, essayist, and poet. Intellectu-
ally precocious, he was admitted to Trinity College, Dublin, while
only thirteen, and completed his M.A. when he was twenty-one;
he was ordained four years later, and earned a Doctor of Divinity
from the University of Dublin at the age of thirty-three. Parnell,
who travelled frequently to London after the death of his wife, was
well-connected with Irish and English literary circles: he knew Jon-
athan Swift, Richard Steele and Joseph Addison, Alexander Pope,
John Gay, and other members of the Scriblerus Club of London.
Parnell's struggles with physical and mental health were remarked
by many of his friends, and Samuel Johnson, among others, noted
Parnell's heavy drinking;[1] one modern scholar, Thomas Woodman,

---

1 "Pope represents him as falling from that time [c. 1714] into intemperance of
wine. That in his latter life he was too much a lover of the bottle, is not denied. . . ."
Johnson, *Lives of the Poets* (London: Dove, 1824), I: 342. Oliver Goldsmith's "Life
of Dr. Parnell," which was commonly prefixed to editions of Parnell's works,
observes that, following the death of his wife, Parnell "began therefore to throw

has suggested that Parnell suffered from "an almost manic-depressive temperament."[1] Much of Parnell's literary output was not published until after his death, when Alexander Pope edited the first collection of Parnell's work, *Poems on Several Occasions* (1722, though published in early December 1721).

The "Night-Piece," from *Poems on Several Occasions*, was probably written in 1714, growing out of the grief Parnell felt following the death of his wife in August 1711. It is widely regarded as the very first "Graveyard School" work, though such a claim need be tempered with the understanding that Parnell was drawing on a number of influences and sources ranging from the *memento mori* tradition to Milton's "Il Penseroso" as well as other, more recent literary treatments of night and death. Yet Parnell must also be given his due as an innovator. While critics such as Woodman dismiss the idea of Parnell as a pre-Romantic, Parnell's habit of retreating, during times of mental oppression, to the Irish countryside to write melancholy meditations on the landscape suggests something in him which found great comfort in the connection between literature and emotion. This connection is evident in the "Night-Piece," where the landscape is the graveyard and a powerful emotional response is a key part of the reaction Parnell cultivates in his readers. That emotion is preparatory for the poem's closing gesture of Christian transcendence and consolation, to be sure, but the indelible trace it leaves attracted the notice of many subsequent writers. The poem's influence may be seen in a number of ways: Parnell introduces the use of the graveyard setting itself, the atmosphere of vaguely unsettling gloom created by the presence of discordant rooks and owls, flickering light, and funereal trees, as well as the concluding trope of daybreak as a symbolic figuring of spiritual salvation and resurrection. These images, as well as the themes of death as a great leveller, reducing distinctions of wealth

---

himself into every company, and to seek from wine, if not relief, at least insensibility" (*Poems on Several Occasions*, 1770, xxvii).

1 Thomas M. Woodman, *Thomas Parnell*. Twayne English Authors Series (Boston: Twayne, 1985), 10. Woodman was surely thinking of remarks such as this by Goldsmith: "He wanted that evenness of disposition which bears disappointment with phlegm, and joy with indifference. He was ever very much elated or depressed; and his whole life spent in agony or rapture" (v).

and class to meaninglessness, and of death not as something to be
feared, will occur frequently in the Graveyard School poems of the
following decades. It is Parnell who deserves credit for assembling
those ingredients for the first time.

The text is taken from *Poems on Several Occasions*, London: T.
Davies, 1770.

———

By the blue taper's trembling light,[1]
No more I waste the wakeful night,
Intent with endless view to pore
The schoolmen[2] and the sages o'er:
Their books from wisdom widely stray,   5
Or point at best the longest way.
I'll seek a readier path, and go
Where wisdom's surely taught below.
    How deep yon azure dyes the sky!
Where orbs of gold unnumber'd lye,   10
While thro' their ranks in silver pride
The nether crescent[3] seems to glide.
The slumb'ring breeze forgets to breathe,
The lake is smooth and clear beneath,
Where once again the spangled show[4]   15
Descends to meet our eyes below.
The grounds which on the right aspire,[5]
In dimness from the view retire:
The left presents a place of graves,
Whose wall the silent water laves.   20
That steeple guides thy doubtful sight
Among the livid gleams of night.
    There pass with melancholy state,

———

1 Common in Western European folklore is the belief that a blue flame or blue
light presages someone's death, although blue flames have also been associ-
ated with hidden treasure (as in Bram Stoker's *Dracula*) and with other lucky, if
uncanny, circumstances.
2 *schoolmen*: scholars.
3 *crescent*: the moon.
4 *spangled show*: the stars, here reflected by the lake surface.
5 *aspire*: slope upward.

By all the solemn heaps of fate,
And think, as softly-sad you tread   25
Above the venerable dead,
"Time was, like thee they life possest,
And time shall be, that thou shalt rest."
   Those, with bending osier¹ bound,
That nameless heave the crumbled ground,   30
Quick to the glancing thought disclose,
Where toil and poverty repose.
   The flat smooth stones that bear a name,
The chissel's slender help to fame,
(Which ere our set of friends decay   35
Their frequent steps may wear away;)
A middle race of mortals own,
Men, half ambitious, all unknown.
   The marble tombs that rise on high,
Whose dead in vaulted arches lye,   40
Whose pillars swell with sculptur'd stones,
Arms, angels, epitaphs, and bones,
These, all the poor remains of state,
Adorn the rich, or praise the great;
Who, while on earth in fame they live,   45
Are senseless of the fame they give.
   Ha! while I gaze, pale Cynthia² fades,
The bursting earth unveils the shades!
All slow, and wan, and wrap'd with shrouds,
They rise in visionary crouds,   50
And all with sober accent cry,
"Think, mortal, what it is to die."
   Now from yon black and fun'ral yew,³
That bathes the charnel-house with dew,

---

1 An osier is a willow tree, here depicted as having branches drooping to the
ground of the graveyard.

2 Cynthia is a poetic name for the moon, from Greek myth.

3 Yew trees have long been associated with cemeteries. Folk belief held that yews
had magical properties that could protect against witchcraft, and Christian sym-
bolism associates their very long lifespans with spiritual immortality and their
poisonous berries with (spiritual) life after death.

Methinks, I hear a voice begin;   55
(Ye ravens, cease your croaking din,
Ye tolling clocks, no time resound
O'er the long lake and midnight ground)
It sends a peal of hollow groans,
Thus speaking from among the bones.   60
   "When men my scythe and darts supply,[1]
How great a King of Fears am I!
They view me like the last of things:
They make, and then they dread,[2] my stings.
Fools! if you less provok'd your fears,   65
No more my spectre-form appears.
Death's but a path that must be trod,
If man wou'd ever pass to God;
A port of calms, a state of ease
From the rough rage of swelling seas.   70
   "Why then thy flowing sable stoles,
Deep pendant cypress,[3] mourning poles,[4]
Loose scarfs to fall athwart thy weeds,
Long palls, drawn hearses, cover'd steeds,
And plumes of black, that as they tread,   75
Nod o'er the 'scutcheons[5] of the dead?

---

1 Death was traditionally pictured with a scythe (cf. "the Grim Reaper") and darts (or lances).

2 The 1770 edition has "draw," but "dread" is the authoritative reading; see Rawson and Lock's edition of Parnell. In line 69 "of" appears as "to" in the 1770 edition.

3 Cypress trees, like yews, have a long association with cemeteries, perhaps because the longevity of cypress wood was found suggestive of immortality while their tall columnar form (reminiscent of a church steeple) denotes a heavenward aspiration. In Greek myth, Cyparissus was a young man who accidentally killed a beloved stag; overcome with grief, he asked the god Apollo to be allowed to mourn forever, and Apollo obliged by turning him into a tree, which became known as the cypress tree and which, in some species, forms drops of sap on the trunk, suggestive of tears.

4 Also known as a "mourning staff," a mourning pole is simply a black pole, sometimes decorated, carried in a funeral procession.

5 A scutcheon (more commonly "escutcheon" now) is a shield-shaped coat of arms, which would have been prominently displayed during the funerals and on the tombs of nobility. Lines 71-76 describe the trappings and decorations of an elaborate funeral procession.

"Nor can the parted body know,
Nor wants the soul, these forms of woe;
As men who long in prison dwell,
With lamps that glimmer round the cell,   80
Whene'er their suff'ring years are run,
Spring forth to greet the glitt'ring sun:
Such joy, tho' far transcending sense,
Have pious souls at parting hence.
On earth, and in the body plac'd,   85
A few, and evil years, they waste:
But when their chains are cast aside,
See the glad scene unfolding wide,
Clap the glad wing, and tow'r away,
And mingle with the blaze of day."   90

David Mallet, "The Excursion. A Poem in Two Books" (*excerpt*)

Mallet (1701?-1765) was a Scottish poet, biographer, dramatist, and political writer; he eventually held Bachelor's and Master's degrees from the University of Edinburgh, the University of Aberdeen, and Oxford. Mallet (whose surname was originally Malloch; he Anglicized it after spending time in London) became friends with several important neoclassical literary figures, including James Thomson, Alexander Pope and Edward Gibbon, and was well-connected in London literary circles, although his reputation as something of a freethinker in religious matters led many, including Samuel Johnson, to regard him with some distrust. Yet the moral and religious component of Mallet's verses is hardly muted, as can plainly be seen in the "Funeral Hymn" below (and in the full text of "The Excursion"), even if it never rises to the heights of the poetic sermonizing of Edward Young or Robert Blair or the other clerical members of the Graveyard School.

"The Excursion," begun in 1726 and published anonymously in 1728, is Mallet's second most well-known poem, the first being "William and Margaret," his redaction of an old folk ballad; Mallet's version was frequently reprinted in the 18th century. "The

Excursion" was influenced by his friend James Thomson's *The Seasons*; it is an excursion of the imagination, a flight of Fancy—"at whose Command / Arise unnumber'd Images of Things"—across seasons, landscapes, and nations, a vision of both natural beauty and of vast scenes of destruction, all serving to remind Mallet of "The Sovereign Maker, First, Supreme, and Best, / Who actuates the whole: at whose Command, / Obedient Fire and Flood, tremendous rise, / His Ministers of Vengeance, to reprove, / And scourge the Nations," although the work is more deistic than is typical of Graveyard School verse.

The excerpt below is from Book One, which begins with a survey of natural beauties in a "cheerful Morn" before moving to the more sublime and disturbing manifestations of natural power. In Book Two Mallet's "excursion" is through the heavens, a trope that prefigures the conclusion of Edward Young's *Night Thoughts*.

The text is taken from the first edition of 1728.

And see! ascending in the distant North,
And rolling gloomy on, collected Clouds,
Broad, o'er the World, draw deep a dreadful Night.   105
The Winds are hush'd; the homeward Birds on Wing
Haste the Hour of Terror and of Storm.
Now, thro' the louring¹ Air, the Lightning's Flash,
Quick-glancing, darts a Moment's horrid Day:
The Thunder now, rous'd in his dark Abode,   110
First in faint Mutterings grumbles from afar,
Awfully heard, awakning dismal Thought!
Dumb Sadness fills the nether World; and fast
The Darkness doubles, and the Tempest swells:
Till, bursting from on high, a mingled Flood,   115
Far-sounding e'er it falls, of Hail and Rain
Pours on the Plains, impetuous, heavy, loud,
Drenching the hoary Head of slow-pac'd Age,
O'ertaken on his chearless Way alone.

---

1 *louring*: lowering.

Again the Thunder, bellowing over-head   120
In broken Peals, rolls hoarse from Cloud to Cloud,
Roar hurrying after Roar, and loudning still
At each last Burst, which rocks the hollow Vault
Of Heaven. Again the nimble Lightning flames,
Incessant, thwarting, thro' th' expansive Dark   125
On all Sides burning; now the Face of Things
Disclosing, swallow'd now at once in Night.
Horror sits shuddering in the guilty Breast,
And feels the deathful Flash before it flies:
Each sleeping Sin, excited, starts to View,   130
And all is Storm within. The Murderer,
Roaming and restless in the deepest Shade,
Hears and flies wild, pursu'd by all his Fears:
And sees the bleeding Shadow of the Slain
Rise hideous, glaring on Him thro' the Gloom!   135

Appeas'd at last, the Tumult of the Skies
Subsides, the Thunder's falling Roar is hush'd:
At once the Clouds fly scattering, and the Sun
Flashes a boundless Splendor o'er the World.
Parent of Light and Joy! to all Things He   140
New Life restores, and from each drooping Field
Draws the redundant Rain, in climbing Mists
Fast-rising to his Ray; till every Flower
Lifts up its Head, and Nature smiles reviv'd.

At first 'tis awful Silence over all,   145
From Sense of late-felt Danger: but at length,
Confirm'd, the brute Creation, in mix'd Quire,[1]
Rejoice aloud to Heaven; and on each Hand,
The Woodlands warble, and the Vallies low.[2]
So pass the songful Hours: and now the Sun,   150
Declin'd, hangs verging on the western Main,
Whose fluctuating Bosom, blushing red
The Space of many Seas beneath his Force,

---

1 *Quire*: choir.
2 *low*: the mooing sound of cattle.

Heaves in soft Swellings murmuring to the Shore,
A circling Glory glows around his Disk   155
Of milder Beams: part, streaming o'er the Sky,
Inflame the distant Azure: part below
Shoot thro' the waving Wood in level Lines,
Tinging the Green with Gold. The gather'd Clouds,
Lucid or dusk, with shadow'd Light distain'd,[1]   160
Float in gay Pomp along th' Horizon's Bound,
Amusive, changeful, shifting into Shapes
Of pleasing Imagery, transient Towers,
And Hills of white Extent, that rise and sink
As sportful Fancy lists; till late the Sun   170
Withdrawing, all th' aerial Landscape fades.

Distinction fails; and in the darkning West,
The last Light, quivering, dimly dies away.
And now th' illusive Flame, oft seen at Eve,
Glides o'er the Lawn, betokning Night's Approach: 175
Onward She comes with silent Step and slow,
In her brown Mantle wrapt, and brings along
The serious Hour, and solemn Thoughtfulness.

Musing, in sober Mood, of Time and Life,
That fly with unreturning Wing away   180
To far Eternity, the World unknown
Where Vision reigns, thro' desert Ways I walk:
Or to the Cypress-Grove, at Twilight shun'd
By passing Swains.[2] The chill Breeze murmurs low,
And the Boughs rustle round me where I stand,   185
With Fancy all-arous'd.——Far on the Left,
Shoots up a shapeless Rock of dusky Height,
The Raven's Haunt: and down its woody Steep,
A dashing Flood in headlong Torrent hurls
His sounding Waters; white on every Cliff,   190
Hangs the light Foam, and sparkles thro' the Gloom.

---

1 *distain'd*: stained, stippled.
2 A swain is a young male of the country, typically understood, in eighteenth-century poetry, as a young lover.

Behind me rises huge an awful Pile,[1]
Sole on this blasted Heath, a Place of Tombs,
Waste, desolate, where Ruin dreary dwells,
Brooding o'er sightless Sculls, and crumbling Bones.   195
Ghastful He sits, and eyes with stedfast Glare
The Column grey with Moss, the falling Bust,
The Time-shook Arch, the monumental Stone,
Impair'd, effac'd, and hastening into Dust,
Unfaithful to their Charge of flattering Fame.   200
All is dread Silence here, and undisturb'd,
Save what the Wind sighs, and the wailing Owl
Screams solitary to the mournful Moon,
Glimmering her western Ray thro' yonder Isle,
Where the sad Spirit walks with shadowy Foot   205
His wonted Round, or lingers o'er his Grave.

Hail Midnight-Shades! hail venerable Dome!
Sure, last Retreat from all the ceaseless Ills,
Fears for th' uncertain Future, present Woes,
A numerous Band! that wait on human Life.   210
The Weary are at Rest; the Small and Great
Meet at their Journey's End, and mingle here.
Here sleeps the Prisoner safe, thro' Death's long Night,
Nor hears th' Oppressor's voice. The Poor and Old,
With all the Sons of Mourning, fearless now   215
Of Want or Woe, find unalarm'd Repose.
Proud Greatness too, the Tyranny of Power,
The Grace of Beauty, and the Force of Youth,
And Name and Place, are here,——for ever lost![2]

Here, humbled in the Dust, forgotten lies,   220
Whom Wealth and outward Beauty join'd to raise
Conspicuous; but ill-match'd his groveling Soul,
The Scourge of Worth, the friendless Good Man's Foe,

---

1 *Pile*: any large and stately building.
2 The egalitarianism of Death is of course a standard feature of Graveyard
School poetry beginning with Parnell's "Night-Piece on Death."

Unletter'd Nireus.[1] Once how basely fear'd,
And honour'd, by the fawning Tribe He fed!   225
Now scorn'd his fallen Name, his Ashes spurn'd:
Such Recompence awaits the worthless Great
From the mean Flatterer, trusted and belov'd.
Ill-judging Mind! presumptuous, wild of Head,
From Reason sunk into the bestial Life!   230
Thy Flow of Riot; thy unlicens'd Joys,
Led on by gay Desire, and smiling Hope,
False Promiser! but follow'd by Distaste,
Remorse, and ruthless Bitterness of Soul,
Urg'd Thee, unmourn'd, inglorious, to thy End.   235

But, at near Distance, on the mouldering Wall
Behold a Monument, with Emblem grac'd,
And fair Inscription: where with Head declin'd,
And folded Arms, the Vertues weeping round
Lean o'er a beauteous Youth who dies below.   240
Thyrsis![2]——'tis He! the Wisest and the Best!
Lamented Shade! whom every Gift of Heaven
Profusely blest: all Learning was his own.
Pleasing his Speech, by Nature taught to flow,
Persuasive Sense and strong, sincere and clear.   245
His Manners greatly Plain; a noble Grace,
Self-taught, beyond the Reach of mimic Art,
Adorn'd him: his calm Temper winning mild;
Nor Pity softer, nor was Truth more bright.
Constant in doing well, He neither sought,   250
Nor shun'd Applause. No bashful Merit sigh'd
Near him neglected: sympathizing He
Wept for the Woe Himself had never known,
And often wip'd the Tear from Sorrow's Eye
With kindly Hand, and taught her Heart to smile.   255

---

1 Nireus was a Greek king who fought in the Trojan War; he was renowned for
his physical beauty.
2 A poet-shepherd from Virgil's pastoral *Eclogues*, Thyris also became a generic
name for any dead poet. Cf. Matthew Arnold's poem of that name (1865) com-
memorating his friend and fellow-poet Arthur Hugh Clough.

'Tis Morning; and the Sun, his welcome Light,
Swift, from beyond dark Ocean's orient Stream,
Casts thro' the Air, enlightening Nature's Face
With new-born Beauty. O'er her ample Breast,
O'er Sea and Shore, light Fancy speeds along,   260
Quick as the darted Beam, from Pole to Pole,
Excursive Traveller. Now beneath the North,
Alone with Winter in his Frost-bound Realm!
Where, a white Waste of Ice, the Polar Sea
Casts cold a chearless Light: where Hills of Snow,   265
Pil'd up from eldest Ages, Hill on Hill,
In blue, bleak Precipices rise to Heaven.
Yet here, even here in this unjoyous World,
Adventrous Mortals, urg'd by Thirst of Gain,
Thro' floating Isles of Ice and fighting Storms,   270
Roam the wild Waves, in Search of doubtful Shores,
By West or East, a Path yet unexplor'd.

Hence eastward to the Tartar's cruel Coast,[1]
By utmost Ocean wash'd, on whose last Wave
The blue Sky leans her Breast, diffus'd immense   275
In solitary Length the Desert lies,
Where Desolation keeps his empty Court.
No Bloom of Spring, o'er all the thirsty Vast,
Nor spiry Grass is found; but Sands instead
In sterile Hills, and rough Rocks rising grey.   280

A Land of Fears! where visionary Forms
Of grisly Spectres from Air, Flood, and Fire,
Swarm——and before them speechless Horror stalks!
To Mischief prone, unfriendly to Mankind,
Oft on the Border of the Waste they stand,   285
Waiting the Traveller who unwary turns
This Way his Step, and with false Objects shewn,
Unreal and enchanting, draw Him on

---

1 Tartar—more properly Tatar—was used to refer to any indigenous peoples of
Central Asia.

Within their Verge: then call the Winds to blow
A blinding Tempest, and around his Head   290
Whirl a whole Plain——o'erwhelm'd he dies unknown,
Unpity'd, far from Aid and Eye of Man.

Here, Night by Night, beneath the starless Dusk,
Crowding in Troops, the Sorcerer and the Witch,
Their Rites Hell-taught perform, and Spells compose.   295
Late, at the Hour that severs Night from Morn,
When Sleep has silenc'd every Thought of Man,
They to their Revels fall, infernal Throng!
And as they mix in circling Dance, or turn
To the four Winds of Heaven with haggard Gaze,   300
Shot streaming from the Bosom of the North,
Opening the hollow Gloom, red Meteors blaze
To lend them Light, and sudden Thunders roll,
Rumbling in broken Murmurs over-head.

From these sad Plains, the waste Abodes of Death,   305
With devious Wing to fairer Climes remote
Southward I stray; where Caucasus in View,[1]
Bulwark of Nations, in broad Eminence
Stretches from Realm to Realm a hundred Hills,
Pale-glittering with eternal Snows to Heaven.   310

David Mallet, "A Funeral Hymn"

From *Poems on Several Occasions* (1763)

I.

Ye midnight shades, o'er Nature spread!
Dumb silence of the dreary hour!
In honor of th'approaching Dead,

---

1 The Caucasus region lies between the Black Sea and the Caspian Sea, north of present-day Turkey and Iran and lying mostly within Russia. In the eighteenth century (and beyond) it was often regarded as the "birthplace of humanity."

Around your awful terrors pour.
   Yes, pour around,   5
   On this pale ground,
Thro' all this deep surrounding gloom,
   The sober thought,
   The tear untaught,
Those meetest[1] mourners at a tomb.   10

II.

Lo! as the surplic'd train[2] draw near
  To this last mansion of mankind,
The slow sad bell, the sable bier,[3]
  In holy musings wrap the mind!
    And while their beam,   15
    With trembling stream,
Attending tapers faintly dart,
    Each mouldering bone,
    Each sculptor'd stone,
Strikes mute instruction to the heart!   20

III.

Now, let the sacred organ blow,
With solemn pause, and sounding slow:
Now, let the voice due measure keep,
In strains that sigh, and words that weep;
Till all the vocal current blended roll,   25
Not to depress, but lift the soaring soul.

IV.

To lift it in the Maker's praise,
  Who first inform'd our frame with breath;

---

1 *meetest*: most appropriate, fitting.
2 The clerical members of a funeral, who would be wearing the loose-fitting white surplice over their ecclesiastical gowns.
3 *bier*: the supporting framework for a coffin.

And after some few stormy days,
   Now, gracious, gives us o'er to Death.   *30*
     No King of Fears
     In him appears,
Who shuts the scene of human woes:[1]
     Beneath his shade
     Securely laid,   *35*
The Dead alone find true repose.

V.

Then, while we mingle dust with dust,
   To One, supremely good and wise,
Raise hallelujahs! God is just,
   And Man most happy, when he dies!   *40*
     His winter past,
     Fair spring at last
Receives him on her flowery shore;
     Where Pleasure's rose
     Immortal blows,   *45*
And sin and sorrow are no more!

Elizabeth Carter, "Ode To Melancholy"

Carter (1717-1806) was an English poet and translator, well-known for her mastery of foreign languages, particularly Greek, and her intellect. She was one of the most important early figures of female literary achievement in British culture (one of the "Bluestockings," a group of educated, literary, upper-middle-class women who met to discuss literary and cultural issues; they were widely mocked by the male intellectual establishment). Her father was a curate and linguist who strongly encouraged education in all of his children, male and female; Carter's intellectual gifts proved to be substantial, and her devotion to study almost obsessive. (Her father once congratulated her on sticking with her plan of not staying

---

1 Compare this description of Death to that in Parnell's "Night-Piece on Death."

up past midnight to study; she arranged to wake up between four and five every morning to study by having a bell installed at the head of her bed, to be rung by the local sexton when he awoke to begin his duties. She became addicted to snuff and green tea, which she took to stay awake in order to study, and suffered from painful headaches her entire adult life as a result.) Like most of the Bluestockings Carter was by no means an early feminist; she advocated female propriety and decorum—although along with female education in intellectual and cultural fields, not merely in "accomplishments"—competence in if not mastery of domestic arts, and support of dominant mainstream ideologies. She was deeply religious, which kept her well within the prevailing frames of reference of eighteenth-century culture.[1] The precarious position of such women in Carter's time is evidenced in two remarks on Carter by Samuel Johnson, the leading intellectual figure of his age. He once praised Carter's knowledge of Greek as being better than that of anyone he knew, but also once said, after hearing another woman praised for her learning, "A man is in general better pleased when he has a good dinner upon his table, than when his wife talks Greek. My old friend, Mrs. Carter, could make a pudding as well as translate Epictetus from the Greek, and work a handkerchief as well as compose a poem." Carter—who never married; Johnson's "Mrs." was a token of respect—today is remembered more for her poems than for her handkerchiefs, and her translations more than her puddings.

Carter's appreciation of the "sweet sadness" of eighteenth-century melancholy, evident in the first poem below, in combination with her own piety, led her to write several poems which may be regarded as lying within the lightly shaded side of the Graveyard School; her commitment to dominant formulations of propriety generally kept her from the more emotionally powerful images and tropes employed by male writers of the Graveyard School, although the opening image in *Rambler* 44 is in a decidedly Gothic vein.

The "Ode to Melancholy" (first published in 1739) incorporates

---

1 Judith Hawley, "Carter, Elizabeth (1717-1806)." *Oxford Dictionary of National Biography*. Edited by H. C. G. Matthew and Brian Harrison. Oxford: Oxford University Press, 2004. Web. 2 Nov. 2012.

much of the language and imagery that will become standard ele-
ments of Graveyard School verse: the "dark grove of mournful
yews", the "midnight horrors! awful gloom!", the worms and the
waiting tomb are all essential provocations to an appropriately
receptive frame of mind, and Carter will follow Parnell, and pre-
figure Blair, in following an opening invocation of graveyard atmo-
sphere with a redemptive message of religious faith and Christian
salvation cast in terms of the breaking light of a new day.

   The text of Carter's poems is taken from *Memoirs of the Life of
Mrs. Elizabeth Carter, with a New Edition of Her Poems*, by the Rev.
Montagu Pennington, 4th edition, vol. 2, London: James Cawthorn,
1825.

———————

> *Alas! shades of night, my day,*
> *O darkness, light to me,*
> *Take, oh take me away to dwell with you,*
> *Take me away.——*[1]

Come Melancholy! silent Pow'r,
Companion of my lonely hour,
   To sober thought confin'd:
Thou sweetly-sad ideal guest,
In all thy soothing charms confest,   5
   Indulge my pensive mind.

No longer wildly hurried thro'
The tides of Mirth, that ebb and flow,
   In Folly's noisy stream:
I from the busy crowd retire,   10
To court the objects that inspire
   Thy philosophic dream.

Thro' yon dark grove of mournful yews
With solitary steps I muse,
   By thy direction led: 15

———————

1 The epigraph, in Greek in Carter's text, is from Sophocles' drama *Ajax*; the
translation is Carter's.

Here, cold to Pleasure's tempting forms,
Consociate with my sister-worms,
  And mingle with the dead.

Ye midnight horrors! awful gloom!
Ye silent regions of the tomb,   20
  My future peaceful bed:
Here shall my weary eyes be clos'd,
And ev'ry sorrow lie repos'd
  In Death's refreshing shade.

Ye pale inhabitants of night,   25
Before my intellectual sight
  In solemn pomp ascend:
O tell how trifling now appears
The train of idle hopes and fears
  That varying life attend.   30

Ye faithless idols of our sense,
Here own how vain your fond pretence,
  Ye empty names of joy!
Your transient forms like shadows pass,
Frail offspring of the magic glass,   35
  Before the mental eye.

The dazzling colours, falsely bright,
Attract the gazing vulgar sight
  With superficial state:
Thro' Reason's clearer optics view'd,   40
How stript of all its pomp, how rude
  Appears the painted cheat.

Can wild Ambition's tyrant pow'r,
Or ill-got Wealth's superfluous store,
  The dread of death controul?   45
Can Pleasure's more bewitching charms
Avert, or sooth the dire alarms
  That shake the parting soul?

Religion! e'er the hand of Fate
Shall make Reflection plead too late,   50
   My erring senses teach,
Amidst the flatt'ring hopes of youth,
To meditate the solemn truth,
   These awful relics preach.

Thy penetrating beams disperse   55
The mist of error, whence our fears
   Derive their fatal spring:
'Tis thine the trembling heart to warm,
And soften to an angel form
   The pale terrific King.[1]   60

When sunk by guilt in sad despair,
Repentance breathes her humble pray'r,
   And owns thy threat'nings just:
Thy voice the shudd'ring suppliant chears,
With Mercy calms her tort'ring fears,   65
   And lifts her from the dust.

Sublim'd by thee, the soul aspires
Beyond the range of low desires,
   In nobler views elate:
Unmov'd her destin'd change surveys,   70
And, arm'd by Faith, intrepid pays
   The universal debt.

In Death's soft slumber lull'd to rest,
She sleeps, by smiling visions blest,
   That gently whisper peace: 75
'Till the last morn's fair op'ning ray
Unfolds the bright eternal day
   Of active life and bliss.

---

1 Death.

Elizabeth Carter, "Thoughts at Midnight"

This poem was first published in 1739. It is in the mode of Milton's "Il Penseroso" and similar works of melancholic musing, here expressly Christianized and largely skirting Graveyard School rhetoric and imagery, although the poem does end with a reference to Judgment Day that includes, as does "Ode to Melancholy," the image of resurrection as daybreak.

———

While Night in solemn shade invests the Pole,
And calm reflection soothes the pensive soul;
While Reason undisturb'd asserts her sway,
And life's deceitful colours fade away:
To thee! all-conscious presence! I devote   5
This peaceful interval of sober thought,
Here all my better faculties confine,
And be this hour of sacred silence thine.
   If by the day's illusive scenes misled,
My erring soul from Virtue's path has stray'd;   10
If by example snar'd, by passion warm'd,
Some false delight my giddy sense has charm'd,
My calmer thoughts the wretched choice reprove,
And my best hopes are center'd in thy love.
Depriv'd of this, can life one joy afford?   15
Its utmost boast a vain unmeaning word.
   But ah! how oft my lawless passions rove,
And break those awful precepts I approve!
Pursue the fatal impulse I abhor,
And violate the virtue I adore!   20
Oft when thy gracious Spirit's guardian care
Warn'd my fond soul to shun the tempting snare,
My stubborn will his gentle aid represt,
And check'd the rising goodness in my breast,
Mad with vain hopes, or urg'd by false desires,   25
Still'd his soft voice, and quench'd his sacred fires,
   With grief opprest, and prostrate in the dust,
Should'st thou condemn, I own the sentence just.

But oh thy softer titles let me claim,
And plead my cause by mercy's gentle name.   30
Mercy, that wipes the penitential tear,
And dissipates the horrors of despair:
From rig'rous Justice steals the vengeful hour:
Softens the dreadful attribute of power;
Disarms the wrath of an offended God,   35
And seals my pardon in a Saviour's blood.
   All pow'rful Grace, exert thy gentle sway,
And teach my rebel passions to obey:
Lest lurking Folly with insidious art
Regain my volatile inconstant heart.   40
Shall ev'ry high resolve devotion frames,
Be only lifeless sounds and specious names?
Or rather while thy hopes and fears controul,
In this still hour each motion of my soul,
Secure its safety by a sudden doom,   45
And be the soft retreat of sleep my tomb.
Calm let me slumber in that dark repose,
'Till the last morn its orient beam disclose:
Then, when the great Archangel's potent sound,
Shall echo thro' Creation's ample round,   50
Wak'd from the sleep of Death, with joy survey
The op'ning splendors of eternal day.

Elizabeth Carter, *Rambler* 44

The *Rambler* was a twice-weekly magazine produced by Samuel
Johnson from 1750-1752. All of the issues were written entirely by
Johnson except for a handful; Carter, the only author to have more
than one contribution, wrote numbers 44 and 100.

Rambler 44 was published on August 18, 1750, and begins with an
image that would be at home in any of the more horrific Graveyard
School poems, or in a tale by Poe. Employing the strategy developed
by Robert Blair and other Graveyard School writers, Carter begins
with a compelling set of graveyard images in order to rivet our
attention, at which point the work shifts to its religious message.

Dreams descend from Jove.

Pope[1]

SIR,

I had lately a very remarkable dream, which made so strong an impression on me, that I remember it every word; and if you are not better employed, you may read the relation of it as follows:

Methought I was in the midst of a very entertaining set of company, and extremely delighted in attending to a lively conversation, when on a sudden I perceived one of the most shocking figures imagination can frame, advancing towards me. She was drest in black, her skin was contracted into a thousand wrinkles, her eyes sunk deep in her head, and her complexion pale and livid as the countenance of death. Her looks were filled with terror and unrelenting severity, and her hands armed with whips and scorpions.[2] As soon as she came near, with a horrid frown, and a voice that chilled my very blood, she bid me follow her. I obeyed, and she led me through rugged paths, beset with briars and thorns, into a deep solitary valley. Wherever she passed, the fading verdure withered beneath her steps; her pestilential breath infected the air with malignant vapours, obscured the lustre of the sun, and involved the fair face of Heaven in universal gloom. Dismal howlings resounded through the forest, from every baleful tree the night-raven uttered his dreadful note, and the prospect was filled with desolation and horror. In the midst of this tremendous scene my execrable guide addressed me in the following manner:

"Retire with me, O rash unthinking mortal, from the vain allurements of a deceitful world, and learn that pleasure was not designed the portion of human life. Man was born to mourn and to be wretched; this is the condition of all below the stars, and whoever endeavours to oppose it, acts in contradiction to the will

---

1 The essay begins with a line from Homer's *Iliad*, in Greek, which is followed by the translation by Alexander Pope.

2 See 1 Kings 12.11: "And now whereas my father did lade you with a heavy yoke, I will add to your yoke: my father hath chastised you with whips, but I will chastise you with scorpions."

of Heaven. Fly then from the fatal enchantments of youth, and social delight, and here consecrate the solitary hours to lamentation and woe. Misery is the duty of all sublunary beings, and every enjoyment is an offence to the Deity, who is to be worshipped only by the mortification of every sense of pleasure, and the everlasting exercise of sighs and tears."

This melancholy picture of life quite sunk my spirits, and seemed to annihilate every principle of joy within me. I threw myself beneath a blasted yew, where the winds blew cold and dismal round my head, and dreadful apprehensions chilled my heart. Here I resolved to lie till the hand of death, which I impatiently invoked, should put an end to the miseries of a life so deplorably wretched. In this sad situation I espied on one hand of me a deep muddy river, whose heavy waves rolled on in slow sullen murmurs. Here I determined to plunge, and was just upon the brink, when I found myself suddenly drawn back. I turned about, and was surprised by the sight of the loveliest object I had ever beheld. The most engaging charms of youth and beauty appeared in all her form; effulgent glories sparkled in her eyes, and their awful splendours were softened by the gentlest looks of compassion and peace. At her approach the frightful spectre who had before tormented me, vanished away, and with her all the horrors she had caused. The gloomy clouds brightened into cheerful sunshine, the groves recovered their verdure, and the whole region looked gay and blooming as the garden of Eden. I was quite transported at this unexpected change, and reviving pleasure began to glad my thoughts, when, with a look of inexpressible sweetness my beauteous deliverer thus uttered her divine instructions:

"My name is Religion. I am the offspring of Truth and Love, and the parent of Benevolence, Hope, and Joy. That monster from whose power I have freed you is called Superstition; she is the child of Discontent, and her followers are Fear and Sorrow. Thus different as we are, she has often the insolence to assume my name and character, and seduces unhappy mortals to think us the same, till she, at length, drives them to the borders of Despair, that dreadful abyss into which you were just going to sink.

"Look round and survey the various beauties of the globe, which heaven has destined for the seat of the human race, and consider whether a world thus exquisitely framed could be meant for the abode of misery and pain. For what end has the lavish hand of Providence diffused such innumerable objects of delight, but that all might rejoice in the privilege of existence, and be filled with gratitude to the beneficent author of it? Thus to enjoy the blessings He has sent is virtue and obedience; and to reject them merely as means of pleasure, is pitiable ignorance or absurd perverseness. Infinite goodness is the source of created existence; the proper tendency of every rational being, from the highest order of raptured seraphs, to the meanest rank of men, is to rise incessantly from the lower degrees of happiness to higher. They have each faculties assigned them for various orders of delights."

"What," cried I, "is this the language of Religion? Does she lead her votaries through flowery paths, and bid them pass an unlaborious life? Where are the painful toils of virtue, the mortifications of penitents, the self-denying exercises of saints and heroes?"

"The true enjoyments of a reasonable being," answered she mildly, "do not consist in unbounded indulgence, or luxurious ease, in the tumult of passions, the languor of indolence, or the flutter of light amusements. Yielding to immoral pleasure corrupts the mind, living to animal and trifling ones debases it; both in their degree disqualify it for its genuine good, and consign it over to wretchedness. Whoever would be really happy, must make the diligent and regular exercise of his superior powers his chief attention, adoring the perfections of his Maker, expressing good-will to his fellow-creatures, cultivating inward rectitude. To his lower faculties he must allow such gratifications as will, by refreshing him, invigorate his nobler pursuits. In the regions inhabited by angelic natures, unmingled felicity for ever blooms, joy flows there with a perpetual and abundant stream, nor needs there any mound to check its course. Beings conscious of a frame of mind originally diseased, as all the human race has cause to be, must use the regimen of a stricter self-government. Whoever has been guilty of voluntary excesses must patiently submit both to the painful workings of nature and needful severities of medicine, in order to his cure. Still he is entitled to a moderate share of whatever alleviating accommodations this fair mansion of his merciful Parent affords, consistent with his recovery. And in proportion as this recovery advances, the liveliest joy will spring from his secret sense of an amended and improving heart. So far from the horrors of despair is the condition even of the guilty. Shudder, poor mortal, at the thought of the gulf into which thou wast but now going to plunge.

"While the most faulty have every encouragement to amend, the more innocent soul will be supported with still sweeter consolations under all its experience of human infirmities; supported by the gladdening assurances that every sincere endeavour to outgrow them shall be assisted, accepted, and rewarded. To such a one the lowliest self-abasement is but a deep-laid foundation for the most elevated hopes; since they who faithfully examine and acknowledge what they are, shall be enabled under my conduct to become what they desire. The Christian and the hero are inseparable; and to aspirings of unassuming trust, and filial confidence, are set no bounds. To him who is animated with a view of obtaining approbation from the Sovereign of the universe, no difficulty is insurmountable. Secure in this pursuit of every needful aid, his conflict with the severest pains and trials, is little more than the vigorous exercises of a mind in health. His patient dependence on that Providence which looks through all eternity, his silent resignation, his ready accommodation of his thoughts and behaviour to its inscrutable ways, is at once the most excellent sort of self-denial, and a source of the most exalted transports. Society is the true sphere of human virtue. In social, active life, difficulties will perpetually be met with; restraints of many kinds will be necessary; and studying to behave right in respect of these is a discipline of the human heart, useful to others, and improving to itself. Suffering is no duty, but where it is necessary to avoid guilt, or to do good; nor pleasure a crime, but where it strengthens the influence of bad inclinations, or lessens the generous activity of virtue. The happiness allotted to man in his present state, is indeed faint and low, compared with his immortal prospects and noble capacities; but yet whatever portion of it the distributing hand of heaven offers to each individual, is a needful support and refreshment for the present moment, so far as it may not hinder the attaining of his final destination.

"Return then with me from continual misery to moderate enjoyment and grateful alacrity. Return from the contracted views of solitude to the proper duties of a relative and dependent being. Religion is not confined to cells and closets, nor restrained to sullen retirement. These are the gloomy doctrines of Superstition, by which she endeavours to break those chains of benevolence and social affection, that link the welfare of every particular with that of the whole. Remember that the greatest honour you can pay to the Author of your being is by such a cheerful behaviour, as discovers a mind satisfied with his dispensations."

Here my preceptress paused, and I was going to express my acknowledgments for her discourse, when a ring of bells from the neighbouring village, and a new-risen sun darting his beams through my windows, awaked me.

I am, Yours, &c.

Robert Blair, "The Grave"

Blair (1699-1746) was a Scottish minister and poet, one of the "founders" of the Graveyard School. Educated at the University of Edinburgh and in Holland, Blair wrote and published very little in his lifetime, perhaps troubled by the perceived incompatibility, among those who shared his rather austere religious beliefs, of literary pursuits and strict living. But "The Grave," first published in March 1743 (although much of it was composed by the early 1730s), became hugely popular by the final decades of the eighteenth century, going through nearly fifty editions by 1798; the poem continued to be widely read well into the nineteenth century.

Blair's poem—presented in its entirety here—is indebted to various sources, perhaps most notably Parnell's "Night Thoughts" (1722), for it borrows all of Parnell's major themes: the invocation of a sublime horror in the graveyard imagery, including the manifestion of ghosts and the yew trees of the churchyard; the description of funereal pomp and pageantry; the grave as the great leveller of class distinction. Both poems even begin by the light of a "sickly taper." Blair's contribution, beyond the expansion of those themes (Parnell's poem of 90 lines is extended to over 760 by Blair), is the much fuller elaboration, in an evangelical mode that Parnell did not share, of Christian piety. As noted in this volume's introduction, Blair somewhat calculatedly included gothic elements in this poem in order to enhance its popularity among a reading audience that Blair felt urgently needed to hear his evangelical message. He largely limited his gothic effects to the early part of the work, "hooking" his readers, in journalistic parlance, with sensationalist imagery in order to more effectively make his spiritual points later in the poem; "The Grave," in the words of one scholar, "drove home its morality with a grim insistence on the horror of physical corruption."[1] In his forceful development of those points Blair goes well beyond Parnell, strenuously encouraging a focus on the spiritual by vigorously reminding us that the grave negates worldly glory and status, beauty, strength, wisdom, and all other material achievements, and that violations of Christian virtue—vainglory, suicide—are a sure path to spiritual failure. The poem concludes with a survey of human sufferings before celebrating the resurrection of the dead into eternal Christian salvation.

The text is taken from the first edition: *The Grave. A Poem,* London: M. Cooper, 1743.

————————

Whilst some affect the sun, and some the shade,
Some flee the city, some the hermitage;
Their aims as various as the roads they take
In journeying thro' life; the task be mine
To paint the gloomy horrors of the tomb;   5
Th' appointed place of rendezvous, where all
These travellers meet. Thy succours I implore,
Eternal King! whose potent arm sustains
The keys of Hell and Death. The Grave, dread thing!
Men shiver, when thou'rt nam'd: Nature appall'd   10
Shakes off her wonted firmness. Ah! how dark
Thy long-extended realms, and rueful wastes!
Where nought but silence reigns, and night, dark night,
Dark as was Chaos, 'ere the infant sun
Was roll'd together, or had try'd his beams   15

1 Charles Peake, *Poetry of the Landscape and the Night* (London: Edward Arnold, 1967), 17.

Athwart the gloom profound![1] The sickly taper
By glimmering thro' thy low-brow'd misty vaults,
(Furr'd round with mouldy damps, and ropy slime,)
Lets fall a supernumerary[2] horror,
And only serves to make thy night more irksome.   20
Well do I know thee by thy trusty yew,
Chearless, unsocial plant! that loves to dwell
'Midst sculls and coffins, epitaphs and worms:
Where light-heel'd ghosts, and visionary shades,
Beneath the wan cold moon (as fame reports)   25
Embody'd thick, perform their mystick rounds.
No other merriment, dull tree! is thine.

   See yonder hallow'd fane![3] the pious work
Of names once fam'd, now dubious or forgot,
And buried 'midst the wreck of things which were: 30
There lie interr'd the more illustrious dead.
The wind is up: hark! how it howls! Methinks
'Till now, I never heard a sound so dreary:
Doors creak, and windows clap, and night's foul bird[4]
Rook'd in the spire screams loud: the gloomy isles[5]   35
Black-plaster'd, and hung round with shreds of 'scutcheons
And tatter'd coats of arms, send back the sound
Laden with heavier airs, from the low vaults
The mansions of the dead. Rous'd from their slumbers
In grim array the grizly spectres rise,   40
Grin horrible, and obstinately sullen
Pass and repass, hush'd as the foot of night.
Again! the screech-owl shrieks: ungracious sound!
I'll hear no more, it makes one's blood run chill.

---

1 A description reminiscent of language used by Milton in *Paradise Lost*, where he
frequently links Chaos with Night (see, for example, Book II: 890-897).

2 *supernumerary*: extra, additional.

3 A fane is a shrine, temple, or church; here it refers to a small chapel with a
crypt.

4 The screech-owl, mentioned again in line 43.

5 That is, the "aisles" of the chapel, decorated for funereal mood and with the
armorial signs ("scutcheons") of those who are buried below.

Quite round the pile[1], a row of reverend elms,   45
Coæval near with that, all ragged shew,
Long lash'd by the rude winds: some rift half down
Their branchless trunks: others so thin at top,
That scarce two crows could lodge in the same tree.
Strange things, the neighbours say,[2] have happen'd here: 50
Wild shrieks have issu'd from the hollow tombs,
Dead men have come again, and walk'd about,
And the great bell has toll'd, unrung, untouch'd.
(Such tales their chear, at wake or gossiping,
When it draws near to witching time of night.)[3]   55

    Oft, in the lone church-yard at night I've seen
By glimpse of moon-shine, chequering thro' the trees,
The school-boy with his satchel in his hand,
Whistling aloud to bear his courage up,
And lightly tripping o'er the long flat stones   60
(With nettles skirted, and with moss o'ergrown,)
That tell in homely phrase who lie below;
Sudden! he starts, and hears, or thinks he hears
The sound of something purring at his heels:
Full fast he flies, and dares not look behind him,   65
'Till out of breath he overtakes his fellows;
Who gather round, and wonder at the tale
Of horrid apparition, tall and ghastly,
That walks at dead of night, or takes his stand
O'er some new-open'd *Grave*; and, strange to tell!   70
Evanishes at crowing of the cock.[4]

---

1 The church which Blair has just been describing.

2 Attributing stories of supernatural manifestation to neighborhood gossip or legend will become a staple of Graveyard School verse and Gothic fiction, allowing even those authors with little taste for the Gothic the opportunity to exploit the heightened emotional register that supernaturalism provides: see, for example, William Wordsworth's "The Thorn" (1798).

3 See *Hamlet* III.2.387: "'Tis now the very witching time of night, / When churchyards yawn and hell itself breathes out contagion to this world."

4 Spirits were commonly supposed to vanish with the rising of the sun. Shakespeare, in *Hamlet*, has the Ghost of Hamlet's father disappear with crowing of a cock, at which Horatio remarks "I have heard, / The cock, that is the trumpet to

The new-made widow too, I've sometimes spy'd,
Sad sight! slow moving o'er the prostrate dead:
Listless, she crawls along in doleful black,
Whilst bursts of sorrow gush from either eye,   75
Fast-falling down her now untasted cheek.
Prone on the lowly grave of the dear man
She drops; whilst busy-meddling memory,
In barbarous succession, musters up
The past endearments of their softer hours,   80
Tenacious of its theme. Still, still she thinks
She sees him, and indulging the fond thought,
Clings yet more closely to the senseless turf,
Nor heeds the passenger who looks that way.

Invidious *Grave*! How dost thou rend in sunder   85
Whom love has knit, and sympathy made one;
A tie more stubborn far than Nature's band!
Friendship! Mysterious cement of the soul!
Sweetner of life! and solder of society!
I owe thee much. Thou hast deserv'd from me,   90
Far, far beyond what I can ever pay.
Oft have I prov'd the labours of thy love,
And the warm efforts of the gentle heart
Anxious to please. Oh! when my friend and I
In some thick wood have wander'd heedless on,   95
Hid from the vulgar eye; and sat us down
Upon the sloping cowslip-cover'd bank,
Where the pure limpid stream has slid along
In grateful errors thro' the under-wood[1]
Sweet-murmuring: methought the shrill-tongu'd thrush   100
Mended his song of love; the sooty black-bird

---

the morn, / Doth with his lofty and shrill-sounding throat / Awake the god of
day; and, at his warning, /Whether in sea or fire, in earth or air, / The extrava-
gant and erring spirit hies / To his confine: and of the truth herein /This present
object made probation" (I.i.149-156).

1 That a stream's meanderings would be considered "errors" reflects neo-classical
sensibility, with its privileging of formality, regularity, and structure, seen in the
geometric forms that dominated the era's landscape design.

Mellow'd his pipe, and soften'd ev'ry note:
The eglantine smell'd sweeter, and the rose
Assum'd a dye more deep; whilst ev'ry flower
Vy'd with its fellow-plant in luxury   105
Of dress. Oh! then the longest summer's day
Seem'd too too much in haste: still the full heart
Had not imparted half: 'twas happiness
Too exquisite to last. Of joys departed
Not to return, how painful the remembrance!   110

    Dull *Grave*! thou spoil'st the dance of youthful blood,
Strik'st out the dimple from the cheek of mirth,
And ev'ry smirking feature from the face;
Branding our laughter with the name of madness.
Where are the jesters now?[1] the men of health   115
Complexionally pleasant? Where the droll?
Whose ev'ry look and gesture was a joke
To clapping theatres and shouting crowds,
And made even thick-lip'd musing melancholy
To gather up her face into a smile   120
Before she was aware? Ah! Sullen now,
And dumb, as the green turf that covers them!

    Where are the mighty thunderbolts of war?
The Roman Cæsars, and the Græcian chiefs,
The boast of story? Where the hot-brain'd youth?   125
Who the tiara at his pleasure tore
From kings of all the then discover'd globe;
And cry'd forsooth, because his arm was hamper'd,
And had not room enough to do its work?[2]
Alas! how slim, dishonourably slim!   130
And cramm'd into a space we blush to name.

---

1 These lines are indebted to the graveyard scene in *Hamlet*: "Where be your
gibes now? your gambols? your songs? your flashes of merriment, that were wont
to set the table on a roar? Not one now, to mock your own grinning? quite chap-
fallen?" (V.i.188-192). Blair returns to this idea in lines 248-250 of this poem.
2 An allusion to Alexander the Great (356-323 BCE), who is said to have wept
when he was told there were no more lands for him to conquer.

Proud royalty! how alter'd in thy looks!
How blank thy features, and how wan thy hue!
Son of the Morning![1] whither art thou gone?
Where hast thou hid thy many-spangled head,   135
And the majestick menace of thine eyes
Felt from afar? Pliant and powerless now,
Like new-born infant wound up in his swathes,
Or victim tumbled flat upon its back,
That throbs beneath the sacrificer's knife: 140
Mute, must thou bear the strife of little tongues,
And coward insults of the base-born crowd;
That grudge a privilege, thou never hadst,
But only hop'd for in the peaceful *Grave*,
Of being unmolested and alone.   145
Arabia's gums and odoriferous drugs,
And honours by the Heralds duly paid
In mode and form, ev'n to a very scruple;
Oh cruel irony! these come too late;
And only mock whom they were meant to honour.   150
Surely there's not a dungeon-slave that's bury'd
In the high-way, unshrouded and uncoffin'd,
But lies as soft, and sleeps as sound as he.[2]
Sorry pre-eminence of high descent
Above the vulgar-born, to rot in state![3]   155

But see! the well-plum'd hearse comes nodding on,
Stately and slow; and properly attended

---

1 Although usually used to refer to Lucifer, "Son of the Morning" here continues
the allusion to Alexander the Great.

2 Alexander the Great is said to have once come upon the philosopher Diogenes
sifting through a pile of bones. When asked what he was doing, Diogenes replied
that he was looking for the bones of Alexander's father, but could not tell them
from the bones of his dungeon-slaves. Blair returns to this idea in lines 229-231.

3 Another allusion to *Hamlet*, this time to that part of the gravedigger scene in
which Hamlet, handed the skull of Yorick and wondering if Alexander the Great
looked (and smelled) as the skull does, remarks to his friend Horatio "To what
base uses we may return, Horatio! Why may not imagination trace the noble
dust of Alexander till 'a find it stopping a bung-hole?" (V.i.202-204). Hamlet devel-
ops this metaphor, and extends it to include Julius Caesar, a few lines further on.

By the whole sable tribe, that painful watch
The sick man's door, and live upon the dead,[1]
By letting out their persons by the hour   160
To mimick sorrow, when the heart's not sad.
How rich the trappings, now they're all unfurl'd,
And glittering in the sun! Triumphant entrys
Of conquerors, and coronation pomps,
In glory scarce exceed. Great gluts of people   165
Retard th' unwieldy show; whilst from the casements
And houses' tops, ranks behind ranks close-wedg'd
Hang bellying o'er. But! tell us, why this waste?
Why this ado in earthing up a carcase
That's fall'n into disgrace, and in the nostril   170
Smells horrible? Ye undertakers! tell us,
'Midst all the gorgeous figures you exhibit,
Why is the principal conceal'd, for which
You make this mighty stir? 'Tis wisely done:
What would offend the eye in a good picture   175
The painter casts discreetly into shades.

   Proud lineage! now how little thou appear'st!
Below the envy of the private man!
Honour! that meddlesome officious ill,
Pursues thee ev'n to death; nor there stops short.   180
Strange persecution! when the *Grave* itself
Is no protection from rude sufferance.

   Absurd! to think to over-reach the *Grave*,
And from the wreck of names to rescue ours!
The best concerted schemes men lay for fame   185
Die fast away: Only themselves die faster.
The far-fam'd sculptor, and the laurell'd bard,
Those bold insurancers of deathless fame,
Supply their little feeble aids in vain.

---

1 Blair is referring in this passage to professional mourners; hiring people to attend funerals and mourn was a custom of long standing in some European countries. The "sable tribe" refers to the black ("sable") clothes these mourners would wear.

The tap'ring pyramid! th' Egyptian's pride,   190
And wonder of the world! whose spiky top
Has wounded the thick cloud, and long out-liv'd
The angry shaking of the winter's storm;
Yet spent at last by th' injuries of heav'n,
Shatter'd with age, and furrow'd o'er with years,   195
The mystick cone, with hieroglyphicks crusted,
Gives way. Oh! lamentable sight! at once
The labour of whole ages lumbers down;
A hideous and mishapen length of ruins.
Sepulchral columns wrestle but in vain   200
With all-subduing time: her cank'ring hand
With calm deliberate malice wasteth them:
Worn on the edge of days, the brass consumes,
The bust moulders, and the deep-cut marble,
Unsteady to the steel, gives up its charge.   205
Ambition! half convicted of her folly,
Hangs down the head, and reddens at the tale.

   Here! all the mighty troublers of the Earth,
Who swam to sov'reign rule thro' seas of blood;
Th' oppressive, sturdy, man-destroying villains!   210
Who ravag'd kingdoms, and laid empires waste,
And in a cruel wantonness of power
Thinn'd states of half their people, and gave up
To want the rest: now like a storm that's spent,
Lye hush'd, and meanly sneak behind thy covert.   215
Vain thought! to hide them from the gen'ral scorn,
That haunts and dogs them like an injur'd ghost
Implacable. Here too the petty tyrant
Of scant domains geographer ne'er notic'd,
And well for neighbouring grounds, of arm as short;   220
Who fix'd his iron talons on the poor,
And grip'd them like some lordly beast of prey;
Deaf to the forceful cries of gnawing hunger,
And piteous plaintive voice of misery:
(As if a slave was not a shred of nature,   225
Of the same common nature with his lord:)

Now! tame and humble, like child that's whipp'd,
Shakes hands with dust, and calls the worm his kinsman;
Nor pleads his rank and birthright. Under ground
Precedency's a jest; vassal and lord   230
Grossly familiar, side by side consume.

When self-esteem, or others' adulation,
Would cunningly persuade us we were something
Above the common level of our kind;
The *Grave* gainsays the smooth-complexion'd flatt'ry,   235
And with blunt truth acquaints us what we are.

Beauty! thou pretty play-thing! dear deceit!
That steals so softly o'er the stripling's heart,
And gives it a new pulse, unknown before!
The *Grave* discredits thee: thy charms expung'd,   240
Thy roses faded, and thy lillies soil'd;
What hast thou more to boast of? Will thy lovers
Flock round thee now, to gaze and do thee homage?
Methinks I see thee with thy head low laid;
Whilst surfeited upon thy damask[1] cheek,   245
The high-fed worm in lazy volumes roll'd,
Riots unscar'd. For this, was all thy caution?
For this, thy painful labours at thy glass?
T' improve those charms, and keep them in repair,
For which the spoiler thanks thee not.[2] Foul-feeder!   250
Coarse fare and carrion please thee full as well,
And leave as keen a relish on the sense.
Look! how the fair one weeps! the conscious tears
Stand thick as dew-drops on the bells of flow'rs:

---

1 The blush or pinkish color of the "damasck rose," a flower originally thought
to have come from Damascus.
2 Again Blair alludes to the graveyard scene in *Hamlet*, in which Hamlet, contem-
plating Yorick's skull and the times when, as a child, he was carried about on Yor-
ick's back, declares that "now, how abhorred my imagination is. My gorge rises at
it. Here hung those lips that I have kissed I know not how oft. . . . Now get you to
my lady's chamber and tell her, let her paint an inch thick, to this favour she must
come" (V.i.186-188, 192-194).

Honest effusion! the swoln heart in vain   255
Works hard to put a gloss on its distress.

   Strength too! thou surly, and less gentle boast
Of those that laugh loud at the village-ring!
A fit of common sickness pulls thee down
With greater ease, than e'er thou didst the stripling   260
That rashly dar'd thee to th' unequal fight.
What groan was that I heard? Deep groan indeed!
With anguish heavy-laden! Let me trace it:
From yonder bed it comes, where the strong man,
By stronger arm belabour'd, gasps for breath   265
Like a hard-hunted beast. How his great heart
Beats thick! his roomy chest by far too scant
To give the lungs full play! What now avail
The strong-built sinewy limbs, and well-spread shoulders?
See! how he tugs for life, and lays about him,   270
Mad with his pain! Eager he catches hold
Of what comes next to hand, and grasps it hard,
Just like a creature drowning! Hideous sight!
Oh! how his eyes stand out, and stare full ghastly
Whilst the distemper's rank and deadly venom[1]   275
Shoots like a burning arrow cross his bowels,
And drinks his marrow up. Heard you that groan?
It was his last. See how the great *Goliath*,[2]
Just like a child that brawl'd itself to rest,
Lies still. What mean'st thou then, O mighty boaster!   280
To vaunt of nerves of thine? What means the bull,
Unconscious of his strength, to play the coward,
And flee before a feeble thing like Man;
That knowing well the slackness of his arm,
Trusts only in the well-invented knife?   285

   With study pale, and midnight vigils spent,
The star-surveying sage, close to his eye

---

1 "Distemper" refers generally to any state of illness.
2 A reference to Goliath, the gigantic champion of the Philistines, defeated by
David in single combat in Samuel 17.4ff.

Applies the sight-invigorating tube[1];
And travelling through the boundless length of space
Marks well the courses of the far-seen orbs,   290
That roll with regular confusion there,
In extasy of thought. But ah! proud man!
Great heights are hazardous to the weak head:
Soon, very soon, thy firmest footing fails;
And down thou dropp'st into that darksome place,   295
Where nor device, nor knowledge ever came.

   Here! the tongue-warrior lies, disabled now,
Disarm'd, dishonour'd, like a wretch that's gagg'd,
And cannot tell his ail to passers by.
Great man of language! whence this mighty change?   300
This dumb despair, and drooping of the head?
Tho' strong persuasion hung upon thy lip,
And sly insinuation's softer arts
In ambush lay about thy flowing tongue;
Alas! how chop-fall'n now? Thick mists and silence   305
Rest, like a weary cloud, upon thy breast
Unceasing. Ah! where is the lifted arm,
The strength of action, and the force of words,
The well-turn'd period,[2] and the well-tun'd voice,
With all the lesser ornaments of phrase?   310
Ah! fled for ever, as they ne'er had been!
Raz'd from the book of fame: or more provoking,
Perchance some hackney hunger-bitten scribbler[3]
Insults thy memory, and blots thy tomb
With long flat narrative, or duller rhymes   315
With heavy-halting pace that drawl along;
Enough to rouse a dead man into rage,
And warm with red resentment the wan cheek.

---

1 Telescope.
2 That is, well-crafted sentences.
3 Although commonly used to denote a horse or carriage for hire, "hackney" also had come to mean, by Blair's time, a person hired to do menial work. The word survives today in the phrase "hack writer," someone turning out mediocre prose for money, which is the sense in which Blair uses the term.

Here! the great masters of the healing art,
These mighty mock-defrauders of the *Tomb*!   320
Spite of their juleps and catholicons[1]
Resign to fate. Proud Æsculapius' son![2]
Where are thy boasted implements of art,
And all thy well-cramm'd magazines[3] of health?
Nor hill, nor vale, as far as ship could go,   325
Nor margin of the gravel-bottom'd brook,
Escap'd thy rifling hand: from stubborn shrubs
Thou wrung'st their shy retiring virtues out,
And vex'd them in the fire: nor fly, nor insect,
Nor writhy snake, escap'd thy deep research.   330
But why this apparatus? Why this cost?
Tell us, thou doughty keeper from the *Grave*!
Where are thy recipes and cordials now,
With the long list of vouchers for thy cures?
Alas! thou speakest not. The bold impostor   335
Looks not more silly, when the cheat's found out.

Here! the lank-sided miser, worst of felons!
Who meanly stole, discreditable shift!
From back and belly too, their proper cheer;
Eas'd of a tax, it irk'd the wretch to pay   340
To his own carcase, now lies cheaply lodg'd,
By clam'rous appetites no longer teaz'd,
Nor tedious bills of charges and repairs.
But ah! where are his rents, his comings in?
Ay! now you've made the rich man poor indeed: 345
Robb'd of his gods, what has he left behind!

---

1 A "julep" would be a sweetened drink with which medicines would be mixed
for palatability; a "catholicon" is a universal remedy or cure.
2 Æsculapius (or Asclepius) was, in Greek myth, the son of Apollo and a nymph,
and was famed for his healing skills. When his skills become so advanced that he
was able to restore the dead to life, he was killed by Zeus at the request of Hades,
god of the underworld, who feared that he would lose his subjects. The modern
symbol of medicine, the staff entwined by a snake, is based on the staff of Æscu-
lapius (and is not to be confused with the caduceus, or staff of Hermes, which is
winged and has two snakes entwined).
3 Small containers for valuables.

Oh! cursed lust of gold! when for thy sake
The fool throws up his int'rest in both worlds,
First starv'd in this, then damn'd in that to come.

How shocking must thy summons be, O Death!   *350*
To him that is at ease in his possessions;
Who counting on long years of pleasure here,
Is quite unfurnish'd for that world to come!
In that dread moment, how the frantick soul
Raves round the walls of her clay tenement,   *355*
Runs to each avenue, and shrieks for help,
But shrieks in vain! How wishfully she looks
On all she's leaving, now no longer hers!
A little longer, yet a little longer,
Oh! might she stay, to wash away her stains,   *360*
And fit her for her passage! mournful sight!
Her very eyes weep blood; and every groan
She heaves is big with horror: but the foe,
Like a stanch murth'rer steady to his purpose,
Pursues her close through ev'ry lane of life,   *365*
Nor misses once the track, but presses on;
Till forc'd at last to the tremendous verge,
At once she sinks to everlasting ruin.

Sure! 'tis a serious thing to die! My soul!
What a strange moment must it be, when near   *370*
Thy journey's end, thou hast the gulf in view?
That awful gulf, no mortal e'er repass'd
To tell what's doing on the other side!
Nature runs back, and shudders at the sight,
And every life-string bleeds at thoughts of parting!   *375*
For part they must: body and soul must part;
Fond couple! link'd more close than wedded pair.
This wings its way to its almighty source,
The witness of its actions, now its judge:
That drops into the dark and noisome *Grave*,   *380*
Like a disabled pitcher of no use.

   If Death was nothing, and nought after Death;
If when men dy'd, at once they ceas'd to be,
Returning to the barren womb of nothing
Whence first they sprung; then might the debauchee   *385*
Untrembling mouth the heav'ns: Then might the drunkard
Reel over his full bowl, and when 'tis drain'd,
Fill up another to the brim, and laugh
At the poor bug-bear Death: then might the wretch
That's weary of the world, and tir'd of life,   *390*
At once give each inquietude the slip
By stealing out of being, when he pleas'd,
And by what way; whether by hemp, or steel:
Death's thousand doors stand open. Who could force
The ill-pleas'd guest to sit out his full time,   *395*
Or blame him if he goes? Sure! he does well
That helps himself as timely as he can,
When able. But if there is an hereafter,
And that there is, conscience, uninfluenc'd
And suffer'd to speak out, tells ev'ry man;   *400*
Then must it be an awful thing to die:
More horrid yet, to die by one's own hand.[1]
Self-murther! name it not: Our island's shame!
That makes her the reproach of neighbouring states.
Shall nature, swerving from her earliest dictate   *405*
Self-preservation, fall by her own act?
Forbid it Heav'n! Let not upon disgust
The shameless hand be foully crimson'd o'er
With blood of its own lord. Dreadful attempt!
Just reeking from self-slaughter, in a rage   *410*
To rush into the presence of our judge!
As if we challeng'd him to do his worst,
And matter'd not his wrath. Unheard of tortures
Must be reserv'd for such: these herd together;
The common damn'd shun their society,   *415*

---

1 Blair again echoes Shakespeare, for Hamlet twice refers to suicide: first, in Act
1, scene 2, when he momentarily wishes "that the Everlasting had not fixed /
His canon 'gainst self-slaughter!" (131-132), and again in the "To be or not to be"
soliloquy (III.i.57ff).

And look upon themselves as fiends less foul.
Our time is fix'd, and all our days are number'd;[1]
How long, how short, we know not: This we know,
Duty requires we calmly wait the summons,
Nor dare to stir 'till Heav'n shall give permission: 420
Like centrys that must keep their destin'd stand,
And wait th' appointed hour, till they're reliev'd.
Those only are the brave, that keep their ground,
And keep it to the last. To run away
Is but a coward's trick: To run away   425
From this world's ills, that at the very worst
Will soon blow o'er, thinking to mend ourselves
By boldly vent'ring on a world unknown,
And plunging headlong in the dark; 'tis mad:
No frenzy half so desperate as this.   430

  Tell us! ye dead! Will none of you in pity
To those you left behind, disclose the secret?
Oh! that some courteous ghost would blab it out!
What 'tis you are, and we must shortly be.
I've heard, that souls departed have sometimes   435
Forewarn'd men of their death: 'Twas kindly done
To knock, and give th' alarum. But what means
This stinted charity? 'tis but lame kindness
That does its work by halves. Why might you not
Tell us what 'tis to die? Do the strict laws   440
Of your society forbid your speaking
Upon a point so nice? I'll ask no more;
Sullen, like lamps in sepulchres, your shine
Enlightens but yourselves: well,—'tis no matter;
A very little time will clear up all,   445
And make us learn'd as you are, and as close.[2]

  Death's shafts fly thick! Here falls the village swain,
And there his pamper'd lord! The cup goes round;

---

1 See Psalm 90.12: "Teach us to number our days aright, that we may gain a heart
of wisdom."
2 Close-mouthed, secretive.

And who so artful as to put it by?
'Tis long since *Death* had the majority;   450
Yet strange! the living lay it not to heart.
See! yonder maker of the dead man's bed,
The sexton! hoary-headed chronicle,
Of hard unmeaning face, down which ne'er stole
A gentle tear; with mattock in his hand   455
Digs through whole rows of kindred and acquaintance,
By far his juniors! Scarce a scull's cast up,
But well he knew its owner, and can tell
Some passage of his life.[1] Thus hand in hand
The sot has walk'd with *Death* twice twenty years;   460
And yet ne'er yonker[2] on the green laughs louder,
Or clubs[3] a smuttier tale: when drunkards meet
None sings a merrier catch, or lends a hand
More willing to his cup. Poor wretch! he minds not,
That soon some trusty brother of the trade   465
Shall do for him what he has done for thousands.

   On this side, and on that, men see their friends
Drop off, like leaves in autumn; yet launch out
Into fantastic schemes, which the long livers,
In the world's hale and undegenerate days,[4]   470
Could scarce have leisure for! Fools that we are!
Never to think of Death, and of ourselves
At the same time! As if to learn to die
Were no concern of ours. Oh! more than sottish!
For creatures of a day, in gamesome mood   475
To frolick on eternity's dread brink,
Unapprehensive; when for ought we know
The very first swoln surge shall sweep us in.
Think we, or think we not, time hurries on
With a resistless unremitting stream,   480

---

1 Yet another moment recalling the gravedigger scene in *Hamlet*.
2 "Yonker" was a generic term for a young man of fashion.
3 Tells among one's friends.
4 A reference to Biblical figures, such as Methuselah, to whom extremely long
lives were attributed (see Genesis 5).

Yet treads more soft than e'er did midnight thief,
That slides his hand under the miser's pillow,
And carries off his prize. What is this world?
What? but a spacious burial-field unwall'd,
Strew'd with Death's spoils, the spoils of animals   485
Savage and tame, and full of dead men's bones?
The very turf on which we tread, once liv'd;
And we that live must lend our carcases
To cover our own offspring: In their turns
They too must cover theirs. 'Tis here all meet!   490
The shiv'ring Icelander, and sun-burnt Moor;[1]
Men of all climes, that never met before;
And of all creeds, the Jew, the Turk, and Christian.
Here the proud prince, and favourite yet prouder,
His sov'reign's keeper, and the people's scourge,   495
Are huddled out of sight. Here lie abash'd
The great negotiators of the Earth,
And celebrated masters of the ballance,
Deep read in stratagems, and wiles of courts:
Now vain their treaty-skill! *Death* scorns to treat.   500
Here the o'er-loaded slave flings down his burthen
From his gall'd shoulders; and when the cruel tyrant,
With all his guards and tools of pow'r about him,
Is meditating new unheard-of hardships,
Mocks his short arm, and quick as thought escapes   505
Where tyrants vex not, and the weary rest.
Here the warm lover leaving the cool shade,
The tell-tale echo, and the babbling stream,
Time out of mind the fav'rite seats of love,
Fast by his gentle mistress lay him down   510
Unblasted by foul tongue. Here friends and foe
Lie close; unmindful of their former feuds.
The lawn-rob'd prelate, and plain presbyter,[2]

---

1 Although specifically referring to an inhabitant of Mauritania (now Morocco
and Algeria) , "Moor" was often used loosely in the eighteenth century (and ear-
lier), typically denoting anyone from Northern Africa.
2 While "plain Presbyter" denoted a rank in the Presbyterian church, Blair here
is contrasting the simple clothing of presbyterian clergy with the more elaborate

E'er while that stood aloof, as shy to meet,
Familiar mingle here, like sister-streams   515
That some rude interposing rock had split.
Here is the large-limb'd peasant: Here the child
Of a span long, that never saw the sun,
Nor press'd the nipple, strangled in life's porch.[1]
Here is the mother with her sons and daughters;   520
The barren wife; and long-demurring maid,
Whose lonely unappropriated sweets
Smil'd like yon knot of cowslips on the cliff,
Not to be come at by the willing hand.
Here are the prude severe, and gay coquet,   525
The sober widow, and the young green virgin,
Cropp'd like a rose, before 'tis fully blown,
Or half its worth disclos'd. Strange medley here!
Here garrulous old age winds up his tale;
And jovial youth of lightsome vacant heart,   530
Whose ev'ry day was made of melody,
Hears not the voice of mirth: The shrill-tongu'd shrew,
Meek as the turtle-dove, forgets her chiding.
Here are the wise, the generous, and the brave;
The just, the good, the worthless, the prophane,   535
The downright clown, and perfectly well-bred;
The fool, the churl, the scoundrel, and the mean,
The supple statesman, and the patriot stern;
The wrecks of nations, and the spoils of time,
With all the lumber[2] of six thousand years.   540

    Poor Man! how happy once in thy first state!
When yet but warm from thy great Maker's hand,
He stamp'd thee with his image, and well-pleas'd

---

garment of a prelate, an official in the Anglican Church. "Lawn" is a fine linen,
often reserved for ceremonial or formal clothing.

1 A span is an old unit of measure, typically measured from thumb-tip to little
finger-tip at full extension, customarily regarded as nine inches, according to the
OED. Blair may be using the word more figuratively, but since he is referring to a
stillborn or miscarried fetus, he could well mean the word in its most literal sense.

2 That is, miscellaneous leftovers. "Six thousand years" was considered the age of
the earth by many in Blair's time.

Smil'd on his last fair work. Then all was well.
Sound was the body, and the soul serene;   545
Like two sweet instruments, ne'er out of tune,
That play their several parts. Nor head, nor heart,
Offer'd to ache: nor was there cause they should;
For all was pure within: no fell remorse,
Nor anxious castings up of what might be,   550
Alarm'd his peaceful bosom: summer seas
Shew not more smooth, when kiss'd by southern winds
Just ready to expire. Scarce importun'd
The generous soil with a luxuriant hand
Offer'd the various produce of the year,   555
And every thing most perfect in its kind.
Blessed! thrice blessed days! But ah, how short!
Bless'd as the pleasing dreams of holy men;
But fugitive like those, and quickly gone.
Oh! slipp'ry state of things! What sudden turns?   560
What strange vicissitudes, in the first leaf
Of man's sad history? To-day most happy,
And 'ere to-morrow's sun has set, most abject!
How scant the space between these vast extremes!
Thus far'd it with our sire:[1] not long he enjoy'd   565
His paradise! Scarce had the happy tenant
Of the fair spot due time to prove its sweets,
Or sum them up; when strait he must be gone
Ne'er to return again. And must he go?
Can nought compound for the first dire offence   570
Of erring man? Like one that is condemn'd
Fain would he trifle time with idle talk,
And parley with his fate. But 'tis in vain.
Not all the lavish odours of the place
Offer'd in incense can procure his pardon,   575
Or mitigate his doom. A mighty angel
With flaming sword forbids his longer stay,[2]

---

1 Adam.
2 Blair's invocation of Genesis 3.24: "So he drove out the man; and he placed at
the east of the garden of Eden Cherubims, and a flaming sword which turned
every way, to keep the way of the tree of life."

And drives the loiterer forth; nor must he take
One last and farewel round. At once he lost
His glory and his God. If mortal now,   *580*
And sorely maim'd, no wonder! Man has sinn'd.
Sick of his bliss, and bent on new adventures,
Evil he wou'd needs try: nor try'd in vain.
(Dreadful experiment! destructive measure!
Where the worst thing could happen, is success.)   *585*
Alas! too well he sped: the good he scorn'd
Stalk'd off reluctant, like an ill-us'd ghost,
Not to return; or if it did, its visits
Like those of angels short, and far between:
Whilst the black dæmon with his hell-'scap'd train,   *590*
Admitted once into its better room,
Grew loud and mutinous, nor would be gone;
Lording it o'er the man, who now too late
Saw the rash error, which he could not mend:
An error fatal not to him alone,   *595*
But to his future sons, his fortune's heirs.
Inglorious bondage! Human nature groans
Beneath a vassalage so vile and cruel,
And its vast body bleeds through ev'ry vein.

   What havock hast thou made? Foul monster, Sin!   *600*
Greatest and first of ills! The fruitful parent
Of woes of all dimensions! But for thee
Sorrow had never been. All noxious thing!
Of vilest nature! Other sorts of evils
Are kindly circumscrib'd and have their bounds.   *605*
The fierce volcano, from his burning entrails
That belches molten stone and globes of fire,
Involv'd in pitchy clouds of smoke and stench,
Marrs the adjacent fields for some leagues round,
And there it stops. The big-swoln inundation,   *610*
Of mischief more diffusive, raving loud,
Buries whole tracts of country, threat'ning more;
But that too has its shore it cannot pass.
More dreadful far than these! sin has laid waste

Not here and there a country, but a world: 615
Dispatching at a wide extended blow
Entire mankind; and for their sakes defacing
A whole creation's beauty with rude hands;
Blasting the foodful grain, the loaded branches,
And marking all along its way with ruin.   620
Accursed thing! Oh, where shall fancy find
A proper name to call thee by, expressive
Of all thy horrors? Pregnant womb of ills![1]
Of temper so transcendently malign,
That toads and serpents of most deadly kind   625
Compar'd to thee are harmless. Sicknesses
Of ev'ry size and symptom, racking pains,
And bluest plagues, are thine! See! how the fiend
Profusely scatters the contagion round!
Whilst deep-mouth'd slaughter bellowing at her heels 630
Wades deep in blood new-spilt; yet for to-morrow
Shapes out new work of great uncommon daring,
And inly pines 'till the dread blow is struck.

    But hold! I've gone too far; too much discover'd
My father's nakedness,[2] and nature's shame.   635
Here let me pause! and drop an honest tear,
One burst of filial duty, and condolance,
O'er all those ample deserts Death hath spread,
This chaos of mankind. O great man-eater!
Whose ev'ry day is Carnival, not sated yet!   640
Unheard of epicure! without a fellow!
The veryest gluttons do not always cram;
Some intervals of abstinence are sought

---

1 Blair may here be alluding to Milton's *Paradise Lost* (1667, 1674), which portrays
Sin as the direct offspring of Lucifer, springing fully formed from his head, whom
Lucifer then impregnates. The offspring of their union is Death, who in turn
rapes his mother; she gives birth to hell-hounds, which frequently return to her
womb and gnaw her entrails. See Book II, 648-814. Milton's description of Sin in
turn echoes Edmund Spenser's description of Error in Book One of *The Faerie
Queene* (1590, 1596).
2 See Genesis 9.23 and Leviticus 18.8 for some of Blair's biblical sources.

To edge the appetite: *Thou* seekest none.
Methinks! the countless swarms thou hast devour'd,   645
And thousands that each hour thou gobblest up;
This, less than *this*, might gorge thee to the full!
But Ah! rapacious still, thou gap'st for more:
Like one, whole days defrauded of his meals,
On whom lank hunger lays her skinny hand,   650
And whets to keenest eagerness his cravings.
(As if diseases, massacres, and poison,
Famine, and war, were not thy caterers!)[1]

But know! that thou must render up thy dead,
And with high int'rest too! They are not thine;   655
But only in thy keeping for a season,
'Till the great promis'd day of restitution;
When loud diffusive sound from brazen trump
Of strong-lung'd cherub shall alarm thy captives,
And rouse the long, long sleepers into life,[2]   660
Day-light, and liberty.————
Then must thy gates fly open, and reveal
The mines, that lay long forming under ground,
In their dark cells immur'd; but now full ripe,
And pure as silver from the crucible,   665
That twice has stood the torture of the fire,
And inquisition of the forge. We know,
Th' illustrious deliverer of mankind,
The Son of God, thee foil'd. Him in thy pow'r
Thou couldst not hold: self-vigorous he rose,   670
And, shaking off thy fetters, soon retook

---

1 Milton portrays Death as particularly ravenous: ". . . and Death / Grinn'd horri-
ble a ghastly smile, to hear / His famine should be fill'd" (*Paradise Lost* II:845-847).
2 See, for example, 1 Corinthians: "Behold, I shew you a mystery; We shall not all
sleep, but we shall all be changed, in a moment, in the twinkling of an eye, at the
last trump: for the trumpet shall sound, and the dead shall be raised incorruptible,
and we shall be changed. For this corruptible must put on incorruption, and this
mortal must put on immortality. So when this corruptible shall have put on incor-
ruption, and this mortal shall have put on immortality, then shall be brought to
pass the saying that is written, Death is swallowed up in victory. O death, where
is thy sting? O grave, where is thy victory?" (15.51-55).

Those spoils, his voluntary yielding lent.
(Sure pledge of our releasment from thy thrall!)
Twice twenty days he sojourn'd here on earth,
And shew'd himself alive to chosen witnesses   675
By proofs so strong, that the most slow-assenting
Had not a scruple left. This having done,
He mounted up to heav'n. Methinks! I see him
Climb the aerial heights, and glide along
Athwart the severing clouds: but the faint eye   680
Flung backwards in the chase, soon drops its hold;
Disabled quite, and jaded with pursuing.
Heaven's portals wide expand to let him in;
Nor are his friends shut out: as some great prince
Not for himself alone procures admission,   685
But for his train: It was his royal will,
That where He is, there should his followers be.
Death only lies between! A gloomy path!
Made yet more gloomy by our coward fears!
But nor untrod, nor tedious: the fatigue   690
Will soon go off. Besides, there's no by-road
To bliss. Then why, like ill-condition'd children,
Start we at transient hardships, in the way
That leads to purer air, and softer skies,
And a ne'er setting sun? Fools that we are!   695
We wish to be, where sweets unwith'ring bloom;
But strait our wish revoke, and will not go.
So have I seen upon a summer's even,
Fast by the riv'let's brink, a youngster play:
How wishfully he looks! To stem the tide   700
This moment resolute, next unresolv'd:
At last! he dips his foot; but as he dips,
His fears redouble, and he runs away
From th' inoffensive stream, unmindful now
Of all the flow'rs, that paint the further Bank,   705
And smil'd so sweet of late. Thrice welcome Death!
That after many a painful bleeding step
Conducts us to our home, and lands us safe
On the long-wish'd for shore. Prodigious change!

Our bane turn'd to a blessing! Death disarm'd   710
Loses her fellness quite: All thanks to him
Who scourg'd the venom out. Sure! the last end
Of the good man is peace. How calm his exit!
Night-dews fall not more gently to the ground,
Nor weary worn out winds expire so soft.   715
Behold him! in the evening-tide of life,
A life well-spent, whose early care it was
His riper years should not upbraid his green:
By unperceiv'd degrees he wears away;
Yet like the sun seems larger at his setting!   720
High in his faith and hopes, look! how he reaches
After the prize in view! and, like a bird
That's hamper'd, struggles hard to get away!
Whilst the glad gates of sight are wide-expanded
To let new glories in, the first fair fruits   725
Of the fast-coming harvest. Then! Oh then!
Each earth-born joy grows vile, or disappears,
Shrunk to a thing of nought. Oh! how he longs
To have his passport sign'd, and be dismiss'd!
'Tis done; and now he's happy: the glad soul   730
Has not a wish uncrown'd. Ev'n the lag[r] flesh
Rests too in hope of meeting once again
Its better half, never to sunder more.
Nor shall it hope in vain: the time draws on
When not a single spot of burial-earth,   735
Whether on land, or in the spacious sea,
But must give back its long-committed dust
Inviolate: and faithfully shall these
Make up the full account; not the least atom
Embezzl'd, or mislaid, of the whole tale.   740
Each soul shall have a body ready furnish'd;
And each shall have his own. Hence ye prophane!
Ask not, how this can be? Sure the same pow'r
That rear'd the piece at first, and took it down,
Can re-assemble the loose scatter'd parts,   745

---

1 Laggard, weary.

And put them as they were. Almighty God
Has done much more; nor is his arm impair'd
Thro' length of days: And what he can, he will:
His faithfulness stands bound to see it done.
When the dread trumpet sounds, the slumb'ring dust,   750
Not unattentive to the call, shall wake;
And ev'ry joint possess its proper place,
With a new elegance of form, unknown
To its first state. Nor shall the conscious soul
Mistake its partner; but amidst the crowd   755
Singling its other half, into its arms
Shall rush, with all th' impatience of a man
That's new-come home; who having long been absent
With haste runs over ev'ry different room,
In pain to see the whole. Thrice happy meeting!   760
Nor Time, nor Death, shall ever part them more.

   'Tis but a night, a long and moonless night,
We make the *Grave* our bed, and then are gone.

   Thus at the shut of ev'n, the weary bird
Leaves the wide air, and in some lonely brake   765
Cow'rs down, and dozes 'till the dawn of day,
Then claps his well-fledg'd wings, and bears away. [1]

Edward Young, *The Complaint, and The Consolation; or, Night Thoughts On Life, Death, And Immortality: In Nine Nights* (excerpts)

Young (1683-1765) was an Oxford-educated English clergyman, dramatist, satirist, and poet. His *Night Thoughts*, as the work is most commonly known, was an instant success when its first part (Nights 1 through 5) was published in 1742-43. The book was written, most scholars agree, as Young's response to the death of his

---

[1] This final image, of a flight into daylight, closely mirrors the ending of Parnell's "A Night-Piece on Death" (1722).

step-daughter, wife, and son-in-law in the span of less than three years. Young brought out more of the poem until it was complete (a total of nine Nights) in 1746, at which point it ran to nearly 10,000 lines. The work was, despite its length, quite popular throughout the eighteenth century and into the early nineteenth, coming out in over one hundred editions and translations in its first fifty years; some of those editions, such as the one William Blake was hired to illustrate, were quite lavish. Young's popularity waned with the rise of a more "authentic," Wordsworthian poetics and with arguments that Young's personal life, particularly his worldliness and ecclesiastical power-seeking, undermined his spiritual authority. Yet the work by which Young is known today was, in the words of one scholar, "for over a century one of the most influential, praised and well-known poems in the English language".[1] The "Complaint" —meaning a lament rather than an expression of dissatisfaction— takes up the first eight books of this work, and is Young's treatise on the sorrows and misguided aspirations of human life; the "Consolation," Night Nine, is the elucidation of Christian consolation in a divinely ordered universe.

Although Young's purpose was to move his audience with a dramatically powerful portrayal of Christian revelation, many readers—and even some of Young's translators—approached the book as "a seminal work in a secular cult of sepulchral melancholy."[2] Although Young would no doubt be troubled by his association with visceral Gothic horrors, it remains the case that he cultivated for his work a powerful emotional impact on his readers, and while much of that impact is the result of a preacher's declamatory, almost evangelical pulpit style deliberately in pursuit of the sublime and coupled with a fervent Christian didacticism, much is also due to Young's adept handling of imagery that was indelibly associated with the "Graveyard School" even in the early 1740s, as the

---

1 Stephen Cornford, *Edward Young: Night Thoughts* (Cambridge: Cambridge University Press, 1989), ix. Cornford's scholarly edition of *Night Thoughts* is extensively annotated, and includes a discussion of the work's publication history.
2 Cornford ix. Cornford goes on to explain, in a remark that points to the tension between Gothic and Christian tendencies in early Graveyard School poetry, that, "Contemplation of death was a frequently recommended Christian duty for Young's contemporaries, and not a source of gothic *frisson*" (14).

excerpts below will indicate. To see Young's work as solely a work of midnight melancholy would be to distort it beyond recognition and out of all character, but it is equally true that *Night Thoughts*, like Parnell's "Night-Piece on Death" and Blair's *The Grave*, is a work that, if it can never be fully contained by the "Graveyard School" label, cannot be fully understood without it.[1]

The text of this poem is taken from the 1773 edition published in London by Rivington et al.

———

Sunt lachrymæ rerum, et mentem mortalia tangunt.[2]

—*Virgilius.*

PREFACE.

As the occasion of this poem was real, not fictitious; so the method pursued in it was rather imposed by what spontaneously arose in the author's mind on that occasion, than meditated or designed: which will appear very probable from the nature of it; for it differs from the common mode of poetry, which is from long narrations to draw short morals. Here, on the contrary, the narrative is short, and the morality arising from it makes the bulk of the poem. The reason of it is, that the facts mentioned did naturally pour these moral reflections on the thought of the writer.

NIGHT THE FIRST.

ON LIFE, DEATH, AND IMMORTALITY

Tired Nature's sweet restorer, balmy sleep!
He, like the world, his ready visit pays
Where Fortune smiles; the wretched he forsakes;

———

1 Cornford points out that Young personally approved a frontispiece to one edition of Night V which showed "a figure leaning on a tombstone in a moonlit churchyard" (18). Young, like Robert Blair before him, was not averse to using "graveyard imagery . . . to lure impressionable readers towards orthodoxy" (18).
2 "There are tears for human affairs, and mortal fate moves the mind to pity." From Virgil's *Aeneid* I:462.

Swift on his downy pinions flies from woe,
And lights on lids unsullied with a tear.   5
    From short (as usual) and disturb'd repose
I wake: how happy they who wake no more!
Yet that were vain, if dreams infest the grave.[1]
I wake, emerging from a sea of dreams
Tumultuous; where my wreck'd desponding thought,   10
From wave to wave of fancied misery,
At random drove, her helm of reason lost:
Though now restored, 'tis only change of pain,
(A bitter change!) severer for severe.
The Day too short for my distress; and Night,   15
E'en in the zenith of her dark domain,
Is sunshine to the colour of my fate.
    Night, sable goddess! from her ebon throne,
In rayless majesty, now stretches forth
Her leaden sceptre o'er a slumb'ring world.   20
Silence, how dead! and darkness, how profound!
Nor eye, nor listening ear, an object finds;
Creation sleeps. 'Tis as the general pulse
Of life stood still, and Nature made a pause;
An awful pause! prophetic of her end.   25
And let her prophecy be soon fulfill'd:
Fate! drop the curtain; I can lose no more.
    Silence and Darkness! solemn sisters! twins
From ancient Night, who nurse the tender thought
To reason, and on reason build resolve,   30
(That column of true majesty in man)
Assist me: I will thank you in the grave;
The grave, your kingdom: *there* this frame shall fall
A victim sacred to your dreary shrine.
But what are ye?—Thou,[2] who didst put to flight   35
Primeval Silence, when the morning stars,
Exulting, shouted o'er the rising ball;—

---

1 An allusion to Shakespeare's *Hamlet*: "To die, to sleep; / To sleep: perchance to
dream: ay, there's the rub; / For in that sleep of death / What dreams may come
/ When we have shuffled off this mortal coil / Must give us pause" (III.i.65-69).
2 God.

O Thou, whose Word from solid darkness struck
That spark, the sun, strike wisdom from my soul;
My soul, which flies to Thee, her trust, her treasure,   40
As misers to their gold, while others rest.
   Thro' this opaque of Nature, and of soul,
This double night, transmit one pitying ray,
To lighten and to cheer. O lead my mind,
(A mind that fain would wander from its woe,)   45
Lead it thro' various scenes of life and death;
And from each scene the noblest truths inspire.
Nor less inspire my conduct, than my song:
Teach my best reason, reason; my best will
Teach rectitude; and fix my firm resolve   50
Wisdom to wed, and pay her long arrear:
Nor let the phial of thy vengeance, pour'd
On this devoted head, be pour'd in vain.
   The bell strikes *one*. We take no note of time,
But from its loss. To give it then a tongue   55
Is wise in man. As if an angel spoke,
I feel the solemn sound. If heard aright,
It is the knell of my departed hours:
Where are they? with the years beyond the flood.
It is the signal that demands dispatch: 60
How much is to be done! My hopes and fears
Start up alarm'd, and o'er life's narrow verge
Look down—on what? A fathomless abyss;
A dread eternity! how surely *mine*!
And can eternity belong to me,   65
Poor pensioner[1] on the bounties of an hour?
   How poor, how rich, how abject, how august,
How complicate, how wonderful is man![2]
How passing wonder He who made him such!
Who centred in our make such strange extremes!   70
From different natures marvellously mixt,

---

1 Recipient of an annuity, in this case of time.
2 Compare to Hamlet's "What a piece of work is a man!" speech (II.ii.304ff):
"How noble in reason, how infinite in faculties, in form and moving how express
and admirable, in action how like an angel, in apprehension how like a god!"

Connexion exquisite of distant worlds!
Distinguish'd link in being's endless chain![1]
Midway from nothing to the Deity!
A beam ethereal, sullied and absorb'd!   75
Tho' sullied and dishonour'd, still divine!
Dim miniature of greatness absolute!
An heir of glory! a frail child of dust!
Helpless immortal! insect infinite!
A worm! a god!——I tremble at myself,   80
And in myself am lost! at home a stranger,
Thought wanders up and down, surpriz'd, aghast,
And wond'ring at her own. How reason reels!
O what a miracle to man is man,
Triumphantly distress'd! what joy! what dread!   85
Alternately transported, and alarm'd!
What can preserve my life? or what destroy?
An angel's arm can't snatch me from the grave;
Legions of angels can't confine me there.
 'Tis past conjecture; all things rise in proof: 90
While o'er my limbs Sleep's soft dominion spread,
What tho' my soul fantastic measures trod
O'er fairy fields; or mourn'd along the gloom
Of pathless woods; or down the craggy steep
Hurl'd headlong, swam with pain the mantled[2] pool;   95
Or scaled the cliff; or danced on hollow winds,
With antic shapes, wild natives of the brain?
Her ceaseless flight, tho' devious, speaks her nature
Of subtler essence than the trodden clod;
Active, aerial, tow'ring, unconfin'd,   100
Unfetter'd with her gross companion's fall.
E'en silent Night proclaims my soul immortal:
E'en silent Night proclaims eternal day.
For human weal,[3] Heaven husbands[4] all events;
Dull sleep instructs, nor sport vain dreams in vain. 105

---

1 A reference to the doctrine of the Great Chain of Being.
2 Fringed with vegetation.
3 Well-being.
4 Directs.

Why then *their* loss deplore, that are not lost?
Why wanders wretched thought their tombs around,
In infidel distress? Are angels there?
Slumbers, rak'd up in dust, ethereal fire?
   They live! they greatly live a life on earth   110
Unkindled, unconceiv'd; and from an eye
Of tenderness, let heav'nly pity fall
On me, more justly number'd with the dead.
This is the desert, *this* the solitude:
How populous! how vital is the grave!   115
This is creation's melancholy vault,
The vale funereal, the sad cypress gloom;
The land of apparitions, empty shades!
All, all on earth is shadow, all beyond
Is substance; the reverse is Folly's creed:[1]   120
How solid all, where change shall be no more!
   This is the bud of being, the dim dawn,
The twilight of our day, the vestibule:
Life's theatre as yet is shut, and Death,
Strong Death, alone can heave the massy bar,   125
This gross impediment of clay remove,
And make us embryos of existence free.
From real life, but little more remote
Is he, not yet a candidate for light,
The future embryo, slumb'ring in his sire.   130
Embryos we must be, till we burst the shell,
Yon ambient azure shell, and spring to life,
The life of gods, O transport! and of man.
   Yet man, fool man! *here* buries all his thoughts;
Inters celestial hopes without one sigh.   135
Pris'ner of earth, and pent beneath the moon,
Here pinions all his wishes; wing'd by Heaven
To fly at infinite; and reach it there,
Where seraphs gather immortality,
On life's fair tree, fast by the throne of God.   140

---

1 Compare these lines to the speech given by Death in Parnell's "Night-Piece on Death."

What golden joys ambrosial clust'ring glow
In His full beam, and ripen for the just,
Where momentary ages are no more!
Where Time, and Pain, and Chance, and Death expire!
And is it in the flight of threescore years   145
To push eternity from human thought,
And smother souls immortal in the dust?
A soul immortal, spending all her fires,
Wasting her strength in strenuous idleness,
Thrown into tumult, raptur'd, or alarm'd,   150
At aught this scene can threaten, or indulge,
Resembles ocean into tempest wrought,
To waft a feather, or to drown a fly.
    Where falls this censure? It o'erwhelms myself.
How was my heart incrusted by the world!   155
O how self-fetter'd was my grovelling soul!
How, like a worm, was I wrapt round and round
In silken thought, which reptile Fancy spun,
Till darken'd Reason lay quite clouded o'er
With soft conceit of endless comfort *here*,   160
Nor yet put forth her wings to reach the skies!
    Night visions may befriend (as sung above):
Our *waking* dreams are fatal. How I dreamt
Of things impossible! (Could sleep do more?)
Of joys perpetual in perpetual change!   165
Of stable pleasures on the tossing wave!
Eternal sunshine in the storms of life!
How richly were my noon-tide trances hung
With gorgeous tapestries of pictured joys!
Joy behind joy, in endless perspective!   170
Till at Death's toll, whose restless iron tongue
Calls daily for his millions at a meal,
Starting I woke, and found myself undone.
Where now my frenzy's pompous furniture?
The cobwebb'd cottage, with its ragged wall   175
Of mouldering mud, is royalty to me!
The spider's most attenuated thread
Is cord, is cable, to man's tender tie

On earthly bliss; it breaks at every breeze.

[. . .]

Death! great proprietor of all! 'tis thine
To tread out empire, and to quench the stars.   205
The sun himself by thy permission shines;
And, one day, thou shalt pluck him from his sphere.
Amid such mighty plunder, why exhaust
Thy partial quiver on a mark so mean?
Why thy peculiar rancour wreak'd on me?   210
Insatiate archer! could not *one* suffice?
Thy shaft flew *thrice*; and thrice my peace was slain;[1]
And thrice, ere thrice yon moon had fill'd her horn.
O Cynthia! why so pale? Dost thou lament
Thy wretched neighbour? grieve to see thy wheel   215
Of ceaseless change out-whirl'd in human life?
How wanes my borrow'd bliss! from Fortune's smile,
Precarious courtesy! not Virtue's sure,
Self-given, solar ray of sound delight.
    In ev'ry vary'd posture, place, and hour,   220
How widow'd ev'ry thought of ev'ry joy!
Thought, busy thought! too busy for my peace!
Through the dark postern[2] of time long elapsed,
Led softly, by the stillness of the night,
Led, like a murderer, (and such it proves!)   225
Strays, (wretched rover!) o'er the pleasing past;
In quest of wretchedness perversely strays;
And finds all desert now; and meets the ghosts
Of my departed joys; a num'rous train!
I rue the riches of my former fate;   230
Sweet comfort's blasted clusters I lament;
I tremble at the blessings once so dear;
And ev'ry pleasure pains me to the heart.

---

1 A reference to the death of Young's stepdaughter (October 1737), wife (January
1740), and son-in-law (August 1740). Young implies, in the next line, that all these
deaths took place within three months of each other.
2 A back or side door.

[. . .]

Lorenzo,[1] Fortune makes her court to thee.   321
Thy fond heart dances, while the syren sings.
Dear is thy welfare; think me not unkind;
I would not damp, but to secure thy joys.
Think not that fear is sacred to the storm.   325
Stand on thy guard against the smiles of Fate.
Is Heav'n tremendous in its frowns? Most sure;
And in its favours formidable too:
Its favours here are trials, not rewards;
A call to duty, not discharge from care;   330
And should alarm us, full as much as woes;
Awake us to their cause, and consequence;
And make us tremble, weigh'd with our desert;
Awe Nature's tumult, and chastise her joys,
Lest while we clasp, we kill them; nay, invert   335
To worse than simple misery their charms.
Revolted joys, like foes in civil war,
Like bosom friendships to resentment sour'd,
With rage invenom'd rise against our peace.
Beware what earth calls happiness; beware   340
All joys, but joys that never can expire.
Who builds on less than an immortal base,
Fond as he seems, condemns his joys to death.
    Mine died with thee, Philander![2] thy last sigh
Dissolved the charm; the disenchanted earth   345
Lost all her lustre. Where, her glitt'ring towers?
Her golden mountains, where? All darken'd down
To naked waste; a dreary vale of tears:
The great magician's dead! Thou poor, pale piece
Of out-cast earth, in darkness! what a change   350
From yesterday! Thy darling hope so near,

---

1 The fictional young man, representing aspects of a life not sufficiently informed
and guided by Christian value and belief, to whom *Night Thoughts* is addressed
throughout.

2 A generic Greek name, here standing for Young's much-beloved son-in-law and
longtime friend, Henry Temple, who died suddenly in August 1740.

(Long-labour'd prize!) O how ambition flush'd
Thy glowing cheek! Ambition, truly great,
Of virtuous praise. Death's subtle seed within,
(Sly, treacherous miner!) working in the dark,   355
Smil'd at thy well-concerted scheme, and beckon'd
The worm to riot on that rose so red,
Unfaded ere it fell; one moment's prey!

[. . .]

Not e'en Philander had bespoke his shroud.
Nor had he cause; a warning was deny'd:
How many fall as sudden, not as safe!
As sudden, tho' for years admonish'd home!   385
Of human ills the last extreme beware;
Beware, Lorenzo! a slow-sudden death.
How dreadful that deliberate surprise!
Be wise to-day, 'tis madness to defer;
Next day the fatal precedent will plead;   390
Thus on, till wisdom is push'd out of life.
Procrastination is the thief of time;[1]
Year after year it steals, till all are fled,
And to the mercies of a moment leaves
The vast concerns of an eternal scene.   395
If not so frequent, would not this be strange?
That 'tis so frequent, this is stranger still.
Of man's miraculous mistakes, this bears
The palm, "That all men are about to live,"
For ever on the brink of being born.   400
All pay themselves the compliment to think
They one day shall not drivel; and their pride
On this reversion takes up ready praise,
At least their own; their future selves applauds;
How excellent that life they ne'er will lead!   405
Time lodg'd in their own hands is folly's vails;
That lodg'd in Fate's, to wisdom they consign;

---

1 This well-known proverb was coined by Young.

The thing they can't but purpose, they postpone.
'Tis not in folly, not to scorn a fool;
And scarce in human wisdom to do more.   410
All promise is poor dilatory man,
And that through every stage: when young, indeed,
In full content we sometimes nobly rest,
Unanxious for ourselves; and only wish,
As duteous sons, our fathers were more wise.   415
At thirty, man suspects himself a fool;
Knows it at forty, and reforms his plan;
At fifty, chides his infamous delay,
Pushes his prudent purpose to resolve;
In all the magnanimity of thought   420
Resolves; and re-resolves; then dies the same.
    And why? Because he thinks himself immortal.
All men think all men mortal, but themselves;
Themselves, when some alarming shock of Fate
Strikes through their wounded hearts the sudden dread;   425
But their hearts wounded, like the wounded air,
Soon close; where past the shaft, no trace is found.
As from the wing no scar the sky retains,
The parted wave no furrow from the keel,
So dies in human hearts the thought of death.   430
E'en with the tender tear which Nature sheds
O'er those we love, we drop it in their grave.
Can I forget Philander? That were strange.
O my full heart!——But should I give it vent,
The longest night, tho' longer far, would fail,   435
And the lark listen to my midnight song.

NIGHT THE FIFTH.

THE RELAPSE.

[. . .]
Night is fair Virtue's immemorial friend;
The conscious Moon, thro' ev'ry distant age,

Has held a lamp to Wisdom, and let fall
On Contemplation's eye, her purging ray.   *180*
The fam'd Athenian,[1] he who woo'd from heav'n
Philosophy the fair, to dwell with men,
And form their manners, not inflame their pride,
While o'er his head, as fearful to molest
His lab'ring mind, the stars in silence slide,   *185*
And seem all gazing on their future guest,
See him soliciting his ardent suit
In private audience: all the live-long night,
Rigid in thought, and motionless, he stands;
Nor quits his theme, or posture, till the sun   *190*
(Rude drunkard! rising rosy from the main!)
Disturbs his nobler intellectual beam,
And gives him to the tumult of the world.
Hail, precious moments! stol'n from the black waste
Of murder'd Time! auspicious Midnight, hail!   *195*
The world excluded, ev'ry passion hush'd,
And open'd a calm intercourse with Heaven,
Here the soul sits in council; ponders *past*,
Predestines *future* action; sees, not feels,
Tumultuous life, and reasons with the storm;   *200*
All her lies answers, and thinks down her charms.
   What awful joy! what mental liberty!
I am not pent in darkness: rather say,
(If not too bold,) in darkness I'm embow'r'd.
Delightful gloom! the clust'ring thoughts around   *205*
Spontaneous rise, and blossom in the shade;
But droop by day, and sicken in the sun.
Thought borrows light elsewhere; from that first fire,
Fountain of animation! whence descends
Urania,[2] my celestial guest! who deigns   *210*
Nightly to visit me, so mean; and now,
Conscious how needful discipline to man,
From pleasing dalliance with the charms of Night,

---

1 Socrates.
2 Greek muse of astronomy.

My wand'ring thought recalls, to what excites
Far other beat of heart; Narcissa's[1] tomb!   215
   Or is it feeble Nature calls me back,
And breaks my spirit into grief again?
Is it a Stygian[2] vapour in my blood?
A cold, slow puddle, creeping thro' my veins?
Or is it thus with all men?—Thus with all.   220
What are we? how unequal! now we soar,
And now we sink; to be the same, transcends
Our present prowess. Dearly pays the soul
For lodging ill; too dearly rents her clay.
Reason, a baffled counsellor! but adds   225
The blush of weakness, to the bane of woe.
The noblest spirit, fighting her hard fate,
In this damp, dusky region, charg'd with storms,
But feebly flutters, yet untaught to fly;
Or, flying, short her flight, and sure her fall.   230
Our utmost strength, when down, to rise again;
And not to yield, tho' beaten, all our praise.
  'Tis vain to seek in men for more than man.
Tho' proud in promise, big in previous thought,
Experience damps our triumph. I, who late,   235
Emerging from the shadows of the grave,
Where Grief detain'd me prisoner, mounting high,
Threw wide the gates of everlasting day,
And call'd mankind to glory, shook off pain,
Mortality shook off, in ether pure,   240
And struck the stars; now feel my spirits fail:
They drop me from the zenith; down I rush,
Like him whom Fable fledged with waxen wings,[3]

---

1 A generic Greek name which Young has been using throughout to refer to his dead step-daughter.

2 Having to do with the river Styx, which in Greek and Roman myth separates the underworld from the world of the living.

3 Icarus, who with his father Daedalus sought to escape from imprisonment by building wings of wax and feathers and flying to freedom. Although warned not to fly too close to the sun, Icarus ignored his father's advice and died when his wings melted and he fell into the sea.

In sorrow drown'd——but not in sorrow lost.
How wretched is the man who never mourn'd!   245
I dive for precious pearl in sorrow's stream:
Not so the thoughtless man that only grieves;
Takes all the torment, and rejects the gain,
(Inestimable gain!) and gives Heaven leave
To make him but more wretched, not more wise.   250

[. . .]

Say, on what themes shall puzzled choice descend?
"Th' importance of contemplating the tomb;   295
Why men decline it; Suicide's foul birth;
The various kinds of Grief; the faults of Age;
And Death's dread character,"—invite my song.
And, first, th' importance of our end survey'd.
Friends counsel quick dismission of our grief.   300
Mistaken kindness! our hearts heal too soon.
Are they more kind than He who struck the blow,
Who bid it do His errand in our hearts,
And banish peace, till nobler guests arrive,
And bring it back a true and endless peace?   305
Calamities are friends: as glaring day
Of these unnumber'd lustres robs our sight,
Prosperity puts out unnumber'd thoughts
Of import high, and light Divine, to man.
The man how bless'd, who, sick of gaudy scenes,   310
(Scenes apt to thrust between us and ourselves!)
Is led by choice to take his fav'rite walk
Beneath Death's gloomy, silent, cypress shades,
Unpierc'd by Vanity's fantastic ray;
To read his monuments, to weigh his dust,   315
Visit his vaults, and dwell among the tombs!
Lorenzo! read with me Narcissa's stone;
(Narcissa was thy fav'rite) let us read
Her moral stone: few doctors¹ preach so well;

---

1 i.e. doctors of divinity; clergymen.

Few orators so tenderly can touch   320
The feeling heart. What pathos in the date!
Apt words can strike; and yet in them we see
Faint images of what we here enjoy.
What cause have we to build on length of life?
Temptations seize, when Fear is laid asleep,   325
And Ill foreboded is our strongest guard.
   See, from her tomb, as from an humble shrine,
Truth, radiant goddess, sallies on my soul,
And puts Delusion's dusky train to flight;
Dispels the mists our sultry passions raise,   330
From objects low, terrestrial, and obscene;
And shows the real estimate of things;
Which no man, unafflicted, ever saw;
Pulls off the veil from Virtue's rising charms;
Detects Temptation in a thousand lies.   335
Truth bids me look on men, as autumn leaves,
And all they bleed for, as the summer's dust,
Driv'n by the whirlwind. Lighted by her beams,
I widen my horizon, gain new powers,
See things invisible, feel things remote,   340
Am present with futurities; think nought
To man so foreign as the joys possess'd,
Nought so much his, as those beyond the grave.

                        [. . .]

   What grave prescribes the best?——A friend's; and yet
From a friend's grave how soon we disengage!
E'en to the dearest, as his marble, cold.
Why are friends ravisht from us? 'tis to bind,
By soft affection's ties, on human hearts,   375
The thought of death, which Reason, too supine,
Or misemploy'd, so rarely fastens there.
Nor Reason, nor Affection, no, nor both
Combin'd, can break the witchcrafts of the world.
Behold th' inexorable hour at hand!   380
Behold th' inexorable hour forgot!

And to forget it, the chief *aim* of life,
Though well to ponder it is life's chief *end*.

NIGHT THE NINTH AND LAST.

THE CONSOLATION.

Containing, Among Other Things,
1.—A Moral Survey Of The Nocturnal Heavens.
2.—A Night-Address To The Deity.

Fatis contraria fata rependens.[1]   Virgil

As when a traveller, a long day past
In painful search of what he cannot find,
At night's approach, content with the next cot,
There ruminates, awhile, his labour lost;
Then cheers his heart with what his fate affords,   5
And chants his sonnet to deceive the time,
Till the due season calls him to repose:
Thus I, long-travell'd in the ways of men,
And dancing, with the rest, the giddy maze
Where disappointment smiles at hope's career;   10
Warn'd by the languor of life's evening ray,
At length have housed me in an humble shed;
Where, future wandering banish'd from my thought,
And waiting, patient, the sweet hour of rest,
I chase the moments with a serious song.   15
Song soothes our pains; and age has pains to soothe.
   When age, care, crime, and friends embrac'd at heart
Torn from my bleeding breast, and Death's dark shade,
Which hovers o'er me, quench th' ethereal fire;
Canst thou, O Night! indulge one labour more?   20

---

1 From Virgil's *Aeneid* (I.239): "countering fate with better fate"—the idea here
is that the sorrow and gloom which have been dominant elements in the *Night
Thoughts* up to this point will be balanced with the positive view of human spiri-
tual possibility presented in Book 9.

One labour more indulge! Then sleep, my strain!
Till, haply, waked by Raphael's[1] golden lyre,
Where night, death, age, care, crime, and sorrow cease;
To bear a part in everlasting lays,
Though far, far higher set, in aim, I trust,   25
Symphonious to this humble prelude here.

[. . .]

Where, the prime actors of the last year's scene?
Their port so proud, their buskin, and their plume![2]
How many sleep, who kept the world awake
With lustre and with noise! Has Death proclaim'd
A truce, and hung his sated lance on high?   60
'Tis brandish'd still, nor shall the present year
Be more tenacious of her human leaf,
Or spread of feeble life a thinner fall.
But needless monuments to wake the thought;
Life's gayest scenes speak man's mortality;   65
Though in a style more florid, full as plain
As mausoleums, pyramids, and tombs.
What are our noblest ornaments, but Deaths
Turn'd flatterers of Life, in paint, or marble,
The well-stain'd canvas, or the featur'd stone?   70
Our fathers grace, or rather haunt, the scene.
Joy peoples her pavilion from the dead.

[. . .]

---

1 One of the archangels of Judeo-Christian and Islamic tradition, associated with
healing. In Islamic tradition Raphael is the archangel who will blow a trumpet to
signal the coming of Judgment Day, but Young's treatment here has him playing
a lyre.
2 Port is one's bearing or manner of holding oneself; a buskin is a type of boot
traditionally worn by actors in Greek tragedy; the plume refers to a feather or
horse-hair decorative element on a helmet or cap. Young's metaphor here is that
life on earth is like a play, with humans as strutting actors in elaborate costume,
and he contrasts this display with death. This metaphor may well be indebted to
Jacques' famous "All the world's a stage" soliloquy in Shakespeare's *As You Like It*
(Act II, scene vii).

Lorenzo! such the glories of the world!   90
What is the world itself? thy world?—A grave.
Where is the dust that has not been alive?
The spade, the plough, disturb our ancestors;
From human mould we reap our daily bread.
The globe around Earth's hollow surface shakes,   95
And is the ceiling of her sleeping sons.
O'er devastation we blind revels keep;
Whole buried towns support the dancer's heel.
The moist of human frame the sun exhales;[1]
Winds scatter, through the mighty void, the dry;   100
Earth repossesses part of what she gave,
And the freed spirit mounts on wings of fire;
Each element partakes our scatter'd spoils;
As Nature, wide, our ruins spread: man's death
Inhabits all things, but the thought of man!   105
  Nor man alone; his breathing bust expires,
His tomb is mortal; empires die: where, now,
The Roman? Greek? They stalk, an empty name!
Yet few regard them in this useful light;
Tho' half our learning is their epitaph.   110
When down thy vale, unlock'd by midnight thought,
That loves to wander in thy sunless realms,
O Death! I stretch my view; what visions rise!
What triumphs! Toils imperial! Arts Divine!
In wither'd laurels glide before my sight!   115
What lengths of far-fam'd ages, billow'd high
With human agitation, roll along
In unsubstantial images of air!
The melancholy ghosts of dead renown,
Whispering faint echoes of the world's applause;   120
With penitential aspect, as they pass,
All point at earth, and hiss at human pride,
The wisdom of the wise, and prancings of the great.

---

1 That is, the sun's heat draws from the ground the moisture released by decaying human corpses.

[. . .]

What then am I?—
                    Amidst applauding worlds,
And worlds celestial, is there found on earth
A peevish, dissonant, rebellious string,
Which jars in the grand chorus, and complains?   370
Censure on thee, Lorenzo! I suspend,
And turn it on myself; how greatly due!
All, all is right, by God ordain'd or done;
And who, but God, resum'd the friends He gave?
And have I been complaining, then, so long?   375
Complaining of His *favours*, Pain and Death?
Who, without Pain's advice, would e'er be good?
Who, without Death, but would be good in vain?
Pain is to save from pain; all punishment,
To make for peace; and Death, to save from death;   380
And second death, to guard immortal life;
To rouse the careless, the presumptuous awe,
And turn the tide of souls another way;
By the same tenderness Divine ordain'd,
That planted Eden, and high-bloom'd for man   385
A fairer Eden, endless, in the skies.

[. . .]

This final effort of the moral Muse,   2371
How justly titled![1] Nor for me alone;
For all that read! What spirit of support,
What heights of Consolation, crown my song!
    Then farewell, Night! of darkness, now, no more: 2375
Joy breaks, shines, triumphs; 'tis eternal day.
Shall that which rises out of nought complain
Of a few evils, paid with endless joys?
My soul! henceforth, in sweetest union join
The two supports of human happiness,   2380

---

1 The Consolation. [Young's note.]

Which some erroneous think can never meet;
True taste of life, and constant thought of death;
The thought of death, sole victor of its dread!
Hope be thy joy, and probity thy skill;
Thy patron He, whose diadem has dropp'd   2385
Yon gems of heaven; eternity, thy prize:
And leave the racers of the world their own,
Their feather, and their froth, for endless toils:
They part with all for that which is not bread;
They mortify, they starve, on wealth, fame, power;   2390
And laugh to scorn the fools that aim at more.
How must a spirit, late escaped from earth,
Suppose Philander's, Lucia's, or Narcissa's,[1]
The truth of things new-blazing in its eye,
Look back, astonish'd, on the ways of men,   2395
Whose lives' whole drift is to forget their graves!
And when our present privilege is pass'd,
To scourge us with due sense of its abuse,
The same astonishment will seize us all.
What *then* must pain us, would preserve us *now*.   2400
Lorenzo! 'tis not yet too late; Lorenzo!
Seize wisdom, ere 'tis torment to be wise;
That is, seize wisdom, ere she seizes thee.
For what, my small philosopher, is Hell?
'Tis nothing, but full knowledge of the Truth,   2405
When Truth, resisted long, is sworn our foe,
And calls Eternity to do her right.
   Thus, darkness aiding intellectual light,
And sacred silence whispering truths divine,
And truths divine converting pain to peace,   2410
My song the midnight raven has outwing'd,
And shot, ambitious of unbounded scenes,
Beyond the flaming limits of the world,
Her gloomy flight. But what avails the flight
Of fancy, when our hearts remain below?   2415
Virtue abounds in flatterers and foes;

---

1 Young's son-in-law, wife, and step-daughter, respectively.

'Tis pride, to praise her; penance, to perform.
To more than words, to more than worth of tongue,
Lorenzo! rise at this auspicious hour;
An hour when Heaven's most intimate with man;   2420
When, like a falling star, the ray divine
Glides swift into the bosom of the just;
And just are all, determined to reclaim;
Which sets that title high, within thy reach.
Awake then; thy Philander calls; awake!   2425
Thou, who shalt wake, when the creation sleeps;
When, like a taper, all these suns expire;
When Time, like him of Gaza,[1] in his wrath,
Plucking the pillars that support the world,
In Nature's ample ruins lies entomb'd;   2430
And Midnight, universal Midnight, reigns.

Mark Akenside, *The Pleasures of Imagination: A Poem in Three Books* (excerpt)

Akenside (1721-1770) was an English physician and poet best known in his lifetime for *The Pleasures of Imagination*, first published in 1744; Akenside began, but did not complete before his death, an expanded revision of this poem. A Dissenter, Akenside entered Edinburgh University intending to become a minister, but was drawn to medical study as his spiritual views were increasingly influenced by deism.

The Pleasures of Imagination was significantly shaped by the thought and writings of Joseph Addison, and records in no uncertain terms Akenside's mistrust of the supernatural and the powerful emotions it can raise, as we see at the end of this excerpt. His remarks on superstition and the supernatural, however, are themselves influenced by Graveyard School tropes—note, for example, the "sickly taper" in line 249 below—and by Akenside's own recognition of the power of the dark imaginative. So while Akenside in many respects stands outside the Graveyard School, his major

---

1 Samson, who destroys a pagan temple in Gaza for revenge after being blinded and captured by the Philistines. See Judges 16.

work nonetheless attests—as do the Graveyard School parodies—
to the alluring potency of its cultural presence.

The text is from the first edition of *The Pleasures of Imagination:
A Poem in Three Books* (London, 1744). The excerpts below are from
Book One.

[At this point in the poem Akenside is remarking on novelty and its
energizing effect on the human mind and spirit.]

For, such the bounteous providence of heav'n,
In every breast implanting this desire   240
Of objects new and strange, to urge us on
With unremitted labour to pursue
Those sacred stores that wait the ripening soul,
In truth's exhaustless bosom. What need words
To paint its power? For this the daring youth   245
Breaks from his weeping mother's anxious arms,
In foreign climes to rove: the pensive sage,
Heedless of sleep, or midnight's harmful damp,
Hangs o'er the sickly taper; and untir'd
The virgin follows, with inchanted step,   250
The mazes of some wild and wondrous tale,
From morn to eve; unmindful of her form,
Unmindful of the happy dress that stole
The wishes of the youth, when every maid
With envy pin'd. Hence, finally, by night   255
The village matron, round the blazing hearth,
Suspends the infant-audience with her tales,
Breathing astonishment! of witching rhymes,
And evil spirits; of the death-bed call
Of him who robb'd the widow, and devour'd   260
The orphan's portion; of unquiet souls
Risen from the grave to ease the heavy guilt
Of deeds in life conceal'd; of shapes that walk
At dead of night, and clank their chains, and wave
The torch of hell around the murderer's bed.   265
At every solemn pause the crowd recoil
Gazing each other speechless, and congeal'd

With shivering sighs: till eager of th' event,
Around the beldame all erect they hang,
Each trembling heart with grateful terrors quell'd.   270

[In the intervening lines, Akenside has been effusing on the joys
and delights of Beauty, particularly as it is expressed in female
attractiveness.]

                    Ye smiling band   335
Of youths and virgins, who thro' all the maze
Of young desire with rival steps pursue
This charm of beauty; if the pleasing toil
Can yield a moment's respite, hither turn
Your favourable ear, and trust my words.   340
I do not mean to wake the gloomy form
Of superstition dress'd in wisdom's garb,
To damp your tender hopes; I do not mean
To bid the jealous thund'rer[1] fire the heavens,
Or shapes infernal rend the groaning earth   345
To fright you from your joys; my cheerful song
With better omens calls you to the field
Pleas'd with your generous ardour in the chase,
And warm as you. Then tell me, for you know,
Does beauty ever deign to dwell where health   350
And active use are strangers? Is her charm
Confess'd in aught, whose most peculiar ends
Are lame and fruitless? Or did nature mean
This awful stamp the herald of a lie;
To hide the shame of discord and disease,   355
And catch with fair hypocrisy the heart
Of idle faith? O no! with better cares
The indulgent mother, conscious how infirm
Her offspring tread the paths of good and ill,
By this illustrious image, in each kind   360
Still most illustrious where the object holds
Its native powers most perfect, she by this

---

1 Zeus.

Illumes the headstrong impulse of desire,
And sanctifies his choice. The generous glebe[1]
Whose bosom smiles with verdure, the clear tract   365
Of streams delicious to the thirsty soul,
The bloom of nectar'd fruitage ripe to sense,
And every charm of animated things,
Are only pledges of a state sincere,
The integrity and order of their frame,   370
When all is well within, and every end
Accomplish'd. Thus was beauty sent from heaven,
The lovely ministress of truth and good
In this dark world: for truth and good are one,
And beauty dwells in them, and they in her,   375
With like participation. Wherefore then,
O sons of earth! would ye dissolve the tie?
O wherefore, with a rash, imperfect aim,
Seek you those flow'ry joys with which the hand
Of lavish fancy paints each flatt'ring scene   380
Where beauty seems to dwell, nor once enquire
Where is the sanction of eternal truth,
Or where the seal of undeceitful good,
To save your search from folly! Wanting these,
Lo! beauty withers in your void embrace,   385
And with the glittering of an idiot's toy
Did fancy mock your vows. Nor let the gleam
Of youthful hope that shines upon your hearts,
Be chill'd or clouded at this awful task,
To learn the lore of undeceitful good,   390
And truth eternal. Tho' the pois'nous charms
Of baleful superstition guide the feet
Of servile numbers, thro' a dreary way
To their abode, through deserts, thorns and mire;
And leave the wretched pilgrim all forlorn   395
To muse at last, amid the ghostly gloom
Of graves, and hoary vaults, and cloister'd cells;
To walk with spectres thro' the midnight shade,

---

1 A cultivated field.

And to the screaming owl's accursed song
Attune the dreadful workings of his heart;   *400*
Yet be not ye dismay'd. A gentler star
Your lovely search illumines. From the grove
Where wisdom talk'd with her Athenian sons,
Could my ambitious hand intwine a wreath
Of Plato's olive with the Mantuan bay,   *405*
Then should my powerful verse at once dispell
These monkish horrors: then in light divine
Disclose the Elysian prospect, where the steps
Of those whom nature charms, through blooming walks,
Thro' fragrant mountains and poetic streams,   *410*
Amid the train of sages, heroes, bards,
Led by their winged Genius and the choir
Of laurell'd science and harmonious art,
Proceed exulting to th' eternal shrine,
Where truth inthron'd with her celestial twins,   *415*
The undivided partners of her sway,
With good and beauty reigns.

James Hervey, *Meditations Among the Tombs. In a Letter to a Lady* (excerpts)

Hervey (1714-1758) was an English clergyman and writer, earning his B.A. at Oxford and his M.A. at Cambridge. Although he remained throughout his life an Anglican clergyman, Hervey was strongly influenced by his Oxford classmate John Wesley, one of the founders of Methodist Christianity (though the two would later feud over doctrinal matters), and Hervey was more tolerant of, and in some ways closer to the views of, evangelical Christianity than was the case with most of his Anglican colleagues. Indeed, the remarkable popularity of his writings, particularly the *Meditations*, is attributable to his works' appeal to evangelical sensibilities. The *Meditations*, Hervey's most significant work—and one which was significantly influenced by Young's *Night Thoughts*—was first published in 1745, went through twenty-five editions before the end of the century, and continued to be popular well into the nineteenth century, even inspiring a blank verse "transposition," by George Cocking, in 1819. (Hervey, true to his principles, gave to charity all of the proceeds from his writings.) Hervey's delineations of "the dreadful pleasure inspired by gazing at fallen monuments and mouldering tombs"[1] will find Gothic expression in Horace Walpole's *The Castle of Otranto* (1764), with its subterranean passages and brooding castle, which of course became instant staples of Gothic literature.

The text is taken from *Meditations and Contemplations. In Two Volumes.* A New Edition Printed from a Copy Corrected by the Author. London: J. Rivington, Jr., 1779.

———

MADAM,

Travelling lately into Cornwall,[2] I happened to alight at a considerable village in that county: where, finding myself under an unexpected necessity of staying a little, I took a walk to the church.[3] The doors, like the heaven to which they lead, were wide open, and readily admitted an unworthy stranger. Pleased with the opportunity, I resolved to spend a few minutes under the sacred roof.

In a situation so retired and awful,[4] I could not avoid falling into a train of meditations, serious and mournfully pleasing. Which I trust, were in some degree profitable to me, while they possessed and warmed my thoughts; and if they may administer any satisfaction to you, Madam, now they are recollected, and committed to writing, I shall receive a fresh pleasure from them.

———

1 Frederick S. Frank, "Appendix C: Aesthetic and Intellectual Backgrounds." Horace Walpole, *The Castle of Otranto and The Mysterious Mother* (Peterborough, Ontario: Broadview, 2003), 315.

2 A large, and largely rural, county or "shire" in southwest England.

3 "I had named, in some former editions, a particular church, viz. Kilkhampton; where several of the monuments, described in the following pages, really exist. But as I thought it convenient to mention some cases here, which are not, according to the best of my remembrance, referred to in any inscriptions there, I have now omitted the name, that imagination might operate more freely, and the improvement of the reader be consulted, without any thing that should look like a variation from truth and fact." [Hervey's note.] Kilkhampton is one of the northernmost towns in Cornwall.

4 Awe-inspiring, moving.

It was an ancient pile, reared by hands, that, ages ago, were mouldered into dust; situate in the centre of a large burial ground; remote from all the noise and hurry of tumultuous life. The body spacious; the structure lofty; the whole magnificently plain. A row of regular pillars extended themselves through the midst, supporting the roof with simplicity, and with dignity. The light, that passed through the windows, seemed to shed a kind of luminous obscurity, which gave every object a grave and venerable air. The deep silence added to the gloomy aspect, and, both heightened by the loneliness of the place, greatly increased the solemnity of the scene.[1] A sort of religious dread stole insensibly on my mind while I advanced, all pensive and thoughtful, along the inmost aisle. Such a dread, as hushed every ruder passion, and dissipated all the gay images of an alluring world.

[. . .]

The next thing which engaged my attention, was the lettered floor. The pavement, somewhat like Ezekiel's roll, was written over from one end to the other. I soon perceived the comparison to hold good in another respect, and the inscriptions to be matter of "mourning, lamentation, and woe."[2] They seemed to court my observation, silently inviting me to read them. And what would these dumb monitors inform me of? "That, beneath their little circumferences, were deposited such and such pieces of clay, which once lived, and moved, and talked: that they had received a charge to preserve their names, and were the remaining trustees of their memory."

Ah! said I, is such my situation? The adorable Creator around me, and the bones of my fellow-creatures under me! Surely, then, I have great reason to cry out, with the revering patriach, How

---

1 Silence, gloom, obscurity, and solitude will become important characteristics of the sublime as developed by Edmund Burke in his *A Philosophical Enquiry into the Origin of our Idea of the Sublime and the Beautiful* (1757), which develops an aesthetic theory of considerable importance to the Gothic literary tradition.

2 Ezekiel 2.10 [Hervey's note.] "And when I looked, behold, an hand was sent unto me; and, lo, a roll of a book was therein; And he spread it before me; and it was written within and without: and there was written therein lamentations, and mourning, and woe." Ezekiel 2.9-10.

dreadful is this place!¹ Seriousness and devotion become this house forever. May I never enter it lightly or irreverently, but with profound awe, and godly fear!

O! that they were wise! said the inspired penman.² It was his last wish for his dear people. He breathed it out, and gave up the ghost. But what is wisdom? It consists not in refined speculations, accurate researches into nature, or an universal acquaintance with history. The divine lawgiver settles this important point in his next aspiration: o! that they understood this! That they had right apprehensions of their spiritual interests, and eternal concerns! That they had eyes to discern, and inclinations to pursue, the things which belong to their peace! But how shall they attain this valuable knowledge? I send them not, adds the illustrious teacher, to turn over all the volumes of literature: they may acquire, and much more expeditiously, this science of life, by considering their latter end. This spark of heaven is often lost under the glitter of pompous erudition, but shines clearly in the gloomy mansions of the tomb. Drowned is this gentle whisper amidst the noise of secular affairs, but speaks distinctly in the retirements of serious contemplation. Behold! how providentially I am brought to the school of wisdom!³ The grave is the most faithful master,⁴ and these instances of mortality the most instructive lessons. Come then, calm attention, and compose my thoughts; come, thou celestial Spirit, and enlighten my mind; that I may so peruse these awful pages as to "become wise unto salvation."⁵

---

1 Genesis 28.17 [Hervey's note.] Jacob makes this remark after awaking from a dream in which God spoke to him.

2 Deuteronomy 32.29 [Hervey's note.]

3 The man how bless'd, who, sick of gaudy scenes, / Is led by choice to take his favourite walk / Beneath Death's gloomy, silent, cypress shades, / Unpierced by Vanity's fantastic ray; / To read his monuments, to weigh his dust, / Visit his vaults, and dwell among the tombs! *Night Thoughts* [Hervey's note.] From Book V, lines 310ff.

4 Wait the great teacher death. [Hervey's note.] This edition omits the attribution, "Pope"; the reference is to Alexander Pope's *Essay on Man*, Epistle I, line 88: "Wait the great teacher, Death, and God adore!"

5 "But continue thou in the things which thou hast learned and hast been assured of, knowing of whom thou hast learned them; And that from a child thou hast known the holy scriptures, which are able to make thee wise unto salvation through faith which is in Christ Jesus." 2 Timothy 3.14-15.

Examining the records of mortality, I found the memorials of a promiscuous multitude.[1] They were huddled, at least they rested together, without any regard to rank or seniority. None were ambitious of the uppermost rooms, or chief seats in this house of mourning. None entertained fond and eager expectations of being honourably greeted in their darksome cells. The man of years and experience, reputed as an oracle in his generation, was content to lie down at the feet of a babe. In this house appointed for all living, the servant was equally accommodated, and lodged in the same story with his master. The poor indigent lay as softly, and slept as soundly, as the most opulent possessor. All the distinction that subsisted, was a grassy hillock, bound with osiers, or a sepulchral stone ornamented with imagery.

Why then, said my working thoughts, O! why should we raise such a mighty stir about superiority and precedence, when the next remove will reduce us all to a state of equal meanness? Why should we exalt ourselves, or debase others, since we must all one day be upon a common level, and blended together in the same undistinguished dust? O! that this consideration might humble my own and others' pride, and sink our imaginations as low as our habitation will shortly be?

Among these confused relics of humanity, there are, without doubt, persons of contrary interests, and contradicting sentiments. But Death, like some able days-man,[2] has laid his hand on the contending parties, and brought all their differences to an amicable conclusion.[3] Here enemies, sworn enemies, dwell together in unity. They drop every imbittered thought, and forget that they once were foes. Perhaps their crumbling bones mix, as they moulder, and those who, while they lived, stood aloof in irreconcileable variance, here fall into mutual embraces, and even incorporate

---

1 Mista senum ac juvenum densentur funera. Horace [Hervey's note.] "Youth jostles age in funeral obsequies." From Horace's *Odes*, 1.28, line 19 (John Conington's translation).

2 A day-laborer.

3 Hi motus animorum atque haec certamina tanta pulveris exigui iactu compressa quiescent. Virgil [Hervey's note.] From Virgil's *Georgics* IV, lines 86-87: "These fiery passions and fierce attacks / Are controlled and quieted by a little scattered dust." In this passage Virgil is talking about ending conflict between bees.

with each other in the grave. O! that we might learn from these friendly ashes, not to perpetuate the memory of injuries, not to foment the fever of resentment, nor cherish the turbulence of passion. That there may be as little animosity and disagreement in the land of the living, as there is in the congregation of the dead! But I suspend for a while such general observations, and address myself to a more particular inquiry.

[. . .]

On this hand is lodged one, whose sepulchral stone tells a most pitiable tale indeed! Well may the little images, reclined over the sleeping ashes, hang down their heads with that pensive air! None can consider so mournful a story, without feeling some touches of sympathizing concern. His age twenty eight; his death sudden; himself cut down in the prime of life, amidst all the vivacity and vigour of manhood, while "his breasts were full of milk, and his bones moistened with marrow."[1] Probably he entertained no apprehensions of the evil hour. And indeed, who could have suspected, that so bright a sun should go down at noon? To human appearance, his hill stood strong. Length of days seemed written in his sanguine countenance. He solaced himself with the prospect of a long, long series of earthly satisfactions. When lo! an unexpected stroke descends! descends from that mighty arm, which "overturneth the mountains by their roots; and crushes the imaginary hero, before the moth"[2] as quickly, and more easily, than our fingers press such a feeble fluttering insect to death.

[. . .]

The only *infallible* way of immortalising our characters; a way equally open to the meanest and most exalted fortune; is, "to make our calling and election sure;"[3] to gain some sweet evidence, that

---

1 Job 21.24.

2 A conflation of Job 4.19 and 9.5. Hervey's footnote, remarking on conflicting scholarly readings of Job 4.19, has been omitted.

3 From 2 Peter 1.10-11: "Wherefore the rather, brethren, give diligence to make your calling and election sure: for if ye do these things, ye shall never fall: For so

our names are written in heaven. Then, however they may be
disregarded or forgotten among men, they will not fail to be had
in everlasting remembrance before the Lord. This is, of all distinc-
tions, far the noblest. Ambition, be this thy object, and every page
of scripture will sanctify thy passion; even grace itself will fan thy
flame. As to earthly memorials, yet a little while, and they are all
obliterated. The tongue of those, whose happiness we have zeal-
ously promoted, must soon be silent in the coffin. Characters cut
with a pen of iron, and committed to the solid rock, will ere long
cease to be legible.[1] But as many as are included "in the Lamb's
book of life,"[2] He himself declares, shall never be blotted out from
those annals of Eternity.[3] When a flight of years has mouldered
the triumphal column into dust: when the brazen statue perishes,
under the corroding hand of time: these honours still continue,
still are blooming and incorruptible, in the world of glory.

> Make the extended skies your tomb;
>   Let stars record your worth;
> Yet know, vain mortals, all must die,
>   As Nature's sickliest birth.
>
> Would bounteous Heav'n indulge my prayer,
>   I frame a nobler choice;
> Nor, living, with the pompous pile;
>   Nor, dead, regret the loss.
>
> In thy fair book of life divine,
>   My God, inscribe my name:

---

an entrance shall be ministered unto you abundantly into the everlasting king-
dom of our Lord and Saviour Jesus Christ."

1 Data sunt ipsis quoque fata sepulchris. Juvenal [Hervey's note.] From the tenth
satire of the Roman poet Juvenal (first century CE), as translated by John Dryden:
"For sepulchres themselves must crumbling fall / In time's abyss, the common
grave of all."

2 Said of the New Jerusalem, in Revelations 21.27: "And there shall in no wise
enter into it any thing that defileth, neither whatsoever worketh abomination, or
maketh a lie: but they which are written in the Lamb's book of life."

3 Revelations 3.5 [Hervey's note.] "He that overcometh, the same shall be clothed
in white raiment; and I will not blot out his name out of the book of life, but I will
confess his name before my Father, and before his angels."

> There let it fill some humble place
> Beneath the slaughtered Lamb.
>
> Thy saints, while ages roll away,
>   In endless fame survive;
> Their glories, o'er the wrongs of time,
>   Greatly triumphant, live.[1]

Yonder entrance leads, I suppose, to the vault. Let me turn aside, and take one view of the habitation, and its tenants. The sullen door grates upon its hinges: not used to receive many visitants, it admits me with reluctance and murmurs. What meaneth this sudden trepidation, while I descend the steps, and am visiting the pale nations of the dead? Be composed, my spirits: there is nothing to fear in these quiet chambers. "Here, even the wicked cease from troubling."[2]

Good Heavens! what a solemn scene! how dismal the gloom! Here is perpetual darkness, and night even at noon-day. How doleful the solitude! Not one trace of cheerful society, but sorrow and terror seem to have made this their dreaded abode. Hark! how the hollow dome resounds, at every tread. The echoes, that long have slept, are awakened; and lament, and sigh, along the walls.

A beam or two finds its way through the grates, and reflects a feebler glimmer from the nails of the coffins. So many of those sad spectacles, half concealed in shades, half seen dimly by the baleful twilight, add a deep horror to these gloomy mansions. I pore upon the inscriptions, and am just able to pick out, that these are the remains of the rich and renowned. No vulgar dead are deposited here. The most illustrious and right honourable, have claimed this for their last retreat. And, indeed, they retain somewhat of a shadowy pre-eminence. They lie, ranged in a mournful order, and in a sort of silent pomp, under the arches of an ample sepulchre, while meaner corpses, without much ceremony, "go down to the stones of the pit."[3]

---

1 This hymn is by Hervey.

2 From Job 3.17: "There the wicked cease from troubling; and there the weary be at rest." Job is cursing the day of his birth and longing for the peace of death.

3 From Isaiah 14.19: "But thou art cast out of thy grave like an abominable branch, and as the raiment of those that are slain, thrust through with a sword,

My apprehensions recover from their surprise. I find, here are
no phantoms, but such as fear raises. However, it still amazes me,
to observe the wonders of this nether world. Those who received
vast revenues, and called whole lordships their own, are here
reduced to half a dozen feet of earth, or confined in a few sheets
of lead. Rooms of state and sumptuous furniture are resigned
for no other ornament than the shroud, for no other apartment
than the darksome niche. Where is the star, that blazed upon the
breast; or coronet, that glittered round the temples? The only
remains of departed dignity are the weather-beaten hatchment,[1]
and the tattered escutcheon.[2] I see no splendid retinue surrounding
this solitary dwelling. The lordly equipage hovers no longer about
the lifeless matter. He has no other attendant than a dusty statue,
which, while the regardless world is as gay as ever, the sculptor's
hand has taught to weep.

Those who gloried in high-born ancestors and noble pedigree
here drop their lofty pretensions. They acknowledge kindred with
creeping things, and quarter arms with the meanest reptiles.[3] They
say to corruption, thou art my father; and to the worm, thou art
my mother, and my sister. Or, should they still assume the style of
distinction, ah! how impotent were the claim! how apparent the
ostentation! It is said by their monument, Here lies the great! How
easily is it replied by the spectator!

> ———— False marble! Where?
> Nothing but poor and sordid dust lies here.[4]

Mortifying truth! Sufficient, one would think, to wean the most

---

that go down to the stones of the pit; as a carcase trodden under feet."
1 "a square or lozenge-shaped tablet exhibiting the armorial bearings of a
deceased person, which is affixed to the front of his dwelling-place." (OED)
2 "The shield or shield-shaped surface on which a coat of arms is depicted; also
in wider sense, the shield with the armorial bearings; a sculptured or painted
representation of this." (OED)
3 To "quarter arms" with someone is to include that person's coat of arms, or
some element of their coat of arms, on one section (or quarter) of one's own
heraldic shield—in other words, an acknowledgment of kinship or close alliance.
4 From "Pindarique Ode, X" by the English poet and courtier Abraham Cowley
(1618-1667): "Here lies the Great — False Marble, where? / Nothing but small and
sordid Dust lies there." (20-21)

sanguine appetite from this transitory state of things, from its sickly satisfactions, its fading glories, its vanishing treasures.

> For now, ye *lying vanities* of life!
> Ye ever tempting, ever-cheating train!
> Where are ye now? and what is your amount?[1]

What is all the world, to these poor breathless beings? What are their pleasures? A bubble broke. What their honours? A dream that is forgotten. What the sum-total of their enjoyments below? Once, perhaps, it appeared to inexperienced and fond desire, something considerable. But now death hath measured it with his line, and weighed it in his scale,[2] what is the upshot? Alas! it is shorter than a span, lighter than the dancing spark, and driven away like the dissolving smoke.

Indulge, my soul, a serious pause. Recollect all the gay things, that were wont to dazzle thy eyes, and inveigle thy affections. Here, examine those baits of sense. Here, form an estimate of their real value. Suppose thyself first among the favourites of fortune, who revel in the lap of pleasure, who shine in the robes of honour; and swim in tides of inexhausted riches. Yet, how soon would the passing-bell proclaim thy exit! And, when once that iron call has summoned thee to thy future reckoning, where would all these gratifications be? At that period, how will all the pageantry of the most affluent, splendid, or luxurious circumstances, vanish into empty air! And is this a happiness so passionately to be coveted?

I thank you, ye relics of sounding titles, and magnificent names. Ye have taught me more of the littleness of the world than all the volumes of my library. Your nobility arrayed in a winding-sheet, your grandeur mouldering in an urn, are the most indisputable

---

1 From James Thomson's "Winter: A Poem," published in 1726, lines 201-203. The phrase "lying vanities" occurs twice in the Bible: in Psalm 31 ("I have hated them that regard lying vanities: but I trust in the Lord" [31:6]) and in Jonah ("They that observe lying vanities forsake their own mercy" [2:8]).

2 Another instance of Hervey's biblical diction. See, for example, 2 Samuel 8.2 ("And he smote Moab, and measured them with a line, casting them down to the ground") and Isaiah 40.12 ("Who hath measured the waters in the hollow of his hand, and meted out heaven with the span, and comprehended the dust of the earth in a measure, and weighed the mountains in scales, and the hills in a balance?")

proofs of the nothingness of created things. Never, surely, did Providence write this important point in such legible characters, as in the ashes of my lord, or on the corpse of his grace.[1] Let others, if they please, pay their obsequious court to your wealthy sons, and ignobly fawn, or anxiously sue, for preferments; my thoughts shall often resort, in pensive contemplation, to the sepulchres of their sires, and learn, from their sleeping dust, to moderate my expectations from mortals, to stand disengaged from every undue attachment to the little interests of time, to get above the delusive amusements of honour, the gaudy tinsels of wealth, and all the empty shadows of a perishing world.

Hark! what sound is that! In such a situation, every noise alarms. Solemn and slow it breaks again upon the silent air! 'Tis the striking of the clock. Designed, one would imagine, to ratify all my serious mediations. Methinks, it says Amen, and sets a seal, to every improving hint. It tells me, that another portion of my appointed time is elapsed. One calls it, "the knell of my departed hours."[2] 'Tis the watch-word to vigilance and activity. It cries in the ear of reason, "Redeem the time. Catch the favourable gales of opportunity: O! catch them, while they breathe, before they are irrecoverably lost. The span of life shortens continually. Thy minutes are all upon the wing, and hastening to be gone. Thou art a borderer upon eternity, and making incessant advances to the state thou art contemplating." May the admonition sink deep, into an attentive and obedient mind! May it teach me that heavenly arithmetic, "of numbering my days, and applying my heart unto wisdom."[3]

I have often walked beneath the impending promontory's craggy cliff; I have sometimes trod the vast spaces of the lonely desert, and penetrated the inmost recesses of the dreary cavern; but never, never beheld nature louring,[4] with so tremendous a form, never felt such impressions of awe striking cold on my heart, as under these

---

1 —— Mors sola fatetur / Quantula sint hominum corpuscula. Juvenal [Hervey's note.] "Death alone reveals how insignificant are the little bodies of men." From Juvenal's *Satire* X, lines 172-173.

2 From Edward Young's *Night Thoughts* (1742), Night I, line 58.

3 Psalm 90.12: "So teach us to number our days, that we may apply our hearts unto wisdom."

4 Appearing gloomy or sullen.

black-browed arches, amidst these mouldy walls, and surrounded by such rueful objects; where melancholy, deepest melancholy, for ever spreads her raven wings. Let me now emerge from the damp and dreadful obscurity. Farewell, ye seats of desolation, and shades of death! Gladly I revisit the realms of day.

Having cast a superficial view upon these receptacles of the dead, curiousity prompts my inquiry to a more intimate survey. Could we draw back the covering of the tomb; could we discern what those are now, who once were mortals—O! how would it surprise and grieve us! Surprise us, to behold the prodigious transformation which has taken place on every individual; grieve us, to observe the dishonor done to our nature in general, within these subterranous lodgments!

Here, the sweet and winning aspect, that were perpetually an attractive smile, grins horribly a naked, ghastly skull. The eye that outshone the diamond's brilliancy, and glanced its lovely lightning into the most guarded heart: alas! where is it? Where shall we find the rolling sparkler? How are all its sprightly beams eclipsed! totally eclipsed! The tongue, that once commanded all the sweetness of harmony, and all the power of eloquence, in this strange land has "forgot its cunning."[1] Where are now those strains of melody, which ravished our ears? Where is that flow of persuasion, which carried captive our judgments? The great master of language, and of song, is become silent as the night that surrounds him. The pampered flesh, so lately clothed in purple[2] and fine linen, how is it covered rudely with clods of clay. There was a time, when the timorously nice creature would scarce "adventure to set a foot upon the ground, for delicateness and tenderness;"[3] but is now enwrapped in clammy earth, and sleeps on no softer a pillow than the ragged gravel-stones. Here, "the strong men bow

---

1 Psalm 137.5: "If I forget thee, O Jerusalem, let my right hand forget her cunning."

2 In classical times purple dyes were very expensive, and so became a color of clothing associated with wealth and status.

3 Deuteronomy 28.56 [Hervey's note.] "The tender and delicate woman among you, which would not adventure to set the sole of her foot upon the ground for delicateness and tenderness, her eye shall be evil toward the husband of her bosom, and toward her son, and toward her daughter."

themselves."[1] The nervous arm[2] is unstrung; the brawny sinews are relaxed; the limbs, not long ago the seats of vigour and activity, lie down motionless; and the bones, which were as bars of iron, are crumbled into dust.

Here, the man of business forgets all his favourite schemes, and discontinues the pursuit of gain. Here, is a total stand[3] to the circulation of merchandise, and the hurry of trade. In these solitary recesses, as in the building of Solomon's temple,[4] is heard no sound of the hammer and ax. The winding-sheet, and the coffin, are the utmost bound of all earthly devices. "Hitherto may they go, but no farther."[5] Here the sons of pleasure take a final farewell of their dear delights. No more is the sensualist anointed with oil, or crowned with rose-buds. He chants no more to the melody of the viol, nor revels any longer, at the banquet of wine. Instead of sumptuous tables, and delicious treats, the poor voluptuary is himself a feast for fattened insects; the reptile riots in his flesh; "the worm feeds sweetly on him."[6] Here also, beauty fails; bright beauty drops her lustre here. O! how her roses fade, and her lilies languish, in this bleak soil! How does the grand leveller pour contempt, upon the charmer of our hearts! how turn to deformity, what captivated the world before!

Could the lover have a sight of his once enchanting fair one, what a startling astonishment would seize him! "Is this the object I not long ago so passionately admired! I said, she was divinely fair, and thought her somewhat more than mortal. Her form was symmetry itself; every elegance breathed in her air; and all the graces

---

1 Ecclesiastes 12.3.

2 "Nervous" not in the modern sense of the word but meaning "sinewy, muscular, strong; vigorous, energetic" (OED).

3 That is, a stop, a cessation.

4 Solomon's temple, the "house of the Lord," was built without the usual noise of craftsmen according to I Kings 6.7: "And the house, when it was in building, was built of stone made ready before it was brought thither: so that there was neither hammer nor axe nor any tool of iron heard in the house, while it was in building."

5 Job 38.11, spoken by Jehovah to the sea as a demonstration of his power: "Hitherto shalt thou come, but no further; and here shall thy proud waves be stayed."

6 Job 24.20 [Hervey's note.] "The womb shall forget him; the worm shall feed sweetly on him; he shall be no more remembered; and wickedness shall be broken as a tree."

waited on her motions. It was music when she spoke: but, when she spoke encouragement, it was little less than rapture. How my heart danced, to those charming accents! And can that, which some weeks ago was to admiration lovely, be now so unsufferably loathsome? Where are those blushing cheeks? Where the coral lips? Where that ivory neck, on which the curling jet, in such glossy ringlets, flowed? With a thousand other beauties of person, and ten thousand delicacies of action?[1] Amazing alteration! Delusory bliss! Fondly I gazed upon the glittering meteor. It shone brightly, and I mistook it for a star, for a permanent and substantial good. But how is it fallen! fallen from an orb not its own! And all that I can trace on earth, is but a putrid mass."[2]

Lie, poor Florella![3] lie deep, as thou dost, in obscure darkness. Let night with her impenetrable shades always conceal thee. May no prying eye be witness to thy disgrace; but let thy surviving sisters think upon thy state, when they contemplate the idol in the glass. When the pleasing image rises gracefully to view, surrounded with a world of charms, and flushed with joy at the consciousness of them all, then, in those minutes of temptation and danger, when vanity uses to steal into the thoughts, then let them remember what a veil of horror is drawn over a face which was once beautiful and brilliant as theirs. Such a seasonable reflection might regulate the labours of the toilet, and create a more earnest solicitude to polish the jewels than to varnish the casket. It might then become their highest ambition to have the mind decked with divine virtues, and dressed after the amiable pattern of their Redeemer's holiness.

And would this prejudice their persons, or depreciate their charms? Quite the reverse! It would spread a sort of heavenly glory over the finest set of features, and heighten the loveliness of

---

1 "Quo fugit Venus? Heu! Quoue color! decens / Quo motus? Quid habis illius, illius, / Quæ spirabat amores, / Quæ me surpuerat mihi?" Horace [Hervey's note.] From Horace, *Odes* IV, stanza 13: "Where has Venus gone? Alas! Where that color? Where the graceful motion? what is left of her, of her who, breathing the spirit of love, robbed me of myself?"

2 This passage in the *Meditations* also recalls, generally, Hamlet's contemplation of Yorick's skull.

3 Poetic name for a beautiful and beloved woman (from the Latin for "blooming" or "flowering").

every other engaging accomplishment. What is yet a more inviting consideration, these flowers would not wither with nature, nor be tarnished by time, but would open continually into richer beauties, and flourish even in the winter of age. But the most incomparable recommendation of these noble qualities is, that from their hallowed relics, as from the fragrant ashes of the phoenix, will ere long arise an illustrious form, bright as the wings of angels, lasting as the light of the new Jerusalem.[1]

[. . .]

Musing upon these melancholy objects, a faithful remembrancer suggested from within, "Must this sad change succeed in me also? Am I to draw my last gasp, to become a breathless corpse, and be what I deplore?[2] Is there a time approaching, when this body shall be carried out upon the bier, and consigned to its clay-cold bed? While some kind acquaintance, perhaps, may drop one parting tear; and cry, Alas! my brother! Is the time approaching?" Nothing is more certain. A decree, much surer than the laws of the Medes and Persians,[3] has irrevocably determined the doom.

Should one of these ghastly figures burst from his confinement, and start up in frightful deformity before me; should the haggard skeleton lift a clattering hand, and point it full in my view; should it open the stiffened jaws, and, with a hoarse tremendous murmur

---

1 A reference to the "new Jerusalem" of Revelations 21-22: "And the city had no need of the sun, neither of the moon, to shine in it: for the glory of God did lighten it, and the Lamb is the light thereof. And the nations of them which are saved shall walk in the light of it: and the kings of the earth do bring their glory and honour into it."

2 I pass, with melancholy state, / By all these solemn heaps of fate; / And think, as soft and sad I tread / Above the venerable dead, / "Time was, like me, they life possess'd, / And time will be when I shall rest." Parnel [sic] [Hervey's note.] This passage is a slight misquotation of Thomas Parnell's "Night-Piece on Death," lines 23-27.

3 "Ancient Indo-European people who established an empire in Media, southwest of the Caspian Sea and including most of Persia (now Iran), in the 7th cent. BC" (OED). "The law of the Medes and the Persians" is proverbial, referring to something as irrevocable and unchangeable; the Medes, and their descendants the Persians, were noted for developing some of the earliest codes of law. The phrase occurs in three times in Chapter 6 of the Book of Daniel.

break this profound silence; should it accost me, as Samuel's appa-
rition addressed the trembling king, "The Lord shall deliver thee
also into the hands of death. Yet a little while, and thou shalt be
with me."[1] The solemn warning, delivered in so striking a manner,
must strongly impress my imagination. A messenger in thunder
would scarce sink deeper. Yet there is abundantly greater reason to
be alarmed by that express declaration of the Lord God Almighty,
"Thou shalt surely die."[2] Well then, since sentence is passed; since I
am a condemned man, and know not when the dead warrant may
arrive, let me die to sin, and die to the world, before I die beneath
the stroke of a righteous God. Let me employ the little uncertain
interval of respite from execution in preparing for a happier state
and a better life. That, when the fatal moment comes, and I am
commanded to shut my eyes upon all things here below, I may
open them again, to see my Saviour in the mansions above.

Since this body, which is so fearfully and wonderfully made,
must fall to pieces in the grave; since I must soon resign all my
bodily powers to darkness, inactivity, and corruption, let it be my
constant care to use them well, while I possess them. . . . May all
my members, devoted entirely to my divine Master, be the willing
instruments of promoting his glory!

Then, ye embalmers, you may spare your pains. These works of
faith and labours of love, these shall be my spices and perfumes.
Enwrapped in these, I would lay me gently down, and sleep
sweetly in the blessed Jesus, hoping that God will "give command-
ment concerning my bones,"[3] and one day fetch them up from the
dust, as silver from the furnace, purified, "I say not seven times,
but seventy times seven."[4]

---

1 1 Samuel xxviii.19. [Hervey's note.]

2 A phrase that appears a number of times in the Old Testament, it is first spoken
by God in Genesis 2:17, warning Adam of the consequences of eating the fruit of
the tree of the knowledge of good and evil.

3 Adapted from Hebrews 11:22: "By faith Joseph, when he died, made mention
of the departing of the children of Israel; and gave commandment concerning
his bones."

4 From Matthew 18:21-22: "Then came Peter to him, and said, Lord, how oft
shall my brother sin against me, and I forgive him? till seven times? Jesus saith
unto him, I say not unto thee, Until seven times: but, Until seventy times seven."

[. . .]

O ye timorous souls, that are terrified at the sound of the pass-
ing bell, that turn pale at the sight of an opened grave, and can
scarce behold a coffin, or a skull, without a shuddering horror; ye
that are in bondage to the grisly tyrant, and tremble at the shaking
of his iron rod, cry mightily to the Father of your spirits, for faith
in his dear Son. Faith will free you from your slavery.[1] Faith will
embolden you to tread on (this fiercest of) serpents. . . .

[The following three paragraphs conclude the *Meditations*:]

Now, madam, lest my meditations set in a cloud, and leave any
unpleasing gloom upon your mind, let me once more turn to the
brightening prospects of the righteous. A view of them and their
delightful expectations may serve to exhilarate the thoughts which
have been musing upon melancholy subjects, and hovering about
the edges of infernal darkness. Just as a spacious field, arrayed
in cheerful green, relieves and reinvigorates the eye which has
fatigued itself by poring upon some minute, or gazing upon some
glaring object.

The righteous seem to lie by, in the bosom of the earth, as a
weary pilot in some well-sheltered creek, till all the alarms which
infest this lower world are blown over. Here they enjoy safe
anchorage, are in no danger of foundering amidst the waves of
prevailing iniquity, or of being shipwrecked on the rocks of any

---

1 "Death's terror is the mountain faith removes; / 'Tis faith disarms destruc-
tion.— / Believe, and look with triumph on the tomb." These, and other quota-
tions, I am proud to borrow from the Night Thoughts, especially from Night the
Fourth. In which energy of language, sublimity of sentiment, and the most exqui-
site beauties of poetry, are the least perfections to be admired. Almost every line
glows with devotion, rises into the most exalted apprehensions of the adorable
Redeemer, and is animated with the most lively faith in His all-sufficient media-
tion. The author of this excellent performance has the peculiar felicity of enno-
bling all the strength of style, and every delicacy of imagination, with the grand
and momentous truths of Christianity. These thoughts give the highest entertain-
ment to the fancy, and impart the noblest improvement to the mind. They not
only refine our taste, but prepare us for death, and ripen us for glory. I never take
up this admirable piece, but I am ready to cry out . . . "Inspire me with such a
spirit, and life shall be delightful, nor death itself unwelcome." [Hervey's note.]

powerful temptation. But ere long we shall behold them hoisting the flag of hope, riding before a sweet gale of atoning merit and redeeming love, till they make, with all the sails of an assured faith, the blessed port of eternal life.

Then, may the honoured friend to whom I am writing, rich in good works, rich in heavenly tempers, but inexpressibly richer in her Saviour's righteousness; O! may she enter the harbour, like a gallant stately vessel, returned successful and victorious from some grand expedition, with acclamations, honour, and joy! While my little bark, attendant on the solemnity, and a partaker of the triumph, glides humbly after, and both rest together in the heaven, the wished for, blissful heaven, of perfect security and everlasting repose.

William Collins, "Ode to Fear"

Collins (1721-1759) was an English poet, educated at Oxford, who published his first poem at the age of eighteen and his first collection of poems by the time he was twenty-one. He was a lifelong friend of the poet Joseph Warton and knew Samuel Johnson and other important cultural figures. Yet Collins's literary output was quite small, and despite several inheritances he was usually in financial difficulty. His second and last collection of poems was published in 1746; it sold so poorly that Collins, in despair, bought the unsold copies himself and burned them. Many of Collins's planned projects never came to fruition, and after receiving a substantial inheritance in 1749 Collins's literary output came almost to a halt, due to a combination of ill health, habitual indolence, and recurring mental illness, for which Collins was briefly institutionalized. His reputation grew significantly after his death; his poetry, with its recurring delineations of powerful emotion, appealed more to Romantic sensibilities than to those which dominated the Augustan period, and the sense of Collins as an under-appreciated poet whose struggles may have resulted from poor reception of his work, and who died tragically young as a result, only added to his appeal in the waning decades of the eighteenth century. It is no surprise to find that Collins is often regarded as a "pre-Romantic" poet.

Yet as "Ode to Fear" shows in its form, Collins registered the influences of his age; this poem shows the influence, even if only casual, of classical Greek forms. Collins has divided the poem into sections—the "strophe" (the first section, which is unlabelled), the "epode," and the "antistrophe," which are adapted from structural elements in some classical Greek verse. An "epode"—from the Greek for "sung after"—most commonly refers to a section of a lyric ode which follows the opening strophe and, typically, antistrophe; Collins arranges his poem differently. An epode will often have a different metrical form, as it does here. A "strophe" originally referred to the opening segment of a choral ode in classical Greek drama; the term is now used much more generally to indicate any section or stanza, particularly of free verse. Originally, the "antistrophe" followed the strophe and employed the same metrical form. As Anna Barbauld pointed out in her introduction to an edition of Collins's poems, such a division has little relevance in English verse. She did, however, identify "Ode to Fear" as "one of the finest in the collection," particularly praising its "spirited" opening invocation of the figure of Fear.[1] Modern critics agree; Patricia Meyer Spacks, in her magisterial study of eighteenth-century supernaturalism, remarks that fear in this poem is "a major source of imaginative richness" and that "Few of his contemporaries . . . succeeded like Collins in projecting rather than merely asserting the imaginative value of the supernatural."[2]

Although not set in a graveyard, the poem's invocation—indeed, celebration—of the unnerving potency of Fear brings it within the emotional range of the Graveyard School, as does its depiction of the disturbing, sublime power of monsters, tempests, shipwreck, and ghosts stalking the Halloween night.

This poem, probably written by summer 1746,[3] was first published in Collins's *Odes on Several Descriptive and Allegoric Subjects*

1 Anna Barbauld, Introduction to *The Poetical Works of Mr. William Collins.* London: Cadell and Davies, 1797, xx.
2 Spacks, *The Insistence of Horror: Aspects of the Supernatural in Eighteenth-Century Poetry* (Cambridge, Mass.: Harvard University Press, 1962), 74.
3 Roger Lonsdale, ed. *The Poems of Gray, Collins, and Goldsmith* (New York: Longman, 1969), 412, 414, 418.

(London: Millar, 1747, although actually published in December 1746), and the text here is taken from that edition.

———————

Thou, to whom the world unknown
With all its shadowy shapes is shown;
Who see'st appall'd th' unreal scene,
While Fancy lifts the veil between:
Ah Fear! Ah frantic Fear!   5
I see, I see thee near.
I know thy hurried step, thy haggard eye!
Like thee I start, like thee disorder'd fly.
For lo, what monsters in thy train appear!
Danger, whose limbs of giant mould   10
What mortal eye can fix'd behold?
Who stalks his round, an hideous form,
Howling amidst the midnight storm;
Or throws him on the ridgy steep
Of some loose hanging rock to sleep;   15
And with him thousand phantoms join'd,
Who prompt to deeds accurs'd the mind;
And those, the fiends who, near allied,
O'er nature's wounds and wrecks preside;
Whilst Vengeance, in the lurid air,   20
Lifts her red arm, expos'd and bare,
On whom that ravening brood of fate,
Who lap the blood of sorrow, wait;
Who, Fear, this ghastly train can see,
And look not madly wild like thee?   25

EPODE

In earliest Greece to thee with partial choice
The grief-full Muse addressed her infant tongue;
The maids and matrons on her awful voice,
Silent and pale, in wild amazement hung.

Yet he, the bard who first invok'd thy name,   30
Disdain'd in Marathon[1] its power to feel:
For not alone he nurs'd the poet's flame,
But reach'd from Virtue's hand the patriot's steel.

But who is he whom later garlands grace,
Who left awhile o'er Hybla's dews to rove,[2]   35
With trembling eyes thy dreary steps to trace,
Where thou and Furies shar'd the baleful grove?

Wrapt in thy cloudy veil th' incestuous queen[3]
Sigh'd the sad call her son and husband heard,
When once alone it broke the silent scene,   40
And he, the wretch of Thebes, no more appear'd.

O Fear, I know thee by my throbbing heart,
Thy withering power inspir'd each mournful line,
Though gentle Pity claim her mingl'd part,
Yet all the thunders of the scene are thine!   45

ANTISTROPHE

Thou who such weary lengths hast past,
Where wilt thou rest, mad nymph, at last?
Say, wilt thou shroud in haunted cell,

---

1 Site of a decisive victory of Greek forces over the invading Persians in 490 BCE, it also gives its name to the modern long-distance race. The great Greek playwright Aeschylus (525-446 BCE), regarded today as the father of tragedy, fought in this battle, as the second stanza of the epode indicates.

2 A reference to the Greek dramatist Sophocles, associated with Hybla (a town in Sicily) because Hybla was famous for its honey, and Sophocles was nicknamed "the Attic [Greek] bee" for the "sweetness" of his verse.

3 In his three plays on the life of Oedipus, Sophocles tells the story of how Queen Jocasta unknowingly married her son, Oedipus (who had unwittingly killed his own father, Jocasta's husband), who thus became King of Thebes, one of the great cities of ancient Greece. Oedipus blinds himself after the truth is revealed, then flees Thebes. He dies at Colonnus, a city sacred to the Furies, the agents of revenge in classical Greek myth.

Where gloomy Rape and Murder dwell?
Or in some hollow'd seat,   50
'Gainst which the big waves beat,
Hear drowning seamen's cries in tempests brought!
Dark power, with shudd'ring meek submitted thought
Be mine to read the visions old,
Which thy awak'ning bards have told: 55
And, lest thou meet my blasted view,
Hold each strange tale devoutly true;
Ne'er be I found, by thee o'eraw'd,
In that thrice-hallow'd eve abroad,[1]
When ghosts, as cottage-maids believe,   60
Their pebbled beds permitted leave,
And goblins haunt, from fire or fen
Or mine or flood, the walks of men!
O thou whose spirit most possest
The sacred seat of Shakspeare's breast!   65
By all that from thy prophet broke,
In thy divine emotions spoke,
Hither again thy fury deal,
Teach me but once like him to feel:
His cypress wreath[2] my meed decree,   70
And I, O Fear, will dwell with thee!

William Collins, "An Ode on the Popular Superstitions of the Highlands of Scotland, Considered as the Subject of Poetry" (excerpts)

This poem, also known by its apparent original title, "Ode to a Friend on His Return etc.," was written in late 1749 or early 1750 but not published until 1788. It offers a survey of various folk beliefs and superstitions encountered in the Scottish Highlands. The friend referred to was the Scottish clergyman and dramatist John Home (1722-1808), to whom Collins had been introduced while

---

1 Halloween.

2 The cypress wreath was associated with Melpomone, the Greek muse of tragedy.

the two were in London; Collins presented the poem to Home shortly before the latter left London to return home to Scotland. The manuscript for the poem was corrupt and incomplete, leading to several attempts on the part of various people to supply the missing sections.[1]

This is a poem that is at some remove from the melancholic musings tradition of the Graveyard School, to be sure, but its energetic presentation of mystic bards and wizards, ghosts and tragic deaths, brings it within the supernaturalist tradition that will develop from both the Graveyard School and the folk ballad tradition in the mid- to late-eighteenth century.

The text of this poem is taken from *The Poetical Works of Milton, Young, Gray, Beattie and Collins* (Philadelphia: Lippincott, 1860), with lines not by Collins removed.

―――――

III.

E'en yet preserved, how often may'st thou hear,
  Where to the pole the Boreal[2] mountains run,
  Taught by the father to his listening son
Strange lays, whose power had charmed a Spenser's ear.
At every pause, before thy mind possessed,   40
  Old Runic[3] bards shall seem to rise around,
With uncouth lyres, in many-coloured vest,
  Their matted hair with boughs fantastic crowned:
Whether thou bid'st the well-taught hind[4] repeat
  The choral dirge that mourns some chieftain brave,   45
When every shrieking maid her bosom beat,
  And strewed with choicest herbs his scented grave!

―――――

1 A substantial discussion of the textual history of this poem is provided in Roger Lonsdale's *The Poems of Gray, Collins, and Goldsmith* (New York: Longman, 1969), 492-501.

2 Northern.

3 Strictly speaking, "runic" refers to ancient Scandinavian or Icelandic writing or, more loosely, culture; Collins is adapting the latter sense of the term to capture a sense of ancientness and mystery for Scottish poetry and culture.

4 Agricultural laborer.

Or whether, sitting in the shepherd's shiel,[1]
   Thou hear'st some sounding tale of war's alarms;
When at the bugle's call with fire and steel,   50
   The sturdy clans poured forth their bonny[2] swarms,
And hostile brothers met to prove each other's arms.

IV

'Tis thine to sing, how, framing hideous spells,
   In Skye's[3] lone isle the gifted wizard-seer,
Lodged in the wintry cave with [. . .]   55
Or in the depth of Uist's[4] dark forest dwells;
How they, whose sight such dreary dreams engross,
   With their own visions oft astonished droop,
When o'er the watery strath[5] or quaggy[6] moss
   They see the gliding ghosts unbodied troop.[7]   60
Or, if in sports, or on the festive green,
   Their [. . .] glance some fated youth descry,
Who now, perhaps in lusty vigour seen,
   And rosy health, shall soon lamented die.
For them the viewless[8] forms of air obey,   65
   Their bidding heed, and at their beck repair;
They know what spirit brews the stormful day,
   And heartless, oft like moody madness, stare
To see the phantom train their secret work prepare.

---

1 Temporary summer hut.
2 Considerable.
3 The Isle of Skye is the largest of the Inner Hebrides, a chain of islands off Scotland's northwest coast; it is known for its rugged beauty and would have served, in the eighteenth century, as an indicator of remoteness and, thus, a "pure" native tradition uncorrupted by civilization.
4 One of two islands in the Outer Hebrides off Scotland's northwest coast, small, rugged, and known for its ancient Celtic and pre-Celtic structures.
5 Wide valley.
6 Boggy, soft.
7 Collins is referring to "second sight," as it was known is his time: the ability to see spirits and catch glimpses of the future, including the fate of particular individuals.
8 Invisible.

VI

[Eight lines are missing.]
What though far off from some dark dell espied,   95
    His glimmering mazes cheer th' excursive[1] sight,
Yet turn, ye wanderers, turn your steps aside,
    Nor choose the guidance of that faithless light;[2]
For watchful, lurking 'mid the unrustling reed,
    At those mirk hours the wily monster lies,[3]   100
And listens oft to hear the passing steed,
    And frequent round him rolls his sullen eyes,
If chance his savage wrath may some weak wretch surprise.

VII

Ah, luckless swain,[4] o'er all unblest indeed!
    Whom late bewildered in the dank, dark fen,   105
    Far from his flocks and smoking hamlet, then!
To that sad spot his [. . .]
On him, enraged, the fiend in angry mood,
    Shall never look with Pity's kind concern,
But instant furious, rouse the whelming flood   110
    O'er its drowned banks, forbidding all return!
Or, if he meditate his wished escape,
    To some dim hill that seems uprising near,
To his faint eye the grim and grisly shape
    In all its terrors clad shall wild appear.   115
Meantime the watery surge shall round him rise,
    Poured sudden forth from every swelling source!
What now remains but tears and hopeless sighs?
    His fear-shook limbs have lost their youthly force,
And down the waves he floats, a pale and breathless corse! 120

---

1 Wandering.
2 Presumably the will o' the wisp, a mysterious light (actually produced by marsh gas) that was said to be used by various supernatural beings to lead wanderers astray.
3 The kelpie, in Scottish folklore a water-spirit, often appearing in the shape of a horse and typically malevolent.
4 Young man.

VIII

For him, in vain, his anxious wife shall wait,
  Or wander forth to meet him on his way;
For him in vain at to-fall[1] of the day,
His bairns[2] shall linger at th' unclosing gate
Ah, ne'er shall he return! Alone, if night   125
  Her travelled limbs in broken slumbers steep!
With dropping willows dressed, his mournful sprite
  Shall visit sad, perhaps, her silent sleep:
Then he, perhaps, with moist and watery hand,
  Shall fondly seem to press her shuddering cheek,   130
And with his blue-swoln face before her stand,
  And, shivering cold, these piteous accents speak:
"Pursue, dear wife, thy daily toils pursue,
  At dawn or dusk, industrious as before;
Nor e'er of me one hapless thought renew,   135
  While I lie weltering on the osiered shore,
Drowned by the Kelpie's wrath, nor e'er shall aid thee more."

IX

Unbounded is thy[3] range; with varied style
  Thy Muse may, like those feathery tribes which spring
  From their rude rocks, extend her skirting wing   140
Round the moist marge of each cold Hebrid isle,
  To that hoar pile which still its ruin shows:
In whose small vaults a pigmy-folk is found,
  Whose bones the delver with his spade upthrows,
And culls them, wondering, from the hallowed ground![4]   145
  Or thither, where beneath the showery west

---

1 Close, end.
2 Children.
3 i.e., John Home.
4 Several islands of the Hebrides had burial sites in which apparently human bones, of a strikingly small size, were found.

The mighty kings of three fair realms are laid;[1]
Once foes, perhaps, together now they rest.
No slaves revere them and no wars invade:
Yet frequent now, at midnight's solemn hour,   150
  The rifted mounds their yawning cells unfold,
And forth the monarchs stalk with sovereign power,
  In pageant robes, and wreathed with sheeny gold,
And on their twilight tombs aerial council hold.

XI

Nor need'st thou blush that such false themes engage
  Thy gentle mind, of fairer stores possessed;
  For not alone they touch the village breast,
But filled in elder time th' historic page.   175
  There, Shakespeare's self, with every garland crowned,
  In musing hour his Wayward Sisters[2] found,
  And with their terrors dressed the magic scene.[3]
From them he sung, when, 'mid his bold design,
  Before the Scot afflicted and aghast,   180
The shadowy kings of Banquo's fated line
  Through the dark cave in gleamy pageant passed.
Proceed! nor quit the tales which, simply told,
  Could once so well my answering bosom pierce;
Proceed, in forceful sounds and colours bold   185
  The native legends of thy land rehearse;
To such adapt thy lyre, and suit thy powerful verse.

---

1 One of the islands of the Hebrides was said to hold the tombs of dozens of kings of Scotland, Ireland, and Norway.

2 The witches in *Macbeth*.

3 The invocation of Shakespeare as a justification for writing about the supernatural is a variant of the final thought in Collins's "Ode to Fear," and presages Horace Walpole's use of Shakespeare for the same purpose in the preface to his *The Castle of Otranto* (1764), the first Gothic novel.

Joseph Warton, "Ode XII. On the Death of ——"

Warton (1722-1800) was an Oxford-educated English clergyman, poet, editor, translator, and literary critic. He and his brother Thomas Warton, a fellow Graveyard School poet, were the sons of Thomas Warton the Elder, a clergyman, poet, and professor of poetry at Oxford. Joseph Warton is often regarded, on the basis of poems such as the early "The Enthusiast" (1744)—a work replete with sensitive descriptions of natural beauty—as a Romantic precursor whose poetry often resisted the practices of mainstream neoclassical literature. Indeed, the "Advertisement" to Warton's *Odes on Various Subjects* begins with his declaration that "The public has been so much accustomed of late to didactic Poetry alone, that any work where the imagination is much indulged, will perhaps not be relished or regarded. But as he is convinced that the fashion of moralizing in verse has been carried too far and as he looks upon Invention and Imagination to be the chief faculties of a Poet, so he will be happy if the following Odes may be look'd upon as an attempt to bring back Poetry into its right channel." Indeed, Warton distanced himself from those neo-classical stalwarts Alexander Pope and Joseph Addison by name in various works. It is this disposition to rejuvenate poetry with imaginative energy that led Warton to incorporate into his verse dramatic, emotive, and supernaturalist elements that bring it within the scope of the Graveyard School. Warton planned a poetic collaboration with his lifelong friend William Collins which never came to fruition, although it did lead to the publication of Warton's *Odes on Various Subjects* (1746), in which all of the selections here were first published. The text presented here is taken from the second edition of *Odes on Various Subjects,* London: Dodsley, 1747.

> No more of mirth and rural joys,
> The gay description quickly cloys,
> In melting numbers, sadly slow,
> I tune my alter'd strings to woe;
> Attend, Melpomene,[1] and with thee bring   5
> Thy tragic lute, Euphranor's[2] death to sing.

---

1 Greek muse of tragedy.
2 Euphranor is a generic Greek name, in this case for the dead man who is the

Fond wilt thou be his name to praise,
For oft' thou heard'st his skilful lays;[1]
Isis[2] for him soft tears has shed,
She plac'd her ivy on his head;   10
Chose him, strict judge, to rule with steady reigns
The vigorous fancies of her listening swains.[3]

With genius, wit, and science blest,
Unshaken Honour arm'd his breast,
Bade him, with virtuous courage wise,   15
Malignant Fortune's darts despise;
Him, ev'n black Envy's venom'd tongues commend,
As Scholar, Pastor, Husband, Father, Friend.

For ever sacred, ever dear,
O much-lov'd shade accept this tear;   20
Each night indulging pious woe,
Fresh roses on thy tomb I strew,
And wish for tender Spenser's moving verse,
Warbled in broken sobs o'er Sidney's hearse;[4]

Let me to that deep cave resort,   25
Where Sorrow keeps her silent court,
For ever wringing her pale hands,
While dumb Misfortune near her stands,
With downcast eyes the Cares around her wait,
And Pity sobbing sits before the gate.   30

Thus stretch'd upon his grave I sung,

---

subject of this elegy: Thomas Warton, Joseph Warton's father.
1 A "lay" is a short poem intended to be sung; here the word is used euphemistically for the poetry of Thomas Warton the Elder.
2 Isis is the river which flows through Oxford.
3 A reference to Thomas Warton the Elder's role as a professor of poetry at Oxford University. A "swain" is a young country male, in pastoral poetry typically portrayed as singing songs to or about his beloved; here it refers more generally to the young poets studying under Warton.
4 A reference to "Astrophel," an elegy on the death of poet and courtier Sir Philip Sidney (1554-1586), by Edmund Spenser (1552-1599).

When strait my ears with murmur rung,
A distant, deaf, and hollow sound
Was heard in solemn whispers round—
Enough, dear Youth!—tho' wrapt in bliss above,   35
Well-pleas'd I listen to thy lays of love.

Joseph Warton, "To Fancy"

This poem is a fairly typical invocation of Fancy, the Muse of
creative power, whom the poet asks to inspire him in writing of
various subjects and themes; the explicit fascination with "Gothic
churches, vaults, and tombs" and with the horrors of war reveal
Warton's interest in powerful emotional states and in the liter-
ary machinery that creates them. Fellow Graveyard School poet
William Shenstone felt that this was the best of the odes inspired
by Milton's "Il Penseroso."

O parent of each lovely Muse,
Thy spirit o'er my soul diffuse,
O'er all my artless songs preside,
My footsteps to thy temple guide,
To offer at thy turf-built shrine,   5
In golden cups no costly wine,
No murder'd fatling of the flock,
But flowers and honey from the rock.[1]
O Nymph, with loosely-flowing hair,
With buskin'd[2] leg, and bosom bare,   10
Thy waist with myrtle-girdle bound,
Thy brows with Indian feathers crown'd,
Waving in thy snowy hand
An all-commanding magic wand,
Of pow'r to bid fresh gardens blow[3]   15

---

1 A reference to Deuteronomy 32.13 and Psalm 81.16.
2 Buskin: a calf-high boot worn by actors in Greek tragedies.
3 Blossom, bloom.

'Mid chearless Lapland's[1] barren snow,
Whose rapid wings thy flight convey
Thro' air, and over earth and sea,
While the vast, various landscape lies
Conspicuous to thy piercing eyes;   20
O lover of the desert, hail!
Say, in what deep and pathless vale,
Or on what hoary[2] mountain's side,
'Midst falls of water you reside,
'Midst broken rocks, a rugged scene,   25
With green and grassy dales between,
'Midst forests dark of aged oak,
Ne'er echoing with the woodman's stroke,
Where never human art appear'd,
Nor ev'n one straw-rooft cott was rear'd,   30
Where Nature seems to sit alone,
Majestic on a craggy throne;
Tell me the path, sweet wand'rer, tell,
To thy unknown sequester'd cell,
Where woodbines cluster round the door,   35
Where shells and moss o'erlay the floor,
And on whose top an hawthorn blows,
Amid whose thickly-woven boughs
Some nightingale still builds her nest,
Each evening warbling thee to rest;   40
Then lay me by the haunted stream,
Wrapt in some wild, poetic dream,
In converse while methinks I rove
With Spenser[3] thro' a fairy grove;
Till suddenly awak'd, I hear   45
Strange whisper'd music in my ear,
And my glad soul in bliss is drown'd,
By the sweetly-soothing sound!

---

1 Lapland (now spanning northern parts of Finland, Norway, Sweden, and Russia) was long associated with gloom (for its lengthy winters) and magic.
2 White, as with snow.
3 Edmund Spenser (1552-1599), best known now for *The Faerie Queene*, an allegorical romance.

Me, Goddess, by the right-hand lead,
Sometimes thro' the yellow mead,   50
Where Joy and white-rob'd Peace resort,
And Venus keeps her festive court,
Where Mirth and Youth each evening meet,
And lightly trip with nimble feet,
Nodding their lily-crowned heads,   55
Where Laughter rose-lip'd Hebe[1] leads;
Where Echo walks steep hills among,
List'ning to the shepherd's song:
Yet not these flowery fields of joy,
Can long my pensive mind employ,   60
Haste, Fancy, from the scenes of folly
To meet the matron Melancholy,
Goddess of the tearful eye,
That loves to fold her arms and sigh;
Let us with silent footsteps go   65
To charnels and the house of Woe,
To Gothic churches, vaults, and tombs,
Where each sad night some virgin comes,
With throbbing breast, and faded cheek,
Her promis'd bridegroom's urn to seek;   70
Or to some Abbey's mould'ring tow'rs,
Where, to avoid cold wint'ry show'rs,
The naked beggar shivering lies,
While whistling tempests round her rise,
And trembles lest the tottering wall   75
Should on her sleeping infants fall.
Now let us louder strike the lyre,
For my heart glows with martial fire,
I feel, I feel, with sudden heat,
My big tumultuous bosom beat;   80
The trumpet's clangors pierce my ear,
A thousand widows' shrieks I hear,
Give me another horse, I cry,

---

1 The goddess of youth, and cupbearer to the gods in Greek myth.

Lo! the base Gallic[1] squadrons fly;
Whence is this rage?——what spirit, say,   85
To battles hurries me away?
'Tis Fancy, in her fiery car,
Transports me to the thickest war,
There whirls me o'er the hills of slain,
Where Tumult and Destruction reign;   90
Where mad with pain, the wounded steed
Tramples the dying and the dead;
Where giant Terror stalks around,
With sullen joy surveys the ground,
And pointing to th' ensanguin'd field,   95
Shakes his dreadful Gorgon-shield![2]
O guide me from this horrid scene
To high-archt walks and alleys green,
Which lovely Laura[3] seeks, to shun
The fervors of the mid-day sun;   100
The pangs of absence, O remove,
For thou can'st place me near my love,
Can'st fold in visionary bliss,
And let me think I steal a kiss,
While her ruby lips dispense   105
Luscious nectar's quintessence!
When young-ey'd Spring profusely throws
From her green lap the pink and rose,
When the soft turtle of the dale
To Summer tells her tender tale,   110
When Autumn cooling caverns seeks,
And stains with wine his jolly cheeks,
When Winter, like poor pilgrim old,
Shakes his silver beard with cold,
At every season let my ear   115

---

1 French.

2 In Greek myth, the Gorgons were female monsters with hair of living snakes;
looking into their eyes turned a person to stone. Medusa is the best known of the
Gorgons. According to Homer's *Iliad*, the Greek king Agamemnon had the image
of a Gorgon on his shield.

3 A generic name for a beloved woman, from the sonnets of Petrarch.

Thy solemn whispers, Fancy, hear.
O warm, enthusiastic maid,
Without thy powerful, vital aid,
That breathes an energy divine,
That gives a soul to every line,   120
Ne'er may I strive with lips profane
To utter an unhallow'd strain,
Nor dare to touch the sacred string,
Save when with smiles thou bid'st me sing.
O hear our prayer, O hither come   125
From thy lamented Shakespeare's tomb,
On which thou lov'st to sit at eve,
Musing o'er thy darling's grave;
O queen of numbers, once again
Animate some chosen swain,   130
Who fill'd with unexhausted fire,
May boldly smite the sounding lyre,
Who with some new, unequall'd song,
May rise above the rhyming throng,
O'er all our list'ning passions reign,   135
O'erwhelm our souls with joy and pain,
With terror shake, and pity move,
Rouse with revenge, or melt with love.
O deign t' attend his evening walk,
With him in groves and grottos talk;   140
Teach him to scorn with frigid art
Feebly to touch th'unraptur'd heart;
Like light'ning, let his mighty verse
The bosom's inmost foldings pierce;
With native beauties win applause,   145
Beyond cold critic's studied laws:
O let each Muse's fame encrease,
O bid Britannia rival Greece!

Joseph Warton, "Against Despair"

Although the arrival of Patience indeed vanquishes despair, the opening stanzas of this poem show Warton's easy command of the Graveyard School's proto-Gothic atmospherics.

> Farewell thou dimpled cherub Joy,
> Thou rose-crown'd, ever-smiling boy,
> Wont thy sister Hope to lead
> To dance along the primrose mead!
> No more, bereft of happy hours,   5
> I seek thy lute-resounding bow'rs,
> But to yon' ruin'd tower repair,
> To meet the god of Groans, Despair;
> Who, on that ivy-darken'd ground,
> Still takes at eve his silent round,   10
> Or sits yon' new-made grave beside,
> Where lies a frantic suicide:
> While lab'ring sighs my heart-strings break,
> Thus to the sullen power I speak:
> "Haste with thy poison'd dagger, haste,   15
> To pierce this sorrow-laden breast!
> Or lead me at the dead of night,
> To some sea-beat mountain's height,
> Whence with headlong haste I'll leap
> To the dark bosom of the deep;   20
> Or shew me far from human eye,
> Some cave to muse in, starve and die,
> No weeping friend or brother near,
> My last, fond, fault'ring words to hear!"
> 'Twas thus with weight of woes opprest,   25
> I sought to ease my bruised breast;
> When straight more gloomy grew the shade,
> And lo! a tall majestic maid!
> Her limbs, not delicately fair,
> Robust, and of a martial air;   30
> She bore of steel a polish'd shield,

Where highly-sculptur'd I beheld
Th' Athenian[1] martyr smiling stand,
The baleful goblet in his hand;
Sparkled her eyes with lively flame,   35
And Patience was the Seraph's name;
Sternly she look'd, and stern began—
"Thy sorrows cease, complaining man,
Rouse thy weak soul, appease thy moan,
Soon are the clouds of sadness gone;   40
Tho' now in Grief's dark groves you walk,
Where grisly fiends around you stalk,
Beyond, a blissful city lies,
Far from whose gates each anguish flies:
Take thou this shield, which once of yore   45
Ulysses and Alcides[2] wore,
And which in later days I gave
To Regulus[3] and Raleigh[4] brave,
In exile or in dungeon drear
Their mighty minds could banish fear;   50
Thy heart no tenfold woes shall feel,
'Twas Virtue temper'd the rough steel,
And, by her heavenly fingers wrought,
To me the precious present brought."

---

1 Socrates [Warton's note.] Socrates, the great figure of classical Greek philosophy, was sentenced to death for corrupting the minds of Athenians and was executed by being given hemlock to drink.

2 Ulysses is the Latin name of Odysseus, the wayfaring hero of Homer's *Odyssey*; Alcides is another name for Hercules.

3 Marcus Atilius Regulus (d. 250 BCE) was a Roman politician and general who spent years as a prisoner of the Spartans; released on parole to serve as an emissary to negotiate with Rome, he instead urged his countrymen to continue their war against the Spartans, then dutifully returned to his captivity. According to the Roman poet Horace, Regulus was then executed by being placed inside a spiked barrel which was rolled downhill.

4 Sir Walter Raleigh (1552-1618) was an English explorer, courtier, and poet. He ran afoul of royal favor three times in his life, each time spending years in prison; his third term ended in his execution.

Joseph Warton, "To Superstition"

"Rome" (line 3) in this poem refers to the Roman Catholic Church, widely regarded in England as a religion of superstition and "monkish" secrecy. Catholic clergy (monks and nuns) would become the standard villains of British Gothic fiction in the late-eighteenth and early-nineteenth centuries. This ode is an *apostrophe*, a direct address to a personified Superstition.

> Hence to some Convent's gloomy isles,
> Where chearful day-light never smiles,
> Tyrant, from Albion[1] haste, to slavish Rome;
> There by dim tapers' livid light,
> At the still solemn hours of night,
> In pensive musings walk o'er many a sounding tomb.

> Thy clanking chains, thy crimson steel,
> Thy venom'd darts, and barbarous wheel,[2]
> Malignant fiend, bear from this isle away,
> Nor dare in Error's fetters bind
> One active, freeborn, British mind,
> That strongly strives to spring indignant from thy sway.

> Thou bad'st grim Moloch's[3] frowning priest
> Snatch screaming infants from the breast,
> Regardless of the frantic mother's woes;
> Thou led'st the ruthless sons of Spain
> To wond'ring India's golden plain,
> From deluges of blood where tenfold harvests rose.[4]

---

1 Poetic name for England.

2 Instruments of torture, an indirect reference to the Spanish Inquisition and other Catholic purges of "heresy."

3 Moloch, also known as Ba'al, was a Phoenician/Eastern Mediterranean deity, demonized by Christian tradition as a devil who torments mothers by stealing their children; Milton's *Paradise Lost* includes just such a depiction.

4 These lines refer to the Goa Inquisition (1560-1812), a "Portuguese Inquisition" conducted in Portugal's territories in India and southeast Asia as an attempt to root out Muslim "heresy." It was infamous for torture. Warton seems to have confused it with the Spanish Inquisition, which did not occur in India.

But lo! how swiftly art thou fled,
When Reason lifts his radiant head;
When his resounding, awful voice they hear,
Blind Ignorance, thy doating sire,
Thy daughter, trembling Fear, retire;
And all thy ghastly train of terrors disappear.

So by the Magi hail'd from far,
When Phoebus[1] mounts his early car,[2]
The shrieking ghosts to their dark charnels flock;
The full-gorg'd wolves retreat, no more
The prowling lionesses roar,
But hasten with their prey to some deep-cavern'd rock.

Hail then, ye friends of Reason hail,
Ye foes to Myst'ry's odious veil,
To Truth's high temple guide my steps aright,
Where Clarke[3] and Woolaston[4] reside,
With Locke[5] and Newton[6] by their side,
While Plato sits above enthron'd in endless light.

---

1 Phoebus was another name for Apollo, Greek god of wisdom and light, and thus often associated with the sun, as here.
2 Chariot; i.e., the rising sun.
3 Samuel Clarke (1675-1729) was an English philosopher and logician who devoted much of his work to a defense of the existence of God.
4 William Wollaston (1659-1724) was an English cleric and moral philosopher.
5 John Locke (1632-1704) was an English philosopher, extremely influential in the development of empiricism and social contract theory.
6 Isaac Newton (1643-1727) was an English scientist, mathematician, astronomer, alchemist, and physicist, inventor of calculus, creator of classical mechanics, and discoverer of the laws of motion and optics. What is notable at the end of Warton's poem is that one line mentions two famous religious philosophers while the next mentions two rationalist philosophers not known for their religious thinking. Clarke in fact wrote against some of Newton's findings and struggled to reconcile them with religious thought.

Thomas Warton, "The Pleasures of Melancholy"

Warton (1728-1790), the brother of Joseph Warton and son of the clergyman, poet, and Oxford professor of poetry Thomas Warton (generally referred to as Thomas Warton the Elder), was himself an Oxford-educated English poet who went on to become a professor of poetry at Oxford and, in 1785, Poet Laureate. *The Pleasures of Melancholy*—written in 1745, when Warton was seventeen, and published anonymously two years later; Warton published a revised version in 1755—opens with an invocation not only of a personified Contemplation, but of the sublime; the depiction of a remote mountaintop in a storm makes use of a number of characteristic elements of sublimity, from which it is only a short step to the "solemn glooms" of the poem's melancholic explorations. Although patterened after Milton's "Il Penseroso," Warton's poem explores a more powerful melancholy that links Warton closely to the Graveyard School.

The text, that of the revised version, is taken from *A Collection of Poems in Six Volumes by Several Hands* compiled and published in 1782 by James Dodsley, the brother and publishing partner of the well-known anthologist, writer, and London bookseller Robert Dodsley, whose first edition of the *Collection*—then only three volumes—appeared in 1748.

Mother of musings, Contemplation sage,
Whose grotto stands upon the topmost rock
Of Teneriff:[1] 'mid the tempestuous night,
On which, in calmest meditation held,
Thou hear'st with howling winds the beating rain   5
And drifting hail descend; or if the skies
Unclouded shine, and thro' the blue serene
Pale Cynthia rolls her silver-axled car,
Whence gazing stedfast on the spangled vault
Raptur'd thou sit'st, while murmurs indistinct   10

---

1 Teneriffe, as it is now commonly spelled, is the largest of the Canary Islands, and features a mountain that reaches over 12,000 feet. Wharton imagines a cave ("grotto") near the summit.

Of distant billows sooth thy pensive ear
With hoarse and hollow sounds; secure, self-blest,
There oft thou listen'st to the wild uproar
Of fleets encount'ring, that in whispers low
Ascends the rocky summit, where thou dwell'st   15
Remote from man, conversing with the spheres![1]
O lead me, queen sublime, to solemn glooms
Congenial with my soul; to cheerless shades,
To ruin'd seats, or twilight cells and bow'rs,
Where thoughtful Melancholy loves to muse,   20
Her fav'rite midnight haunts. The laughing scenes
Of purple Spring, where all the wanton train
Of Smiles and Graces seem to lead the dance
In sportive round, while from their hands they show'r
Ambrosial blooms and flow'rs, no longer charm;   25
Tempe, no more I court thy balmy breeze,[2]
Adieu green vales! ye broider'd meads,[3] adieu!

Beneath yon ruin'd abbey's moss-grown piles
Oft let me sit, at twilight hour of eve,
Where thro' some western window the pale moon   30
Pours her long-levell'd rule of streaming light;
While sullen sacred silence reigns around,
Save the lone screech-owl's note, who builds his bow'r
Amid the mould'ring caverns, dark and damp,
Or the calm breeze, that rustles in the leaves   35
Of flaunting ivy, that with mantle green
Invests some wasted tow'r. Or let me tread
Its neighb'ring walk of pines, where mus'd of old
The cloyster'd brother: thro' the gloomy void
That far extends beneath their ample arch   40
As on I pace, religious horror wraps

---

1 The rotating crystalline spheres to which, in the Ptolemaic model of the universe, the planets and stars are attached.

2 Tempe, a valley in eastern Greece near Mt. Olympus, had since Classical times been associated with Apollo and the Muses, the inspirers of human art and culture.

3 Fields ("meads" or meadows) "embroidered" or covered with flowers.

My soul in dread repose. But when the world
Is clad in Midnight's raven-colour'd robe,
'Mid hollow charnels¹ let me watch the flame
Of taper dim, shedding a livid glare   45
O'er the wan heaps; while airy voices talk
Along the glimm'ring walls; or ghostly shape,
At distance seen, invites with beck'ning hand
My lonesome steps thro' the far-winding vaults.
Nor undelightful is the solemn noon   50
Of night, when haply wakeful from my couch
I start: lo, all is motionless around!
Roars not the rushing wind; the sons of men
And every beast in mute oblivion lie;
All nature's hush'd in silence and in sleep.   55
O then how fearful is it to reflect,
That thro' the still globe's aweful solitude
No being wakes but me! till stealing sleep
My drooping temples bathes in opiate dews.
Nor then let dreams, of wanton folly born,   60
My senses lead through flowery paths of joy;
But let the sacred Genius of the night
Such mystic visions send, as Spenser² saw,
When thro' bewild'ring Fancy's magic maze,
To the fell house of Busyrane he led   65
Th' unshaken Britomart; or Milton knew,³
When in abstracted thought he first conceiv'd
All heav'n in tumult, and the Seraphim
Come tow'ring, arm'd in adamant and gold.

Let others love soft Summer's ev'ning smiles,   70
As, list'ning to the distant water-fall,
They mark the blushes of the streaky west;

---

1 Vaults for holding human remains.
2 Edmund Spenser (1552-1599), best known now for *The Faerie Queene*, an alle-
gorical romance. Britomart, representative of chastity and purity, is one of the
heroines of *The Faerie Queene*, Busyrane one of her antagonists.
3 John Milton (1608-1674), author of *Paradise Lost*, a poetic recounting of Lucifer's
rebellion and the Fall.

I choose the pale December's foggy glooms.
Then, when the sullen shades of ev'ning close,
Where thro' the room a blindly-glimm'ring gleam   75
The dying embers scatter, far remote
From Mirth's mad shouts, that thro' th' illumin'd roof
Resound with festive echo, let me sit,
Blest with the lowly cricket's drowsy dirge.
Then let my thought contemplative explore   80
This fleeting state of things, the vain delights,
The fruitless toils, that still our search elude,
As through the wilderness of life we rove.
This sober hour of silence will unmask
False Folly's smiles, that like the dazzling spells   85
Of wily Comus[1] cheat th' unweeting[2] eye
With blear illusion, and persuade to drink
That charmed cup, which Reason's mintage fair
Unmoulds, and stamps the monster on the man.
Eager we taste, but in the luscious draught   90
Forget the pois'nous dregs that lurk beneath.

Few know that elegance of soul refin'd,
Whose soft sensation feels a quicker joy
From Melancholy's scenes, than the dull pride
Of tasteless splendor and magnificence   95
Can e'er afford. Thus Eloise,[3] whose mind
Had languish'd to the pangs of melting love,
More genuine transport found, as on some tomb
Reclin'd, she watch'd the tapers of the dead;
Or thro' the pillar'd aisles, amid pale shrines   100
Of imag'd saints, and intermingled graves,

---

1 In Greek myth, Comus (son of Circe and Bacchus) was the god of revelry, and
was sometimes associated with beastliness. As such he is the subject of *Comus: A
Masque*, an important poem by Milton.
2 Unwitting, unknowing.
3 The story of Eloise and Abelard is a well-known medieval tale of passion and
thwarted love; it ends with the lovers banished to religious seclusion as punish-
ment for their illicit love. Alexander Pope memorialized their tragic story in his
poem "Eloise to Abelard" (1717).

Mus'd a veil'd votaress; than Flavia[1] feels,
As through the mazes of the festive ball,
Proud of her conquering charms, and beauty's blaze,
She floats amid the silken sons of dress,   105
And shines the fairest of th' assembled fair.

When azure noon-tide cheers the dædal[2] globe,
And the blest regent of the golden day
Rejoices in his bright meridian bow'r,
How oft my wishes ask the night's return,   110
That best befriends the melancholy mind!
Hail, sacred Night! thou too shalt share my song!
Sister of ebon-scepter'd Hecat,[3] hail!
Whether in congregated clouds thou wrap'st
Thy viewless chariot, or with silver crown   115
Thy beaming head encirclest, ever hail!
What tho' beneath thy gloom the sorceress-train,
Far in obscured haunt of Lapland-moors,
With rhymes uncouth the bloody cauldron bless;
Tho' Murder wan, beneath thy shrouding shade   120
Summons her slow-ey'd vot'ries to devise
Of secret slaughter, while by one blue lamp
In hideous conf'rence sits the list'ning band,
And start at each low wind, or wakeful sound:
What tho' thy stay the pilgrim curseth oft,   125
As all benighted in Arabian wastes
He hears the wilderness around him howl
With roaming monsters, while on his hoar head
The black-descending tempest ceaseless beats;
Yet more delightful to my pensive mind   130

---

1 In ancient Rome, Julia Flavia was the niece of the Emperor Domitian; he fell
passionately in love with her and arranged for her husband's death. She may have
been the inspiration for a generic "Flavia," who attracts and distracts men with
her beauty, although Warton is also referencing Alexander Pope's use of Flavia
as the name of figure in his poem "Epistle to a Lady," where she represents an
irrational pursuit of happiness.
2 Variegated, richly adorned.
3 Hecat, or Hecate, is the Greek goddess of crossroads, and also of witches and
ghosts.

Is thy return, than bloomy morn's approach,
Ev'n then, in youthful prime of opening May,
When from the portals of the saffron east
She sheds fresh roses, and ambrosial dews.
Yet not ungrateful is the morn's approach,   135
When dropping wet she comes, and clad in clouds,
While thro' the damp air scowls the louring¹ south,
Blackening the landscape's face, that grove and hill
In formless vapours undistinguish'd swim:
Th' afflicted songsters of the sadden'd groves   140
Hail not the sullen gloom; the waving elms
That hoar thro' time, and, rang'd in thick array,
Enclose with stately row some rural hall,
Are mute, nor echo with the clamors hoarse
Of rooks rejoicing on their airy boughs;   145
While to the shed the dripping poultry crowd,
A mournful train; secure the village-hind
Hangs o'er the crackling blaze, nor tempts the storm;
Fix'd in th' unfinish'd furrow rests the plough:
Rings not the high wood with enliv'ning shouts   150
Of early hunter: all is silence drear;
And deepest sadness wraps the face of things.

Thro' Pope's² soft song though all the Graces breathe,
And happiest art adorn his Attic³ page;
Yet does my mind with sweeter transport glow,   155

---

1 Gloomy, threatening.

2 Alexander Pope (1688-1744), one of the major literary figures of early eighteenth-century literature, whose insistence on elevated diction, poetic formality, classical allusion and didactic intent helped define the Augustan literary mainstream. Warton, along with his brother Joseph and William Cowper, are among the earliest poets to pursue a poetics of feeling and plain language, countering Pope and laying the groundwork for Romanticism, as the passage beginning with this line makes clear. For a fuller examination of Warton's literary-historical engagement with Pope, see Robert J. Griffin, "The Eighteenth-Century Construction of Romanticism: Thomas Warton and the Pleasures of Melancholy," *ELH* 59.4 (1992): 799-815.

3 Attic: specifically, pertaining to Athens; more generally, a reference to the neo-classical principles championed by Pope and other eighteenth-century writers.

As at the root of mossy trunk reclin'd,
In magic Spenser's wildly-warbled song
I see deserted Una[1] wander wide
Thro' wasteful solitudes, and lurid heaths,
Weary, forlorn; than when the fated fair,[2]   160
Upon the bosom bright of silver Thames,
Launches in all the lustre of brocade,
Amid the splendors of the laughing Sun.
The gay description palls upon the sense,
And coldly strikes the mind with feeble bliss.   165

Ye Youths of Albion's beauty-blooming isle,
Whose brows have worn the wreath of luckless love,
Is there a pleasure like the pensive mood,
Whose magic wont to soothe your soften'd souls?
O tell how rapturous the joy, to melt   170
To Melody's assuasive[3] voice; to bend
Th' uncertain step along the midnight mead,
And pour your sorrows to the pitying moon,
By many a slow trill from the bird of woe[4]
Oft interrupted; in embowering woods   175
By darksome brook to muse, and there forget
The solemn dulness of the tedious world,
While Fancy grasps the visionary fair:
And now no more th' abstracted ear attends
The water's murm'ring lapse, th' entranced eye   180
Pierces no longer through th' extended rows
Of thick-rang'd trees; till haply from the depth
The woodman's stroke, or distant-tinkling team,
Or heifers rustling through the brake alarms,
Th' illuded[5] sense, and mars the golden dream.   185

---

1 Una is another of the virtuous heroines in Edmund Spenser's *The Faerie Queene*.
2 The "fated fair" is a reference to the character of Belinda in Pope's "The Rape of the Lock." Warton's preference for Spenser's heroine over Pope's is a mark of his movement away from neo-classical poetics.
3 Soothing.
4 The owl.
5 Tricked, deluded.

These are delights that absence drear has made
Familiar to my soul, e'er since the form
Of young Sapphira,[1] beauteous as the Spring,
When from her vi'let-woven couch awak'd
By frolic Zephyr's hand, her tender cheek   190
Graceful she lifts, and blushing from her bow'r
Issues to cloath in gladsome-glist'ring green
The genial globe, first met my dazzled sight:
These are delights unknown to minds profane,
And which alone the pensive soul can taste.   195

The taper'd choir, at the late hour of prayer,
Oft let me tread, while to th' according[2] voice
The many-sounding organ peals on high,
The clear slow-dittyed chaunt, or varied hymn,
'Till all my soul is bath'd in ecstasies,   200
And lap'd in Paradise. Or let me sit
Far in sequester'd iles of the deep dome,
There lonesome listen to the sacred sounds,
Which, as they lengthen through the Gothic vaults,
In hollow murmurs reach my ravish'd ear.   205
Nor when the lamps expiring yield to night,
And solitude returns, would I forsake
The solemn mansion, but attentive mark
The due clock swinging slow with sweepy sway,
Measuring Time's flight with momentary sound.   210

Nor let me fail to cultivate my mind
With the soft thrillings of the tragic Muse,
Divine Melpomene, sweet Pity's nurse,
Queen of the stately step, and flowing pall.
Now let Monimia[3] mourn with streaming eyes   215

1 A generic name for a beloved woman.
2 Harmonious.
3 A character in Thomas Otway's *The Orphan* (1680). Monimia is beloved by
the brothers Castalio and Polydore; she agrees to marry Castalio but Polydore
deceives them both and spends the wedding night with Monimia. Discovering
the deception the next day, Monimia poisons herself; Polydore kills himself by
running upon his brother's sword, and Castalio then kills himself.

Her joys incestuous, and polluted love:
Now let soft Juliet in the gaping tomb
Print the last kiss on her true Romeo's lips,
His lips yet reeking from the dreadly draught;[1]
Or Jaffier kneel for one forgiving look.[2]   220
Nor seldom let the Moor of Desdemone
Pour the misguided threats of jealous rage.[3]
By soft degrees the manly torrent steals
From my swoln eyes; and at a brother's woe
My big heart melts in sympathizing tears.   225

What are the splendors of the gaudy court,
Its tinsel trappings, and its pageant pomps?
To me far happier seems the banish'd Lord
Amid Siberia's unrejoicing wilds
Who pines all lonesome, in the chambers hoar   230
Of some high castle shut, whose windows dim
In distant ken discover trackless plains,
Where Winter ever whirls his icy car;
While still-repeated objects of his view,
The gloomy battlements, and ivied spires   235
That crown the solitary dome, arise;
While from the topmost turret the slow clock,
Far heard along th' inhospitable wastes,
With sad-returning chime awakes new grief;
Ev'n he far happier seems than is the proud,   240
The potent Satrap,[4] whom he left behind
'Mid Moscow's golden palaces, to drown
In ease and luxury the laughing hours.

---

1 A reference to Shakespeare's *Romeo and Juliet*, in which Juliet feigns death;
Romeo kills himself when he discovers what he believes is her corpse, and Juliet
then commits suicide.

2 Jaffier is the main character in Thomas Otway's *Venice Preserved* (1682). Having
been driven to ruin by the father of the woman he secretly married, Jaffier joins a
band of rebels and, after a series of complications, resorts to suicide.

3 In Shakespeare's *Othello*, the Moor Othello is manipulated into murdering his
wife Desdemona.

4 A provincial governor.

Illustrious objects strike the gazer's mind
With feeble bliss, and but allure the sight,   245
Nor rouse with impulse quick th' unfeeling heart.
Thus seen by shepherd from Hymettus' brow,[1]
What dædal landscapes smile! here balmy groves,
Resounding once with Plato's voice, arise,
Amid whose umbrage green her silver head   250
Th' unfading olive lifts; her vine-clad hills
Lay forth their purple store, and sunny vales
In prospect vast their level laps expand,
Amid whose beauties glistering Athens tow'rs.
Though through the blissful scenes Ilissus[2] roll   255
His sage-inspiring flood, whose winding marge
The thick-wove laurel shades; though roseate Morn
Pour all her splendors on th' empurpled scene;
Yet feels the hoary Hermit truer joys,
As from the cliff that o'er his cavern hangs   260
He views the piles of fall'n Persepolis[3]
In deep arrangement hide the darksome plain.
Unbounded waste! the mould'ring obelisk
Here, like a blasted oak, ascends the clouds;
Here Parian[4] domes their vaulted halls disclose   265
Horrid with thorn, where lurks th' unpitying thief,
Whence flits the twilight-loving bat at eve,
And the deaf adder[5] wreathes her spotted train,
The dwellings once of elegance and art.
Here temples rise, amid whose hallow'd bounds   270
Spires the black pine, while thro' the naked street,
Once haunt of tradeful merchants, springs the grass:

---

1 Hymettus is a mountain near Athens, fabled for its honey and marble, and is used by Warton as part of his description of a sylvan landscape in classical Greece.
2 A river flowing through Athens.
3 Persepolis was an important cultural center in ancient Persia (modern Iran), plundered by Alexander the Great in 330 BCE. Its ruins were a frequent subject of paintings and travel writing.
4 Parian: made of marble from the Greek island of Paros; one of the most sought-after marbles in classical times.
5 Snakes register vibrations, but have no external organs for hearing audible sounds.

Here columns heap'd on prostrate columns, torn
From their firm base, increase the mould'ring mass.
Far as the sight can pierce, appear the spoils   275
Of sunk magnificence! a blended scene
Of moles,[1] fanes,[2] arches, domes, and palaces,
Where, with his brother Horror, Ruin sits.

O come then, Melancholy, queen of thought!
O come with saintly look, and stedfast step,   280
From forth thy cave embower'd with mournful yew,
Where to the distant curfew's solemn sound[3]
List'ning thou sitt'st, and with thy cypress bind
Thy votary's hair, and seal him for thy son.
But never let Euphrósyne[4] beguile   285
With toys of wanton mirth my fixed mind,
Nor in my path her primrose-garland cast.
Though 'mid her train the dimpled Hebe[5] bare
Her rosy bosom to th' enamour'd view;
Though Venus, mother of the Smiles and Loves,   290
And Bacchus, ivy-crown'd, in citron bow'r
With her on nectar-streaming fruitage feast:
What though 'tis hers to calm the low'ring skies,
And at her presence mild th' embattel'd clouds
Disperse in air, and o'er the face of heav'n   295
New day diffusive gleam at her approach;
Yet are these joys that Melancholy gives,
Than all her witless revels happier far;
These deep-felt joys, by Contemplation taught.

---

1 "Moles" typically refers, architecturally, to stone piers or breakwaters, but here is likely to refer to Roman-style mausoleums.

2 Fanes are shrines or temples; this passage echoes, and inverts, a passage from "Summer" in James Thomson's *Summer*: "Where palaces, and fanes, and villas rise" (769).

3 Curfew: the practice, dating from medieval times, of ringing a bell at the onset of evening. Gray's "Elegy Written in a Country Churchyard" will begin, famously, with a reference to the tolling curfew bell; Milton's influential "Il Penseroso" perhaps begins the tradition: "Oft, on a plat of rising ground, / I hear the far-off curfew sound, / Over some wide-watered shore, / Swinging slow with sullen roar" (73-76).

4 In classical Greek myth one of the three Graces, and the goddess of Joy.

5 Greek goddess of youth.

Then ever, beauteous Contemplation, hail!   *300*
From thee began, auspicious maid, my song,
With thee shall end: for thou art fairer far
Than are the nymphs of Cirrha's mossy grot;[1]
To loftier rapture thou canst wake the thought,
Than all the fabling Poet's boasted pow'rs.   *305*
Hail, queen divine! whom, as tradition tells,
Once, in his ev'ning-walk a Druid found,
Far in a hollow glade of Mona's woods;[2]
And piteous bore with hospitable hand
To the close shelter of his oaken bow'r.   *310*
There soon the sage admiring mark'd the dawn
Of solemn musing in your pensive thought;
For when a smiling babe, you lov'd to lie
Oft deeply list'ning to the rapid roar
Of wood-hung Meinai, stream of Druids old,   *315*
That lav'd his hallow'd haunt with dashing wave.

Thomas Gray, "Elegy Written in a Country Churchyard"

Gray (1716-1771) was an English poet, translator, and literary and
historical scholar, educated at Eton and Cambridge, where he was
supposed to be studying law but preferred reading and writing
poetry instead. Gray further deferred his legal studies by touring
through Europe with Horace Walpole, a friend from Eton and
son of the Prime Minister; after two years on the Continent the
two quarrelled and Gray returned separately to England. He spent
almost the entirety of his life at Cambridge, finally abandoning the
study of law when favorable resolution of family financial issues
allowed him to live independently, if modestly. Gray then devoted
himself to literary and historical studies.

---

1 Cirrha (Kirra) was a town in Greece near the temple of Delphi, sacred to Apollo.
2 Mona is the classical name of the island of Anglesey, off the coast of Wales;
it was the site of a battle, recorded by the ancient Roman historian Tacitus, in
which Roman soldiers were awed, briefly, by their encounter with Druid priests.
The Romans overwhelmed the natives, however, and cut down the "groves of
Mona," sacred to the Druid inhabitants of the island. "Meinai" (line 315) refers
to the Menai Strait, the body of water separating Anglesey from the mainland.

Gray published the "Elegy," which he had begun writing in the early or mid-1740s, only reluctantly. The poem had circulated among Gray's friends, and through them among cultured society, in manuscript form for almost a year; upon hearing that someone had submitted the work, in Gray's name, for magazine publication, Gray quickly wrote to Horace Walpole (with whom he had reconciled) requesting his friend's help in having the work published, anonymously, by the eminent London publisher Robert Dodsley. The poem appeared in February 1751, and went through four more editions by the end of the year. Its popularity continued for decades, and led to numerous imitations and parodies. In 1757 Gray was offered the post of Poet Laureate, which he declined.

The "Elegy" is one of the landmarks of Graveyard School poetry—indeed it is often identified as one of the major works of English literature—although it also marks a notable departure from Graveyard tradition in its rejection of the horrific and the supernatural. Despite the fact the first edition of the poem was illustrated with skulls and coffins, the "Elegy" eschews the "hook them with horror" approach of Blair's "The Grave" or even the calmer but still forceful Gothic atmosphere of Parnell's "Night-Piece on Death." It is, almost needless to say, very far in tone from the declamatory sermonizing of Edward Young or James Hervey. Its low key, reflective of Gray's own personality, is the key of pastoral elegy rather than proto-Gothic Graveyard verse, although Gray's elegy is generic rather than personal, and as such reveals a broadly applied pensive melancholy that leads to reflections on compassion and morality, redeemed by Christian faith at its conclusion but in a tone of calm assurance rather than dire warning.

The text is taken from *The Poems of Mr. Gray*, published by James Dodsley, London, 1768; the footnotes of that edition have been removed.

The Curfew tolls the knell of parting day,
The lowing herd wind slowly o'er the lea,[1]
The plowman homeward plods his weary way,
And leaves the world to darkness and to me.

------

1 Field or meadow.

Now fades the glimmering landscape on the sight,   5
And all the air a solemn stillness holds,
Save where the beetle wheels his droning flight,
And drowsy tinklings lull the distant folds;

Save that from yonder ivy-mantled tow'r
The moping owl does to the moon complain   10
Of such, as wand'ring near her secret bow'r,
Molest her ancient solitary reign.

Beneath those rugged elms, that yew-tree's shade,
Where heaves the turf in many a mould'ring heap,
Each in his narrow cell for ever laid,   15
The rude Forefathers of the hamlet sleep.

The breezy call of incense-breathing Morn,
The swallow twitt'ring from the straw-built shed,
The cock's shrill clarion, or the echoing horn,
No more shall rouse them from their lowly bed.   20

For them no more the blazing hearth shall burn,
Or busy housewife ply her evening care:
No children run to lisp their sire's return,
Or climb his knees the envied kiss to share.

Oft did the harvest to their sickle yield,   25
Their furrow oft the stubborn glebe[1] has broke:
How jocund did they drive their team afield!
How bow'd the woods beneath their sturdy stroke!

Let not Ambition mock their useful toil,
Their homely joys, and destiny obscure;   30
Nor Grandeur hear with a disdainful smile
The short and simple annals of the poor.

---

1 The soil of a tilled field.

The boast of heraldry, the pomp of pow'r,
And all that beauty, all that wealth e'er gave,
Awaits alike th' inevitable hour: 35
The paths of glory lead but to the grave.

Nor you, ye Proud, impute to These the fault,
If Memory o'er their Tomb no Trophies raise,
Where through the long-drawn aisle and fretted[1] vault
The pealing anthem swells the note of praise.   40

Can storied urn or animated bust
Back to its mansion call the fleeting breath?
Can Honour's voice provoke the silent dust,
Or Flatt'ry soothe the dull cold ear of death?

Perhaps in this neglected spot is laid   45
Some heart once pregnant with celestial fire;
Hands, that the rod of empire might have sway'd,
Or waked to extasy the living lyre.

But Knowledge to their eyes her ample page
Rich with the spoils of time did ne'er unroll;   50
Chill Penury repress'd their noble rage,
And froze the genial current of the soul.

Full many a gem of purest ray serene
The dark unfathom'd caves of ocean bear:
Full many a flower is born to blush unseen,   55
And waste its sweetness on the desert air.

Some village Hampden[2] that with dauntless breast
The little tyrant of his fields withstood,
Some mute inglorious Milton here may rest,
Some Cromwell[3] guiltless of his country's blood.   60

---

1 Decorated.

2 John Hampden (1594-1643) was an English politician, one of the heroes of the English Civil War for his resistance to Charles I and his championing of the rights of Parliament against excessive royal power.

3 Oliver Cromwell (1599-1658), English political and military figure who led the English Civil War against Charles I.

Th' applause of list'ning senates to command,
The threats of pain and ruin to despise,
To scatter plenty o'er a smiling land,
And read their hist'ry in a nation's eyes,

Their lot forbade: nor circumscrib'd alone   65
Their glowing virtues, but their crimes confin'd;
Forbade to wade through slaughter to a throne,
And shut the gates of mercy on mankind,

The struggling pangs of conscious truth to hide,
To quench the blushes of ingenuous shame,   70
Or heap the shrine of Luxury and Pride
With incense kindled at the Muse's flame.

Far from the madding crowd's ignoble strife,
Their sober wishes never learn'd to stray;
Along the cool sequester'd vale of life   75
They kept the noiseless tenor of their way.

Yet ev'n these bones from insult to protect
Some frail memorial still erected nigh,
With uncouth rhymes and shapeless sculpture deck'd,
Implores the passing tribute of a sigh.   80

Their name, their years, spelt by th' unletter'd muse,
The place of fame and elegy supply:
And many a holy text around she strews,
That teach the rustic moralist to die.

For who, to dumb Forgetfulness a prey,   85
This pleasing anxious being e'er resign'd,
Left the warm precincts of the chearful day,
Nor cast one longing ling'ring look behind?

On some fond breast the parting soul relies,
Some pious drops the closing eye requires;   90
Ev'n from the tomb the voice of Nature cries,
Ev'n in our Ashes live their wonted Fires.

For thee, who mindful of th' unhonour'd Dead
Dost in these lines their artless tale relate;
If chance, by lonely contemplation led,   95
Some kindred spirit shall inquire thy fate,

Haply[1] some hoary-headed Swain may say,
"Oft have we seen him at the peep of dawn
Brushing with hasty steps the dews away
To meet the sun upon the upland lawn.   100

"There at the foot of yonder nodding beech
That wreathes its old fantastic roots so high,
His listless length at noontide would he stretch,
And pore upon the brook that babbles by.

"Hard by yon wood, now smiling as in scorn,   105
Mutt'ring his wayward fancies he would rove,
Now drooping, woeful wan, like one forlorn,
Or craz'd with care, or cross'd in hopeless love.

"One morn I miss'd him on the custom'd hill,
Along the heath and near his fav'rite tree;   110
Another came; nor yet beside the rill,
Nor up the lawn, nor at the wood was he;

"The next with dirges due in sad array
Slow thro' the church-way path we saw him borne.
Approach and read (for thou can'st read) the lay,   115
Grav'd on the stone beneath yon aged thorn."

THE EPITAPH.

Here rests his head upon the lap of Earth
A Youth to Fortune and to Fame unknown.
Fair Science frown'd not on his humble birth,
And Melancholy mark'd him for her own.   120

---

1 Perhaps.

Large was his bounty, and his soul sincere,
Heav'n did a recompense as largely send:
He gave to Mis'ry all he had, a tear,
He gain'd from Heav'n ('twas all he wish'd) a friend.

No farther seek his merits to disclose,   125
Or draw his frailties from their dread abode,
(There they alike in trembling hope repose,)
The bosom of his Father and his God.

Richard Cumberland, "An Elegy Written on Saint Mark's Eve"

Cumberland (1732-1811) was a well-known and popular English novelist, essayist, and dramatist, educated at Cambridge and serving for much of his life in minor political roles assisting several leading political figures of his day. Cumberland's reputation today rests almost entirely on his dramatic works; his prose and poetry seem to garner little critical attention or respect.[1] The example of Cumberland's verse included here may not be a fair representation of his mature capabilities, however; the "Elegy" was Cumberland's first published work—printed when he was twenty-two years old

---

1 Speaking of the "Elegy," the writer and critic William Mudford remarked that Cumberland "wrote An Elegy on St. Mark's Eve, a particular period of time, when it is believed, by the superstitious, that the apparitions of all those who are to die in the course of the ensuing year, will be seen walking across the churchyard at midnight. But the public had no sympathy with so idle a tale, and the piece, which Dodsley published, passed quietly into that oblivion in which, as the author has not drawn it forth, nor I have ever seen it, it may be permitted to remain" (*A Critical Examination of the Writings of Richard Cumberland* [London: Sherwood, Neely, and Jones, 1812], I: 96. Mudford seems to be drawing from Cumberland's own assessment of the poem: "about this time I made my first small offering to the press, following the steps of Gray with another elegy, written on Saint Mark's eve, when, according to rural tradition the ghosts of those, who are to die within the year ensuing, are seen to walk at midnight across the churchyard. I believe the public were very little interested by my plaintive ditty, and Mr. Dodsley, who was publisher, as little profited." (*Memoirs of Richard Cumberland, Written by Himself* [New York: Brisban & Bannan, 1806], p. 75.)

—and, like many initial literary efforts, is strongly shaped by domi-
nant literary trends of the time: in this case, the Graveyard School
and the popularity of Gray's recently published "Elegy Written in
a Country Churchyard," with some additional coloring taken from
Parnell and Blair.[1] Cumberland has increased the Gothic intensity
of Gray's mild melancholy, beginning with his title, which invokes
the British folk superstition—one on which John Keats began, but
did not complete, a poem—that on the Eve of St. Mark (April 24),
the spirits of all who are to die in the coming year will enter the
parish church in the hours around midnight. The Gothic trappings
are, as with Blair and Parnell, concentrated in the opening section
of the poem, as its concluding movement is a lengthy moralized
speech by a ghost who seems to have carefully read Gray's poem.

The text is taken from the anonymous first—and only—edition,
published in London by M. Cooper, 1754.

Fraught with malicious storm a louring cloud
Disrobes the firmament, that glow'd with light,
While from yon rain-beat porch the raven loud
Ushers with hideous shriek the startled night.

The spider ticking from the fretted wall,   5
And humming beetle sing their drowsy knell,
The sightless batts a shrill assembly call,
And dire events in dismal sounds foretell.

To this lone waste, this dark and dreary vale,
Where mould'ring sleeps the once-inspired clay,   10
(If so I read aright the gossip tale,)
Each destin'd shade directs its gloomy way.

How some the churlish and rough whirlwind ride
Mingling I've learnt amid the village throng,

---

[1] It may be noted, however, that Cumberland was known, throughout his entire
professional life, to be a frequent borrower of other writers' work. The play-
wright Richard Sheridan, in his 1779 drama *The Critic*, satirized Cumberland as a
character named Sir Fretful Plagiary.

Others, like sailing meteors, nimbly glide,   15
Or stalk slow-pac'd the thick-strew'd tombs among.

  Each, as her mind presents the varied shape,
With greedy horror tells her heedful friend,
She, o'er the blue and glim'ring lamp agape,
Feels ev'ry magic hair to start on end.   20

  Warn'd by that dying flame at length to part
Each trembling guest slips to her several bed,
Whilst I, fond swain, bewail a slighted heart,
And breathe my sorrows to the senseless dead.

  But thou, that haunt'st the cloister-circled tower,   25
Echo, I ween, dost hear my wailing moan,
For sure as comes this sad and secret hour,
Thy ill-tim'd sympathy returns each groan.

  Thou too, pale cypress, whose forewarning leaf
Strews the dull mansions of th' intombed dead,   30
Say, is it then in friendship to my grief
Thou point'st where soon shall rest this witless head?

  Yet for thou'rt wont my humble brow to crown,
And eke my pipe thy wreathed bows sustain,
If chance my fate should reach some shepherd clown[1]   35
Tell, for you know, the story of my pain.

  Nor may thy bark its many a wound abide,
The name which marreth us shall ruin thee,
Nor shall the wise this simple talk deride,
Can I find ought more stony-deaf than she?   40

  Tho' the proud trunk heaven's full despight doth brave,
Nathless it yieldeth to the subtle wind,
Tho' the rock frown, the patient prostrate wave
By long assault doth sure admittance find:

---

1 Rustic.

Yet she unmov'd my mournful sigh can hear,   45
And sterner than the knotted oak remain,
Yet she remorseless sees my falling tear,
And less than lifeless flint regards my pain.

But strait the sluggish hemlock springing round
Wafts to my slumb'ring sense the loaded gale,   50
While night, who now bad hush each ruder sound,
Soft o'er my temples spreads her sable veil.

The balmy influence of long-lacked sleep
To sweet oblivion lulls my soothed breast,
The winds that erst did lash the vexed deep,   55
The storm of raging troubles sinks to rest.

O Sleep! how near to death art thou allied!
O Death! what art thou but a longer dream?
Nor wot I of the ill that can betide,
When thou so still and so serene dost seem.   60

Strange sights oppress my fancy's wakeful eye,
A gastly troop of meager ghosts appear,
There one in pensive plight I do espy
To close with uncouth gait the creeping rear.

Oh then! thou spirit forlorn, instruct me soon   65
Why shrinks my soul at thy partic'lar sight,
Say why thou visit'st thus the paly moon
Doubling the native horrors of the night.

Still in the most dejected front I see
Some struggling spark, some faint upholding ray,   70
Alas! why comes not the same hope to thee?
Thy mien is sadness, and thy look dismay.

At this he waves his head, and strikes his breast,
And thrice in piteous sort he doth assay,

The eloquence of woe bespeaks the rest,   75
And stops the fault'ring accent on its way.

    At length—"I warn thee, mark you cheerless train,
Know, ere this eve returns, to each is given,
Or to endure the fierce assault of pain,
Or freely tread the star-pav'd courts of heaven.   80

    "See many a faded cheek and furrow'd brow,
That witness dire dismay, and lost estate,
What soul so confident but fears to know
That righteous sentence which must seal its fate?

    "The mimic tyrant whose contemptuous mind   85
Ne'er smil'd in pity on the wretch beneath,
At the last hour in serious truth shall find
No flattery in the chill embrace of death.

    "Awhile he stood in lawless pow'r unharm'd;
What pow'r shall screen him at that vengeful time,   90
When every eye shall wake, each hand be arm'd
To shame his folly, and correct his crime?

    "What tho' the pageantry of labor'd woe
Should bid the marble rise to solemn pride;
Such the false grandeur of its bootless shew,   95
It gilds the glittering slave it meant to hide.

    "The ruddy swain who leaves his quiet sleep,
Chiding with early song the ling'ring dawn,
Whose sober care directs the trooping sheep
Or to the willowy brook, or pastur'd lawn,   100

    "To whom, as mindful of his lowly birth,
Nature an universal blank hath given,
Soon when he quits this dull unfriendly earth,
Shall rest approved by the voice of heaven.

"For his poor steps would ne'er presume to tread   *105*
Those much-worn paths where nobler feet had been,
Dar'd not to follow where they boldly led,
But left to greater souls the privilege to sin.

"The charms of wit, the joys of youth shall fade,
And beauty's early bloom shall wither'd be,   *110*
A killing blast shall strike th' unwary maid,
That heart will bleed, tho' now it tortures thee.

"The noise of sports, the luxury of dress,
All giddy gay desires shall wear away,
Each splendid vanity forget to bless,   *115*
And she all wan with wasting grief decay.

"For neither titled fame, nor hoarded wealth,
Nor beauty's early bloom hath power to save,
Nor sober industry, nor ruddy health
Can hold one victim from th' untimely grave.   *120*

"But idly sure the needful time we spend,
While as more weighty words I should impart,
O let thy reason's dearest thought attend,
And read th' awak'ning lesson to thine heart.

"Far be thy custom'd place where yonder steep   *125*
High over-arch'd surveys the distant stream,
Think what a giddy height it is to leap,
Think, and beware, nor slight your warning dream.

"To cleave the yielding unsubstantial air,—
To light transfixt upon the pointed rock,—   *130*
O think!——Yet, if thy steady sense can dare
To meet with welcome hail this mortal shock.

"Too soon thou wilt regret thine evil plight,
That spirit howe'er resolv'd must needs be griev'd,

When hell's dread regions open to the sight,   135
Regions, which eye ne'er saw, nor heart conceiv'd.

"And well I ween the wretch, whoe'er he be,
That swims that gulph shall never pass it more,
It is a merciless and thwarting sea,
That ne'er will waft him to the once-left shore.   140

"Then rue the hapless while, thou foolish swain,
When thou wast trapped by those witching eyes,
It is the galled conscience gives the pain,
That fell insatiate worm, that never dies.

"To the gross mould, from whence it did begin,   145
After short time the kindred clay returns,
While the more active light which shines within,
The unexhausted lamps for ever burns.

"That quick'ning portion of the Spirit divine
Shall surely last thro' endless time to come,   150
Nor seek her airy motions to confine
Within her shallow limits of the tomb.

"Perchance some fury, like this scornful fair,
May haunt thy walks, and every step attend,
Cloath'd in each frown the same she may appear,   155
Save this a mortal, that a deathless fiend.

"Yet, worthless as I am, I do not mean
With curious and affrontive zeal to pry,
Where heaven hath drawn its curtain o'er the scene,
And shut the clouded prospect from mine eye.   160

"This only and important truth I learn,
When the last trump shall wake the lazy dead,
No vain pretence, no trifling fond concern
Shall rouse the shrouded sinner from his bed.

"Hence then, and mingle in the mirthful train,   165
With them resume thy long-neglected crook,
Awake to sprightly stop the pipe again,
Cheer thy sad heart, and smooth thy love-worn look.

"If so thine hallow'd soul thou e'er didst love,
As heaven in gentle mercy leans to thee,   170
If there be damn'd below, or saints above,
If thou art mock'd of her, or mourn'd of me,

"If ought can move thee——fly this wily snare
That may seduce thee to this fearful end,"
(When strait dissolving in the viewless air)   175
"Awake!" he cries, "bestir thee, and amend!"

Henry Jones, "The Relief; or Day Thoughts. A Poem. Occasioned by The Complaint, or Night Thoughts" (excerpts)

Jones (1721-1770) was an Irish poet and playwright who, despite success with his first volume (published by subscription in 1754 and underwritten by his patron, the English politician Philip Stanhope, 4th Earl of Chesterfield) and with his first play, struggled to remain solvent (and sober) throughout his life.

No exploration of the Graveyard School can be complete without some consideration of various responses to it, and while the host of imitative works that constitute so much of the genre give a fair indication of its popularity and general appeal, there was, as well, a sceptical and negative reaction. That reaction is powerfully illustrated by Jones's "The Relief," which urges in no uncertain terms a rejection of the Gothic horrors and dark emotions exploited by so many Graveyard Poets—and with which Jones was clearly quite familiar—and urges instead both a recognition of Nature's beauty and Life's richness as evidence of the immanent presence of the divine and the understanding that life's sorrows and pains are terrible enough. Jones's passionate rejection, expressed in the language of Christian consolation, of Graveyard School tropes and themes is all the more striking for his secular background.

The text of this poem is taken from its first publication: *The Relief* (London: J. Robinson, 1754).

———

——Assert Eternal Providence,
And justify the ways of God to Men.

Milton[1]

Why all this solemn apparatus? why?
Why all this din, about a worm's concerns?
The child of dust, of misery, of scorn;
The prey of flattery, the food of pride;
Vain expectation's bubble, reason's dupe;   5
By frantic hope misled; and lost in whirls
Of visionary scenes, enchanted piles,[2]
The fancy'd fabricks built by vanity
Upon the vapours of a heated brain;
By craft kept up in injur'd reason's spight,   10
By custom held in reverential awe;
The sacred bugbears of a frighted world;
To serve the purpose of designing knaves,
And yoke the neck of fools?——

The awful temples, tombs, and tolling clocks;   15
The midnight damps that drop from weeping yews,
Beneath th' eclipsed moon, (the Scriech-Owl's Haunt)
Drenching the locks of some night-watching pilgrim,
Who sits, in dismal meditation wrapt,
And brainsick horror, o'er yon mould'ring grave,   20
By time defac'd, and frequent footsteps worn:
No mark remaining, but th' erected stone
Inscrib'd with narratives uncouth, of birth,
Of death, (a mute unmeaning blank between)
The chissel's story to the pensive hind,   25
Who painful pores upon the wasted words,
And puzzling scans th' imperfect characters

---

1 From Milton's *Paradise Lost*, I: 25-26.
2 Extensive buildings.

Half hid in nettles, and perplex'd with thorn.
Here, moping superstition nightly broods;
Here counts the clarion of the bird of dawn,   30
Whose dreary note proclaims the ebbing night,
And drives the frighted goblin to his haunt,
The time-recording cock:[1] or to the winds
Repeats her unavailing vespers o'er;
The winds, that mournful yell, from ecchoing vaults,   35
And broken sepulchres, their groaning accents;
As if they wail'd the long-departed dead,
Who slumber, deep in everlasting night,
Within these dreary mansions, where no dawn
Returns. Thus, hideous Melancholy dips   40
Her pencil, still, in dark delusive tincts,
And paints the face of things; detested groupe!
A landskip fit for Hell: the work of fiends!

Let rescu'd Fancy turn aloft her eye,
And view yon wide extended arch; behold   45
Yon crystal concave, studded with the gems,
The radiant gems of Heav'n, that nightly burn
In golden lamps, and gild th' ætherial space;
That smiling vault, that canopy of stars,
Those cluster'd constellations! Mark yon moon   50
Serenely shine; (her borrow'd lustre full;)
The mountain tops, the rocks, the vales, the lawns,
By her set off, adorn'd, and made delightful:
The boundless main, a polish'd mirror now,
Reflecting, from its bosom, back, the vast,   55
The wonderful, the glorious, glad appearance!
Bright visions echo to th' enchanted eye;
As, on the ear, harmonious sounds return

---

1 An allusion to *Hamlet*, in which the Ghost of Hamlet's father disappears with crowing of a cock, at which Horatio remarks "I have heard, / The cock, that is the trumpet to the morn, / Doth with his lofty and shrill-sounding throat / Awake the god of day; and, at his warning, / Whether in sea or fire, in earth or air, / The extravagant and erring spirit hies / To his confine: and of the truth herein / This present object made probation" (I.i.149-156).

In mimic notes, responsive made to fill,
To charm the fancy, with repeated transport.   60
All these, in their eternal round, rejoice;
All these, with universal praise, proclaim
Their Great Creator; bountiful, benign,
Immensely good, rejoicing in his creatures!

[. . .]

What should we fear? This glorious prospect brings
No dreadful phantom to the frighted eye,   75
No terror to the soul; 'tis transport all!
Here fancy roves, in sweet variety
For ever lost; her native bliss. For her,
The blue ethereal arch expands; her table
Spread out with all the dainties of the sky,   80
Imagination's rich regale. For her
The clouds absorb the ev'ning ray; and drink
The liquid gold, which stains their fleecy sides
With all the tincts of Heav'n, transmitted through
A thousand diff'rent strainers to the eye,   85
And thence upon the ravish'd soul diffus'd.
The blushing beauties of the infant morn,
Aurora's¹ saffron beam; the splendid bow,
Whose copious arch was bent by hands divine,
An emblem form'd of half eternity,   90
By angels robe'd in all the aggregate,
Th' unblended aggregate, of various day,
Of Heav'n's own day; and from its sun-beams drawn,
In all its tinges dipt, its glories dress'd.
For her, the smiling earth puts on her mantle;   95
Her mantle green, with purple mix'd, with gold,
With all the liv'ries of the youthful spring,
To wake new raptures in the heart of man;
And fill his soul with gratitude immense.
All these are Reason's treasures, stores of thought;   100

---

1 Greek goddess of the dawn.

Reflection's unexhausted funds, replete
With matter for her own delightful task.
Here wisdom works at large; here smiling builds,
For sweet content, a homely shed; where joy,
Where gladness, visit oft her temp'rate guests,   105
And make their willing stay: here, undisturb'd,
They reign, they revel, take their fill of all
That Nature (ever bounteous Mother) yields,
For use or pleasure: but excess avoid;
That fiend accurs'd, whose bloated visage wan,   110
And troubled eye, betray her inward pang,
Which shakes severe her paralytic nerve,
Her tott'ring frame; e'er death, by Nature taught,
And time, in season due, with gentle hand
Can cut the wasted thread: excess usurps   115
With force th' abortive task, and vindicates
Her prey——Come all, ye family of Joy;
Ye children of the chearful hour, begot
By wisdom on the virtuous mind; O, come!
Come innocence, in conscious strength secure;   120
Come courage, foremost in the manly train;
Come all; and in the honest heart abide,
Your native residence, your fortress still,
From real or from fancy'd evils free:
O, come; indignant, drive out, far beyond   125
The utmost precincts of the human breast,
Beyond the springs of hope, the cells of joy,
And ev'ry mansion where a virtue lives;
O drive far off, for ever drive that bane,
That hideous pest, engender'd deep in Hell,   130
Where Stygian[1] gloom's condens'd dimension'd darkness
Contains, within its dire embrace, that monster
Horrid to sight, and by the frighted Furies
In their dread pannic Superstition nam'd!

---

1 Stygian refers to the River Styx, which separated the earth from the underworld
in Greek myth.

The close contracted span of human life   135
Is dearly purchas'd by the sons of care;
Since sickness, disappointment, pain, and death,
A thousand vary'd unavoided evils,
Prey hourly on the vexing heart of man,
Like officers of wrath, let loose by pride,   140
To raise the rigid tax on wretched being;
A dreadful int'rest, for a sum so small!
Enough are these, alas, to gall and sting!
What need we then for fancy'd evils seek,
To scare the soul, and harrow up the heart,   145
Already toss'd, and torn, and broken down
By evils of its own contrivance? Evils
Still adverse found, to Nature's wholesome ways;
The bane of ev'ry bliss, and social joy:
Ambition, with her train; and luxury,   150
With custom link'd, with fell corruption join'd,
Led up by fashion in her frantic dance,
Follow'd by misery, despair, and death.
For pity's sake, forbear to haunt the world
With hideous spectres, and fantastic forms;   155
With harpy footed Furies, fearful phantoms,
Everlasting torments, and unquenched fire.
O say, what horrid scenes are these you draw!
What portraits of th' Almighty! hence, away;
See reason turns the face aside, see Nature   160
Start at the monstrous form! and cry aloud
Through all her works, it is not like. Forbear,
Ye croaking ministers of midnight dreams,
Ye madding trumpeters of false report,
Forbear to pour your ghastly images   165
On truth, nor give just Providence the lie.
What's a church-yard, what I pray? This horrid goblin
Array'd in midnight weeds by frantic fancy
I' th' solemn moon-struck hour? A bed prepar'd
For silent unperceiving dust that once   170
To human thought was wedded, vital clay,
Divorc'd by death to join the general mother,

Divided far from its companion dear,
Th' immortal soul, that now above the stars
Forgets this trampled clod, and joins the choirs   175
Of bliss, 'tis gloomy all and solemn. Hark,
Was it the clock that told the passing hour,
And told it too at midnight? when deep silence
And hideous darkness reign o'er half the world:
It was.——What then? it tells it too at noon,   180
Amidst the noise and sunshine of that hour,
The clock that calls to business or to pleasure
The sons of avarice and sensual joy.
What tragic bustle when an engine strikes!
Shall meer negations, unsubstantial shades,   185
Such monsters form, to fright th' unthinking crowd
To fancy tangible, to terror real?
Let monks, let nurses put these vizors[1] on,
To startle bigots and astonish babes;
Reason scorns, and common sense defies 'em;   190
And who so weak to shudder at the sound
Of yon departed moment fled for ever!
Or with his sad foreboding sighs keep time
To each elapsing sand that silent flows
From his exhausting glass with breaking heart   195

[. . .]

Rise up, thou glorious attribute! assert
Thy native dignity; rise up once more,
In injur'd man's defence; rise, Reason, rise;
And with thy ray, invincible, drive far   335
These fancy-form'd, these monster-stalking shades,
These giant shapes, by Melancholy seen,
With horrid strides, to glance athwart the sick
Imagination, curtain'd in already
By superstition's hand, and terrify'd   340
By her magnific glass, reflecting still

---

1 Mask, deception.

The midnight goblin, and the ghastly shade.
In justice to thy Great Creator, rise,
To human nature, and to injur'd truth:
Thou attribute divine! thou ray of God!   345
Immortal reason! come, and with thee bring
In thy exulting train, invincible,
The honest purpose, and the chearful heart;
The joyful fancy, fill'd with images
Of truth, of science, and of social Love.   350
Let friendship too be there; O, closer to
Thy sacred breast embrace her; closer yet:
She comes, she comes, from heav'n, her native place,
And with her see whate'er deserves thy wish,
Whate'er is cordial, comely, and humane,   355
Whate'er is rational, whate'er is pure;
The handmaid of th' Almighty, sent to bless
The suffering sons of men; to soften sorrow;
To sweeten care: seraphic guest! all hail!
Thou, dearer than relations dear; than son,   360
Than father, brother, wife, or tender tye;
Thou child of sweet benevolence, begot
By Reason on the virtuous heart; arise,
Thou best belov'd of Heav'n! thou joy, thou crown
Of man, arise; and from thy sacred presence   365
Drive far each hideous apparition, form'd
By midnight Hags, beneath th' abortive gloom,
The bane of ev'ry social bliss; thy bane.

[. . .]

Why should approaching death affright the soul?
Why reason start, and turn away from him,
Who comes to bring us home from misery,   450
Mistake and fear? the messenger of Heav'n!
No grisly terror to the honest heart,
If God be just.

[. . .]

        Away with such
Contagion from the eyes of man; with tombs,
With church-yards, tolling midnight clocks; away   *490*
With fun'ral pomp, with gloomy mock parade,
With sable hearses, scutcheons, nodding plumes,[1]
And all the dismal pageantry of death.
Let fancy drive these goblins from her sight;
Let mirth, let joy, let transport fill their place;   *495*
Philosophy and faith shall hand them in,
And Nature bid them welcome. O rejoice,
Distinguish'd man! rejoice, how bless'd thy lot,
Whilst reason is thy guide! look up, look up,
O see where hope stands pointing to the sky,   *500*
On sun-beams rais'd, by angels beckon'd on;
See her celestial flight, where thou shalt follow.
Turn thy eyes thither; thither lift thy heart.
Thy gracious God awaits thee there; to Him
Thou shalt return in season due, to taste   *505*
Immortal transports! thy beginning, end,
Thy center, Father, saviour, and thy friend.

---

1 The language of lines 491-492 closely echoes descriptions in Parnell's "Night-Piece on Death" and Blair's "The Grave."

William Mason, "Ode: On Melancholy"

Mason (1725-1797) was a Cambridge-educated English poet, satirist, minister, amateur musician and musical scholar, abolitionist, antiquarian, and innovative landscape designer. Moderate financial independence in middle age gave Mason the leisure to devote much of his later life to literary and landscaping pursuits. He was a close friend of Thomas Gray, for whom he served as literary executor and biographer, and of Horace Walpole until political differences led to their estrangement; he was a lifelong enemy—and satiric and critical target—of Samuel Johnson. Mason, with his strong interest in the picturesque, is often regarded as a transitional figure between mainstream neo-classicism and Romanticism, although he is consistently positioned as a minor poet, too often imitative of Milton and of his eighteenth-century contemporaries, whose appeal was largely to an audience only of his own moment; little interest in his works can be found even in the early Romantic period, and it is not unusual to find anthologies of eighteenth-century verse in which Mason is unrepresented. Yet Mason's interest in the picturesque and in a more emotionally resonant poetics—as well, surely, as his friendship with Gray—led him to compose several works that are firmly within the Graveyard School tradition, though it is certainly true, as one scholar has remarked, that Mason's poetic preference was more for "pensive sentimentalizing on rural scenes, rather than the more strenuous horrors in the style of the Gothic romance."[1]

This elegy, sometimes also known as "Ode: To A Friend," was first published in 1756; the text is from *Odes*, 2nd edition (Cambridge: Bentham, 1756).

I

Ah! cease this kind persuasive strain,
Which, when it flows from Friendship's tongue,
However weak, however vain,

-----

1 John W. Draper, *William Mason: A Study in Eighteenth-Century Culture* (New York: New York University Press, 1924): 157.

O'erpowers beyond the Siren's song:
Leave me, my friend, indulgent go,   5
And let me muse upon my woe.
Why lure me from these pale retreats?
Why rob me of these pensive sweets?
Can Musick's voice, can Beauty's eye,
Can Painting's glowing hand, supply   10
A charm so suited to my mind,
As blows this hollow gust of wind,
As drops this little weeping rill
Soft-tinkling down the moss-grown hill,
Whilst thro' the west, where sinks the crimson Day,   15
Meek Twilight slowly sails, and waves her banners grey?

II

Say, from Affliction's various source
Do none but turbid waters flow?
And cannot Fancy clear their course?
For Fancy is the friend of Woe.   20
Say, mid that grove, in love-lorn state,
When yon poor ringdove mourns her mate,
Is all, that meets the shepherd's ear,
Inspir'd by anguish, and despair?
Ah! no; fair Fancy rules the song: 25
She swells her throat; she guides her tongue;
She bids the waving aspin-spray[1]
Quiver in cadence to her lay;
She bids the fringed osiers bow,
And rustle round the lake below,   30
To suit the tenor of her gurgling sighs,
And sooth her throbbing breast with solemn sympathies.

III

To thee, whose young and polish'd brow
The wrinkling hand of Sorrow spares;

---

1 Leaves of the aspen tree.

Whose cheeks, bestrew'd with roses, know 35
No channel for the tide of tears;
To thee yon abbey dank, and lone,
Where ivy chains each mould'ring stone
That nods o'er many a martyr's tomb,
May cast a formidable gloom. 40
Yet some there are, who, free from fear,
Could wander thro' the cloysters drear,
Could rove each desolated aisle,
Though midnight thunders shook the pile;
And dauntless view, or seem to view, 45
(As faintly flash the lightnings blue)
Thin shiv'ring ghosts from yawning charnels throng,
And glance with silent sweep the shaggy vaults[1] along.

IV

But such terrific charms as these,
I ask not yet: My sober mind 50
The fainter forms of sadness please;
My sorrows are of softer kind.
Through this still valley let me stray,
Wrapt in some strain of pensive GRAY:[2]
Whose lofty genius bears along 55
The conscious dignity of Song;
And, scorning from the sacred store
To waste a note on Pride or Power,
Roves, when the glimmering twilight glooms,
And warbles mid the rustic tombs: 60
He, too, perchance (for well I know,
His heart would melt with friendly woe)
He, too, perchance, when these poor limbs are laid,
Will heave one tuneful sigh, and sooth my hov'ring shade.

---

1 Presumably the vaults are "shaggy" because of moss or algae.
2 Thomas Gray.

William Mason, "Elegy VI: Written in a Church-yard in South Wales, 1787"

Mason's examination of the Welsh practice of planting flowers on graves forms an interesting contrast with Caroline Bowles Southey's later treatment of this folk practice in the first of her "Chapters on Churchyards," included later in this volume.

The text of this poem, written in 1787, is from *The Works of William Mason* (London: Cadell & Davies, 1811), 4 vols.

A custom is prevalent with the peasants in that part of the country, of planting field flowers and sweet herbs on the graves of their relations and friends; a pleasing specimen of this which the Author saw when he was paying a visit to Lord Vernon at Breton Ferry, Glamorganshire, in the summer of the year 1787, occasioned him to write this Elegy, first published 1797. [Mason's note.]

From southern Cambria's[1] richly-varied clime,
   Where grace and grandeur share an equal reign;
Where cliffs o'erhung with shade, and hills sublime
   Of mountain lineage sweep into the main;[2]
From bays, where Commerce furls her wearied sails,   5
   Proud to have dar'd the dangers of the deep,
And floats at anchor'd ease inclos'd by vales,
   To Ocean's verge where stray the vent'rous sheep;
From brilliant scenes like these I turn my eye;
   And, lo! a solemn circle[3] meets its view,
Wall'd to protect inhum'd[4] mortality,
   And shaded close with poplar and with yew.
Deep in that dell the humble fane appears,
   Whence prayers if humble best to Heaven aspire;
No tower embattled, no proud spire it rears,   15

---

1 Poetic name for Wales.
2 Ocean.
3 The churchyard wall.
4 Buried.

A moss-grown croslet[1] decks its lowly choir.
  And round that fane the sons of toil repose,
    Who drove the plough-share, or the sail who spread;
  With wives, with children, all in measur'd rows,
    Two whiten'd flint stones mark the feet and head.   20
While these between full many a simple flow'r,
  Pansy, and pink,[2] with languid beauty smile;
    The primrose opening at the twilight hour,
  And velvet tufts of fragrant chamomile.
For, more intent the smell than sight to please,   25
  Surviving love selects its vernal race;
    Plants that with early perfume feed the breeze
  May best each dank and noxious vapour chase.
The flaunting tulip, the carnation gay,
  Turnsole,[3] and peony, and all the train   30
    That love to glitter in the noontide ray,
  Ill suit the copse where Death and Silence reign.
Not but perchance to deck some virgin's tomb,
  Where violets sweet their twofold purple spread,
    Some rose of maiden blush may faintly bloom,   35
  Or with'ring hang its emblematic head.
These to renew, with more than annual care
  That wakeful love with pensive step will go;
    The hand that lifts the dibble[4] shakes with fear
  Lest haply it disturb the friend below.   40
Vain fear! for never shall disturber come
  Potent enough to wake such sleep profound,
    Till the dread herald to the day of doom
  Pours from his trump[5] the world-dissolving sound.
Vain fear! yet who that boasts a heart to feel,   45
  An eye to pity, would that fear reprove?
    They only who are curst with breasts of steel

---

1 Small cross.
2 "Pink" refers to a large group of flowers, collectively known as "pinks," which includes such well-known flowers as carnations, baby's breath, and Sweet William.
3 Any of a number of plants that "turned" their flower heads to follow the sun.
4 An implement used to dig holes for the planting of bulbs or seeds.
5 Trumpet.

Can mock the foibles of surviving love.
Those foibles far beyond cold Reason's claim
    Have power the social charities to spread;   50
They feed, sweet Tenderness! thy lambent flame,
    Which, while it warms the heart, improves the head.
Its chemic aid a gradual heat applies
    That from the dross of self each wish refines,
Extracts the liberal spirit, bids it rise   55
    Till with primeval purity it shines.
Take then, poor peasants, from the friend of Gray[1]
    His humbler praise; for Gray or fail'd to see,
Or saw unnotic'd, what had wak'd a lay
    Rich in the pathos of true poesy.   60
Yes, had he pac'd this church-way path along,
    Or lean'd like me against this ivied wall,
How sadly sweet had flow'd his Dorian[2] song,
    Then sweetest when it flow'd at Nature's call.
Like Tadmor's king,[3] his comprehensive mind   65
    Each plant's peculiar character could seize;
And hence his moralizing Muse had join'd,
    To all these flow'rs, a thousand similies.
But he, alas! in distant village-grave
    Has mix'd with dear maternal dust his own;   70
Ev'n now the pang, which parting Friendship gave,
    Thrills at my heart, and tells me he is gone.
Take then from me the pensive strain that flows
    Congenial to this consecrated gloom;
Where all that meets my eye some symbol shows   75
    Of grief, like mine, that lives beyond the tomb.
Shows me that you, though doom'd the livelong year
    For scanty food the toiling arm to ply,

---

1 Thomas Gray, author of "Elegy Written in a Country Churchyard" and close friend of Mason's. Mason was roundly criticized for invoking Gray in a poem that is itself something of an imitation of Gray's most famous work.
2 In classical Greek music, "Dorian" referred to simple yet solemn music—and, by extension, poetry.
3 Tadmor was a city constructed by King Solomon, famed for his wisdom. See 1 Kings 9.18 and 2 Chronicles 8.4.

Can smite your breasts, and find an inmate there
   To heave, when Mem'ry bids, the ready sigh.   80
Still nurse that best of inmates, gentle swains!
   Still act as heartfelt sympathy inspires;
The taste, which birth from Education gains,
   Serves but to chill Affection's native fires.
To you more knowledge than what shields from vice   85
   Were but a gift would multiply your cares;
Of matter and of mind let reasoners nice[1]
   Dispute; be Patience, yours, Presumption theirs.
You know (what more can earthly Science know?)
   That all must die; by Revelation's ray   90
Illum'd, you trust the ashes placed below
   These flow'ry tufts, shall rise again to day.
What if you deem, by hoar[2] tradition led,
   To you perchance devolv'd from Druids[3] old,
That parted souls at solemn seasons tread   95
   The circles that their shrines of clay enfold?
What if you deem they some sad pleasure take
   These poor memorials of your love to view,
And scent the perfume for the planter's sake,
   That breathes from vulgar rosemary and rue?[4]   100
Unfeeling Wit may scorn, and Pride may frown;
   Yet Fancy, empress of the realms of song,
Shall bless the decent mode, and Reason own
   It may be right——for who can prove it wrong?[5]

---

1 Particular, precise.
2 White-haired, old.
3 Druids were the priestly class of ancient Celtic peoples in Britain.
4 Rosemary and rue are two of the plants mentioned by Ophelia in *Hamlet* (IV, v), when the death of her father has driven her mad.
5 "Although I run the risk of some imputed vanity, I am induced to add here, the opinion of a too partial friend concerning the foregoing Poem; but shall only extract from the written paper which he gave me, the part that points out the specific differences which occurred to him, when he compared it with another of a very similar title. And this I do merely to obviate a prejudice which some readers might take to it, as supposing from the title and subject that I wrote it to emulate what, I am as ready to own as they are, is *inimitable*. 'Your Elegy, (says this Gentleman) as it relates to a particular and local custom in South Wales, must of course little resemble Mr. Gray's, which is purely of a general kind. He laments

James Beattie, "Elegy [Tir'd with the busy crouds]"

Beattie (1735-1803) was a Scottish poet who earned a B.A. and M.A. at Marischal College (now part of the University of Aberdeen in Scotland). Beattie studied divinity in order to become a clergy-man, but never took orders, instead devoting himself to teaching, quickly becoming a professor at Marischal College and associat-ing with an important circle of Scottish philosophers and writers. A friend of Thomas Gray, Beattie edited an edition of his poems in the late 1760s. Beattie is best known in literary circles for *The Minstrel* (1771, 1774), a semi-autobiographical work describing a shepherd boy's childhood amidst the beauties of nature; this work was significantly influential for Wordsworth and other Romantics. Beattie's philosophical works were often attacks on philosophi-cal scepticism, which Beattie felt was antithetic to religion and morality. Beattie had a somewhat troubled domestic life; while he himself suffered from periodic bouts of depression and inca-pacitating headaches, his wife exhibited increasing symptoms of mental instability, and after 13 years of marriage Beattie found it impossible to remain with her.

Like many "elegies" of the eighteenth century (and later), this poem eulogizes no specific individual; it is, rather, an elegiac

---

the departed peasants; you compassionate those that lament them: he places their former occupations in an honourable light; you view, in an amiable one, the weakness of their surviving friends: in the former Elegy, we find the dead consid-ered with respect to what their possible situation while living might have been, with all the advantages of knowledge; in the latter the living are endeavoured to be consoled for the want of it. In the general church-yard of the one, contempla-tion is more widely extended; in the other particular one, concern is more nearly impressed. His verses inspire a solemnity which awes and arrests the mind; your's breathe a tenderness which softens and attracts the heart: there are stanzas in Gray's Elegy of what, I venture to call, sublime melancholy; in yours of extreme sensibility.—It is a curious circumstance that the writer of the former should be introduced into both these Elegies, but certainly, as reality is superior to fiction, in a more pathetic manner in the latter. The locality of your scene enabled you to open with a picturesque description, which, besides contrasting strongly with the place of interment, is copied from nature, and animated with expression.'—I will add, that it was not so much for the sake of this kind of contrast that I gave the Elegy such an exordium, as to make it appear a day scene, and as such to contrast it with the twilight scene of my excellent Friend's Elegy." [Mason's note.]

reflection on sleep and the varied fancies produced by dreams, the
ephemerality of which are for Beattie models of the transitori-
ness of human life, and with the recognition of similarity Beattie
achieves his closing trope, one directly indebted to Parnell and
other Graveyard school poets.

The poems here were included in Beattie's collection *Original
Poems and Translations*, published in 1760; some of the poems in
this volume had been published a few years earlier in magazines.

Tir'd with the busy crouds, that all the day
Impatient throng where Folly's altars flame,
My languid powers dissolve with quick decay,
Till genial Sleep repair the sinking frame.

Hail kind Reviver! that canst lull the cares,   5
And every weary sense compose to rest,
Lighten th' oppressive load which Anguish bears,
And warm with hope the cold desponding breast.

Touch'd by thy rod, from Power's majestic brow
Drops the gay plume; he pines a lowly clown;   10
And on the cold earth stretch'd the son of Woe
Quaffs Pleasure's draught, and wears a fancy'd crown.

When rous'd by thee, on boundless pinions born
Fancy to fairy scenes exults to rove,
Now scales the cliff gay-gleaming on the morn,   15
Now sad and silent treads the deepening grove;

Or skims the main, and listens to the storms,
Marks the long waves roll far remote away;
Or mingling with ten thousand glittering forms
Floats on the gale, and basks in purest day.   20

Haply, ere long, pierc'd by the howling blast
Through dark and pathless deserts I shall roam,
Plunge down th' unfathom'd deep, or shrink aghast
Where bursts the shrieking spectre from the tomb:

Perhaps loose Luxury's enchanting smile   25
Shall lure my steps to some romantic dale,
Where Mirth's light freaks th' unheeded hours beguile,
And airs of rapture warble in the gale.

Instructive emblem of this mortal state!
Where scenes as various every hour arise   30
In swift succession, which the hand of Fate
Presents, then snatches from our wondering eyes.

Be taught, vain man, how fleeting all thy joys,
Thy boasted grandeur, and thy glittering store;
Death comes, and all thy fancy'd bliss destroys,   35
Quick as a dream it fades, and is no more.

And, sons of Sorrow! though the threatening storm
Of angry Fortune overhang a while,
Let not her frowns your inward peace deform;
Soon happier days in happier climes shall smile.   40

Through earth's throng'd visions while we toss forlorn,
'Tis tumult all, and rage, and restless strife;
But these shall vanish like the dreams of morn,
When Death awakes us to immortal life.

James Beattie, "Epitaph [To this grave is committed]"

This work, also known as "Epitaph on Two Brothers," is dated Nov.
1, 1757, and includes the following note: "This Epitaph is engraven
on a tombstone in the church-yard of Lethnet in the shire of
Angus." Angus is in the east-central part of Scotland.

To this grave is committed
All that the Grave can claim
Of two Brothers —— and —— ————

Who on the vii of October MDCCLVII,
   Both unfortunately perished in the —— water: 5
The one in his xxii, the other in his xviii year.
   Their disconsolate Father —— ——
Erects this monument to the memory of
     These amiable Youths;
      Whose early virtues promised   10
Uncommon comfort to his declining years,
   And singular emolument to society.

   O Thou! whose steps in sacred reverence tread
These lone dominions of the silent Dead;
On this sad stone a pious look bestow,   15
Nor uninstructed read this tale of woe;
And while the sigh of sorrow heaves thy breast,
Let each rebellious murmur be supprest;
Heaven's hidden ways to trace, for us, how vain!
Heaven's wise decrees, how impious, to arraign!   20
Pure from the stains of a polluted age,
In early bloom of life, they left the stage:
Not doom'd in lingering woe to waste their breath
One moment snatch'd Them from the power of Death:
They liv'd united, and united died;   25
Happy the friends, whom Death cannot divide!

John Cunningham, "The Contemplatist: A Night-Piece"

Cunningham (1729?-1773) was an Irish-born poet, playwright, and
actor who spent much of his adult life moving between England
and Scotland as he sought success on the stage and in poetry; it
was in the latter that Cunningham was most effective, particularly
with the publication of *Poems, Chiefly Pastoral* in 1766, which went
through several editions in his lifetime.

   "The Contemplatist" was first published in 1762, and serves as
something of a corrective to the main current of Graveyard School
imagery, making this poem another work in this anthology which
helps to mark the boundaries of the Graveyard School's appeal.

Although Cunningham could, in poems such as "Elegy on a Pile of
Ruins" (not included here), infuse Gothically dramatic landscapes
with emotional power in the service of moral contemplation, he
insistently checks the flow of that emotional energy in "The Con-
templatist," which like Henry Jones' "The Relief; or Day Thoughts,"
reverses and ultimately rejects dominant Graveyard School tropes,
filling their dark vacancies, through the exercise of moral and logi-
cal rigor, with redemption and restoration.

The text is taken from the second edition of *Poems, Chiefly
Pastoral*.

Nox erat ———
Cum tacet omnis ager, pecudes, pictæque volucres.[1]

I

The Queen of Contemplation, Night,
  Begins her balmy reign;
Advancing in their varied light
  Her silver-vested train.

II

'Tis strange, the many marshal'd stars,   5
  That ride yon sacred round,
Should keep, among their rapid cars,
  A silence so profound!

III

A kind, a philosophic calm,
  The cool creation wears!   10
And what Day drank of dewey balm,
  The gentle Night repairs.

---

1 From Virgil's *Aeneid*, Book IV: "It was night . . . while all the countryside was
still, and the beasts, and the colorful birds."

IV

Behind their leafy curtains hid,
  The feather'd race how still!
How quiet now the gamesome kid,   15
  That gambol'd round the hill!

V

The sweets, that bending o'er their banks,
  From sultry Day declin'd,
Revive in little velvet ranks,
  And scent the western wind.   20

VI

The Moon, preceded by the breeze
  That bade the clouds retire,
Appears amongst the tufted trees,
  A Phœnix nest on fire.

VII

But soft——the golden glow subsides!   25
  Her chariot mounts on high!
And now, in silver'd pomp, she rides
  Pale regent of the sky!

VIII

Where Time, upon the wither'd tree
  Hath carv'd the moral chair,   30
I sit, from busy passions free,
  And breathe the placid air.

IX

The wither'd tree was once in prime;
  Its branches brav'd the sky!
Thus, at the touch of ruthless Time,   35
  Shall Youth and Vigour die.

X
I'm lifted to the blue expanse:
  It glows serenely gay!
Come, Science, by my side, advance,
  We'll search the Milky Way.   *40*

XI
Let us descend——The daring flight
  Fatigues my feeble mind;
And Science, in the maze of light,
  Is impotent and blind.

XII
What are those wild, those wand'ring fires,   *45*
  That o'er the moorland ran?
Vapours.¹——How like the vague desires
  That cheat the heart of Man!

XIII
But there's a friendly guide!——a flame,
  That lambent o'er its bed,   *50*
Enlivens, with a gladsome beam,
  The hermit's osier shed.

XIV
Among the russet shades of night,
  It glances from afar!
And darts along the dusk; so bright,   *55*
  It seems a silver star!

---

1 The will o' the wisp, or *ignis fatuus* ("fool's fire"), a glowing light often seen over bogs or marshland and long associated with the supernatural in Western European folk traditions.

XV

In coverts, (where the few frequent)
 If Virtue deigns to dwell,
'Tis thus, the little lamp, Content,
 Gives lustre to her cell. 60

XVI

How smooth that rapid river slides
 Progressive to the deep!
The Poppies, pendent o'er its sides,
 Have charm'd the waves to sleep.

XVII

Pleasure's intoxicated sons! 65
 Ye indolent! ye gay!
Reflect——for as the river runs,
 Life wings its tractless way.

XVIII

That branching grove of dusky green
 Conceals the azure sky; 70
Save, where a starry space between,
 Relieves the darken'd eye.

XIX

Old Error, thus, with shades impure,
 Throws sacred Truth behind:
Yet sometimes, through the deep obscure, 75
 She bursts upon the mind.

XX

Sleep, and her sister Silence reign,
 They lock the Shepherd's fold!
But hark——I hear a lamb complain,
 'Tis lost upon the wold! 80

XXI

To savage herds, that hunt for prey,
　An unresisting prize!
For having trod a devious way,
　The little rambler dies.

XXII

As luckless is the Virgin's lot,　　　　　　　　85
　Whom pleasure once misguides:
When hurried from the halcion cot,
　Where Innocence presides—

XXIII

The passions, a relentless train!
　To tear the victim run:　　　　　　　　　90
She seeks the paths of peace in vain,
　Is conquer'd——and undone.

XXIV

How bright the little insects blaze,
　Where willows shade the way;
As proud as if their painted rays　　　　　　95
　Could emulate the Day!

XXV

'Tis thus, the pigmy sons of pow'r
　Advance their vain parade!
Thus, glitter in the darken'd hour,
　And like the glow-worms[1] fade!　　　　　100

XXVI

The soft serenity of night,
　Ungentle clouds deform!
The silver host that shone so bright,
　Is hid behind a storm!

---

1 The common British term for a species of firefly in which the bioluminescent
female is flightless.

XXVII

The angry elements engage!   *105*
  An oak, (an ivied bower!)
Repels the rough wind's noisy rage,
  And shields me from the shower.

XXVIII

The rancour, thus, of rushing fate,
  I've learnt to render vain: *110*
For whilst Integrity's her seat,
  The soul will sit serene.

XXIX

A raven, from some greedy vault,
  Amidst that cloister'd gloom,
Bids me, and 'tis a solemn thought!   *115*
  Reflect upon the tomb.

XXX

The tomb!——The consecrated dome!
  The temple rais'd to Peace!
The port, that to its friendly home
  Compels the human race!   *120*

XXXI

Yon village, to the moral mind,
  A solemn aspect wears;
Where sleep hath lull'd the labour'd hind,
  And kill'd his daily cares:

XXXII

'Tis but the church-yard of the Night;   *125*
  An emblematic bed!
That offers to the mental sight,
  The temporary dead.

XXXIII

From hence, I'll penetrate, in thought,
  The grave's unmeasur'd deep;   130
And tutor'd, hence, be timely taught,
  To meet my final sleep.

XXXIV

'Tis peace——(The little chaos past!)
  The gracious moon restor'd!
A breeze succeeds the frightful blast,   135
  That through the forest roar'd!

XXXV

The Nightingale, a welcome guest!
  Renews her gentle strains;
And Hope, (just wand'ring from my breast)
  Her wonted seat regains.   140

XXXVI

Yes——When yon lucid orb is dark,
  And darting from on high;
My soul, a more celestial spark,
  Shall keep her native sky.

XXXVII

Fann'd by the light—the lenient breeze,   145
  My limbs refreshment find;
And moral rhapsodies, like these,
  Give vigour to the mind.

George Keate, "The Ruins of Netley Abbey. A Poem"

Keate (1729-1797) was an English writer, painter, and amateur antiquarian. Trained for the law but never practicing, Keate devoted himself to literary and cultural pursuits, travelling extensively in Europe, befriending Voltaire, and becoming an early proponent of the literary treatment of dramatic landscapes in his poem "The Alps" (1763), which Keate dedicated to Edward Young, author of *Night Thoughts*.

Keate's interest in history and culture was manifested, in part, in his interest in architectural artifacts and ruins; his interest in Netley Abbey was shared by many writers and artists in the eighteenth and nineteenth centuries, including Thomas Gray, Horace Walpole, William Lisle Bowles, and John Constable. Located in south-central England, Netley Abbey, established by Cistercian monks in 1239, was dissolved during the reign of Henry VIII and by the eighteenth century was a popular sightseeing destination noted for its picturesque ruins.

Like most "Graveyard" verse published to this point, this poem pursues a moral didacticism in its engagement with the solitude of the ruin and the melancholic reflections it prompts.

This poem was first published in 1764; it was expanded and revised for publication in 1769 as "Netley Abbey: An Elegy." The text here, of the first version, is taken from *The Poetical Works of George Keate, Esq.* (London: J. Dodsley, 1781).

———————

Hence all the trivial pleasures of the crowd,
Folly's vain revel, and that treach'rous art
Which captivates the gay, or sooths the proud,
And steals each better purpose from the heart.

More welcome far the shades of this wild wood   5
Skirting with cheerful green the seabeat sands,
Where Netley, near the margin of the flood[1]
In lone magnificence a ruin stands.

---

1 Netley Abbey is located only a few hundred yards from the sea.

How chang'd alas! from that rever'd abode
Which spread in ancient days so wide a fame,   10
When votive monks these sacred pavements trod,
And swell'd each echo with Jehovah's name!

Now sunk, deserted, and with weeds o'ergrown,
Yon aged walls their better years bewail;
Low on the ground their loftiest spires are thrown,   15
And ev'ry stone points out a moral tale.

Mark how the ivy with luxuriance bends
Its winding foliage through the cloister'd space,
O'er the green window's mould'ring height ascends,
And seems to clasp it with a fond embrace.—   20

With musing step I pace the silent aisle,
Each moss-grown nook, each tangled path explore,
While the breeze whistles through the shatter'd pile,
Or wave light-dashing murmurs on the shore.

No other noise in this calm scene is heard,   25
No other sounds these tranquil vaults molest,
Save the complainings of some mournful bird
That ever loves in solitude to rest.

Haunts such as these delight, and o'er the soul
Awhile their grateful melancholy cast,   30
Since through all periods she can boundless roll,
Enjoy the present, and recall the past!—

Here, pious hermits from the world retir'd
In contemplation wing'd their thoughts to heav'n;
Here, with religion's heart-felt raptures fir'd,   35
Wept o'er their erring days, and were forgiv'n.

Race after race succeeding, in these cells,
Learn'd how to value life, learn'd how to die;
Lost are their names, and no memorial tells
In what lone spot their mould'ring ashes lie!   40

Mute is the matin bell[1] which us'd to call
The wakeful fathers from their humble beds;
No midnight taper glimmers on the wall,
Or o'er the floor its trembling radiance sheds!

No sainted shrine now pours its blaze of light   45
Bidding the zealous bigot[2] hither roam;
No holy relick glads the pilgrim's sight,
Or lures his foot-steps from a distant home!—

Now fainter to the view each object grows,
In the clear west the day's last gleams are seen,   50
On night's dim front the star of ev'ning[3] glows,
And dusky twilight aids the solemn scene.

Again quick fancy peoples all the gloom,
Calls from the dust the venerable dead,
Who ages since lay shrouded in the tomb,   55
And bids them these accustom'd limits tread.

Swift as her wish the shadowy forms appear,
O'er each chang'd path with doubtful step they walk,
From their keen eyes she sees amazement stare,
And hears, or thinks she hears, the spectres talk.   60

E'en now they pass, and fading like a dream
Back to their hallow'd graves again they go;
But first bequeath one pitying sigh, and seem
To mourn with me the fate of all below! —

Disparted roofs that threaten from above,   65
The tott'ring battlement, the rifted tow'r,

---

1 The bell signalling morning prayers, formally known as matins.
2 One who is excessively devoted to a particular religious creed. While Keate
recognized, in print, Catholicism's ability to inspire great art and architecture, he
was, like Anglicans of his time, suspicious of Catholicism as a religion of secrecy,
authority, and superstition.
3 Venus.

With many a scatter'd fragment loudly prove,
All conqu'ring Time, the triumphs of thy pow'r.

These speaking stones one sacred truth maintain,
That dust to dust is man's predestin'd lot;   70
He plans, and labours,——yet how much in vain!—
Himself, his monuments, how soon forgot!—

Forgot on Earth,——but one there sits on high
Who bids our virtues to his throne ascend,
Pleas'd he beholds them with parent's eye,   75
To give our hope new wings, and crown our end!—

And you, ye fair, of gayer scenes the grace,
If chance should lead you from the jocund train,
Curious to visit this sequester'd place,
Amidst its ruins wander not in vain.   80

Whence do they still our silent wonder claim
E'en in this low, this desolated state?
'Tis from remembrance of their former fame:—
They once were beautiful, they once were great!

'Tis goodness best adorns the female heart;   85
Asks a respect which must with years increase,
Lives, when the roses from the cheek depart,
And all the joys of adulation cease!

Forgive the Muse, if with an anxious love
She wooes you to attend her friendly lay;   90
Warns you, lest faithless to yourselves ye prove,
And in false pleasures trifle life away.

Know, in your breasts is lodg'd a spark divine
For ever prompting to each great desire;—
Th' inconstant world must change, that still shall shine,   95
Nor Death's cold hand e'er quench th' immortal fire.

Ne'er may dishonour's blast an entrance find,
O keep it sacred with a vestal's[1] care,
Feed it with all the graces of the mind,
Nor fail to pour the social duties there.　　　*100*

So o'er your forms when Time his veil shall cast,
And ev'ry charm by age shall be decay'd,
Your fair renown shall triumph to the last,
And virtue guard the conquests beauty made.

William Shenstone, "Elegy IV: Ophelia's Urn. To Mr. G—"

Shenstone (1714-1763) was an English poet and landscape gardener (like fellow Graveyardist William Mason) who spent seven years at Oxford (his name was actually on the registrar's books for ten) yet who may have never earned a degree (he claimed not to have one, although records at Pembroke College, Oxford, show him as B.A.) He stood out in other ways as well, such as refusing to wear the wigs that were popular with upper-class men at the time. Although his pastoral and elegiac poetry influenced Thomas Gray (and the "Elegy Written in a Country Churchyard") and others, and despite the fact he had a number of friends in the literary and publishing world, a good deal of Shenstone's poetry was not published until his collected works were issued posthumously in 1764.

Shenstone's elegies were written in the early to mid-1740s[2]; the "Mr G.—" of the title is Shenstone's friend and schoolfellow Richard Graves, himself a writer and cleric. "Ophelia" would of course invoke for Shenstone's readers the pathos of Shakespeare's *Hamlet*, but Shenstone has something more particular in mind. Graves had jilted an early lover, but when she died in March 1743, he had a monument erected in her memory, referring to her by this pseudonym, as he would do in his 1772 novel *The Spiritual*

---

1 In classical Rome, the "Vestal virgins" were in charge of the shrine of Vesta, goddess of the hearth.

2 J. Fisher, "Shenstone, Gray, and the Moral Elegy," *Modern Philology* 34.3 (1937): 273-294. Elegy IV was, according to Fisher, most likely written in early 1743.

Quixote. This poem marks a notable departure from the hortatory moralizing and funerary horrors of much Graveyard verse up to this point. The opening stanzas in fact reject the idea of spectral terrors and explore instead the possibilities of a pensive melancholy, a "haunting" not by grim spectres or by a personified Death but by the awareness and evocation of personal loss.

Shenstone wrote "A Prefatory Essay on Elegy" to accompany his elegies upon their publication, which he was seeing through the press when he died. Shenstone begins his consideration of the genre with a brief overview of the origins of elegy, arguing that its original purpose, to commemorate the death of a beloved or illlustrious person, soon gave way to a sense of the term so broad as to become valueless, including as it did "the facetious mirth and libertine festivity of the votaries of love." Shenstone argued that only works which "diffuse a pleasing melancholy" (6) deserve the label of elegy. Like many of his fellow eighteenth-century poets, Shenstone felt that the purpose of poetry was to cultivate virtue; elegy, he argued, was the poetic form best suited to the cultivation of private virtue. It is not surprising to find that for Shenstone, who spent most of his adult life in rural semi-seclusion, the elegy is "best suited to shew the simplicity and innocence of rural life to advantage" (6), for it does so with a refinement and dignity that pastoral does not achieve. Elegy is best for ridiculing the arrogance of nobility and for inculcating personal virtues, for celebrating liberty and innocence and the cultivation of moral character—the essay, in short, becomes an apologia for Shenstone's own life and a defense of the elegy as he understood and practiced it. For Shenstone, who concludes his essay by explaining how the events and locales of his own life inspired and informed his elegies, the form serves not as a stylized device of cultural achievement or as an occasion for sermonizing, but an expression, in the register of pensive melancholy, of personal emotional and psychological states. He insists on a moral aspect to all poetry, to be sure, but as the "graveyard" examples of his elegies below make clear, Shenstone helped open up possibilities for the Graveyard School, helping point it in a more personal and expressive direction, one that will find its fullest expression in poets of the following decades, with Charlotte Smith being perhaps the most vivid example.

Text: *The Works in Verse and Prose of William Shenstone, Esq.*, 2
vols., London: R. & J. Dodsley, 1764.

Thro' the dim veil of ev'ning's dusky shade,
  Near some lone fane, or yew's funereal green,
What dreary forms has magic fear survey'd!
  What shrouded spectres superstition seen!

But you secure shall pour your sad complaint,   5
  Nor dread the meagre phantom's wan array;
What none but fear's officious hand can paint,
  What none, but superstition's eye, survey.

The glim'ring twilight and the doubtful dawn
  Shall see your step to these sad scenes return: 10
Constant, as crystal dews impearl the lawn,
  Shall Strephon's[1] tear bedew Ophelia's urn!

Sure nought unhallow'd shall presume to stray
  Where sleep the reliques of that virtuous maid:
Nor aught unlovely bend its devious way,   15
  Where soft Ophelia's dear remains are laid.

Haply thy muse, as with unceasing sighs
  She keeps late vigils on her urn reclin'd,
May see light groups of pleasing visions rise;
  And phantoms glide, but of celestial kind.   20

There fame, her clarion pendent at her side,
  Shall seek forgiveness of Ophelia's shade;
"Why has such worth, without distinction, dy'd,
  Why, like the desert's lilly, bloom'd to fade?"

Then young simplicity, averse to feign,   25
  Shall unmolested breathe her softest sigh:

---

1 These are generic Greek names for the lover and the woman he has lost to
death, in this case Richard Graves and the woman he jilted, Utrecia Smith.

And candour with unwonted warmth complain,
  And innocence indulge a wailful cry.

Then elegance with coy judicious hand,
  Shall cull fresh flow'rets for Ophelia's tomb: 30
And beauty chide the fates' severe command,
  That shew'd the frailty of so fair a bloom!

And fancy then with wild ungovern'd woe,
  Shall her lov'd pupil's native taste explain:
For mournful sable[1] all her hues forego,   35
  And ask sweet solace of the muse in vain!

Ah gentle forms expect no fond relief;
  Too much the sacred Nine[2] their loss deplore:
Well may ye grieve, nor find an end of grief—
  Your best, your brightest fav'rite is no more.   40

William Shenstone, "Elegy XXII: Written in the Year —— when the Rights of Sepulture were so Frequently Violated"

"Right of sepulture" refers not only to burial but to the owner-
ship, and thus the presumed inviolability, of a burial plot. Although
grave-robbing is most typically associated with the nineteenth
century and its increased demand for cadavers for use in medical
schools, the eighteenth century saw a notable increase in the prac-
tice as well, particularly in the decade of the 1740s after the rise of
private medical academies.[3]

Say, gentle sleep, that lov'st the gloom of night,
  Parent of dreams! thou great magician, say,
Whence my late vision thus endures the light;
  Thus haunts my fancy thro' the glare of day.

---

1 The black of mourning garb.
2 The Muses of Greek mythology.
3 J. Fisher, "Shenstone, Gray, and the Moral Elegy," *Modern Philology* 34.3 (1937):
284-85. Fisher dates this elegy to 1747, though with some uncertainty.

The silent moon had scal'd the vaulted skies,   5
  And anxious care resign'd my limbs to rest;
A sudden lustre struck my wond'ring eyes,
  And Silvia[1] stood before my couch confest.

Ah! not the nymph so blooming and so gay,
  That led the dance beneath the festive shade!   10
But she that, in the morning of her day,
  Intomb'd beneath the grass-green sod was laid.

No more her eyes their wonted radiance cast;
  No more her breast inspir'd the lover's flame,
No more her cheek the Pæstan[2] rose surpast;   15
  Yet seem'd her lip's etherial smile the same.

Nor such her hair as deck'd her living face;
  Nor such her voice as charm'd the list'ning crowd;
Nor such her dress as heighten'd ev'ry grace;
  Alas! all vanish'd for the mournful shroud!   20

Yet seem'd her lip's etherial charm the same;
  That dear distinction every doubt remov'd;
Perish the lover, whose imperfect flame
  Forgets one feature of the nymph he lov'd.

"Damon," she said, "mine hour allotted flies;   25
  Oh! do not waste it with a fruitless tear!
Tho' griev'd to see thy Silvia's pale disguise,
  Suspend thy sorrow, and attentive hear.

So may thy muse with virtuous fame be blest!
  So be thy love with mutual love repaid!   30
So may thy bones in sacred silence rest,
  Fast by the reliques of some happier maid!

---

1 Generic name for a beloved woman, in this case the narrator's deceased beloved.
2 Paestum, a city in classical Rome, famed for its roses.

Thou know'st, how ling'ring on a distant shore
  Disease invidious nipt my flow'ry prime;
And oh! what pangs my tender bosom tore,   35
  To think I ne'er must view my native clime!

No friend was near to raise my drooping head;
  No dear companion wept to see me die;
Lodge me within my native soil, I said;
  There my fond parents honour'd reliques lie.   40

Tho' now debarr'd of each domestic tear;
  Unknown, forgot, I meet the fatal blow;
There many a friend shall grace my woeful bier,[1]
  And many a sigh shall rise, and tear shall flow.

I spoke, nor fate forbore his trembling spoil;   45
  Some venal[2] mourner lent his careless aid;
And soon they bore me to my native soil,
  Where my fond parents' dear remains were laid.

'Twas then the youths, from ev'ry plain and grove,
  Adorn'd with mournful verse thy Silvia's bier;   50
'Twas then the nymphs their votive garlands wove,
  And strew'd the fragance of the youthful year.

But why alas! the tender scene display?
  Cou'd Damon's foot the pious path decline?
Ah no! 'twas Damon first attun'd his lay,   55
  And sure no sonnet was so dear as thine.

Thus was I bosom'd in the peaceful grave;
  My placid ghost no longer wept its doom;
When savage robbers every sanction brave,
  And with outrageous guilt defraud the tomb!   60

---

1 The frame that supports a coffin at a funeral or wake, or, as here, the coffin and
all its funeral trappings.
2 Hired.

Shall my poor corse, from hostile realms convey'd,
   Lose the cheap portion of my native sands?
Or, in my kindred's dear embraces laid,
   Mourn the vile ravage of barbarian hands?

Say, wou'd thy breast no death-like torture feel,   65
   To see my limbs the felon's grip obey?
To see them gash'd beneath the daring steel?[1]
   To crowds a spectre, and to dogs a prey?

If Pæan's sons[2] these horrid rites require,
   If health's fair science be by these refin'd,   70
Let guilty convicts, for their use, expire;
   And let their breathless corse avail mankind.

Yet hard it seems, when guilt's last fine is paid,
   To see the victim's corse deny'd repose!
Now, more severe! the poor offenceless maid   75
   Dreads the dire outrage of inhuman foes.

Where is the faith of ancient pagans fled?
   Where the fond care the wand'ring manes[3] claim?
Nature, instinctive, cries, Protect the dead,
   And sacred be their ashes, and their fame: 80

Arise, dear youth! ev'n now the danger calls;
   Ev'n now the villain snuffs his wonted prey;
See! See! I lead thee to yon' sacred walls—
   Oh! fly to chase these human wolves away."

---

1 A reference to anatomical research or teaching, for which most corpses were disinterred in the eighteenth and nineteenth centuries.
2 Pæan's sons: doctors and medical students. Pæan ("PEE-uhn") was, in classical Greek myth, a god of healing (and thus was often linked to Apollo, also a healing god). (The word eventually came to mean a song of praise, possibly because of chanted "spells" associated with healing.)
3 Manes ("MAH-nays") were, in ancient Roman mythology, the souls of deceased loved ones.

Susanna Blamire, "Written in a Churchyard, on Seeing a Number of Cattle Grazing in It"

Blamire (1747-1794) was an English poet known as the "Muse of Cumberland" for her birth and lifelong residence in that most northwest of English counties. A prolific poet who co-authored several works with Catherine Gilpin, sister of noted landscape artist and writer William Gilpin, Blamire was also a supporter of the French Revolution and an amateur physician who regularly ministered to the poor.

Although widely known to her friends as an accomplished poet, Blamire published very little during her lifetime, and most of that anonymously. Not until a collection of her work was published in 1842, almost 50 years after her death from rheumatic fever, did Blamire attract wider critical attention.

This poem was written in 1766, one of the earliest of Blamire's works, and is another of the many works inspired by the popularity of Gray's "Elegy Written in a Country Churchyard." Like Gray, Blamire focuses on the levelling aspect of death and on the spiritual, strictly eschewing Gothic atmospherics. Blamire announces her moral intention in the opening quatrain, and remains true to that mission.

The text is taken from *The Poetical Works of Miss Susanna Blamire*, collected by Henry Lonsdale with preface, memoir, and notes by Patrick Maxwell (Edinburgh: John Menzies, 1842). Line spacing has been added between quatrains for ease of readability.

Be still my heart, and let this moving sight
   Whisper a moral to each future lay;
Let this convince how like the lightning's flight
   Is earthly pageantry's precarious stay.

Within this place of consecrated trust   5
   The neighbouring herds their daily pasture find;
And idly bounding o'er each hallow'd bust,
   Form a sad prospect to the pensive mind.

Whilst o'er the graves thus carelessly they tread,
   Allur'd by hunger to the deed profane,   10
They crop the verdure rising from the bed
   Of some fond parent, or some love-sick swain.

No more does vengeance to revenge the deed
   Lodge in their breasts, or vigour aid the blow;
The power to make the sad offenders bleed   15
   The prostrate image ne'er again shall know.

Nor can the time-worn epitaph rehearse
   The name or titles which its owner bore;
No more the sorrow lives within the verse,
   For memory paints the moving scene no more.   20

Perhaps 'tis one whose noble deeds attain'd
   Honour and fame in time of hostile war;—
Whose arm the Captive's liberty regain'd,
   And stamp'd his valour with a glorious scar.

Alas! his widow might attend him here,   25
   And children, too, the slow procession join,
And his fond friends indulge the trickling tear
   O'er his last honours at the awful[1] shrine.

Perhaps some orphan here might see inurn'd
   The only guardian of her orphan years;   30
And, on the precipice of errors turn'd,
   Become reclaim'd by sweet repentant tears.

The lover, too, might strain an eager look,
   Once more attempting to survey the fair
Who, for his sake, her early friends forsook,   35
   With him her days of joy or grief to share.

What beauty or what charms adorn'd the frame
   Of this cold image, now to earth consign'd;

---

1 Awe-inspiring.

Or what just praise the heart's high worth might claim,
  The time-worn letters now no more remind.   40

Then what is honour?—what is wealth or fame?
  Since the possessor waits the common doom!
As much rever'd we find the peasant's name
  As the rich lord's, when in the levelling tomb.

To both alike this tribute we may send,   45
  The heart-swollen sigh, or the lamenting tear;
And without difference o'er their ashes bend,
  For all distinctions find a level here.

For nought avails the marble o'er each head,
  Nor all the art which sculpture can bestow,   50
To save the memory of the honour'd dead,
  Or strike the living with their wonted awe.

Then come, ye vain, whom Fortune deigns to bless,
  This scene at once shall all her frauds expose;
And ye who Beauty's loveliest charms possess   55
  From this may find a moral in the rose.

For soon infirmity shall fix her seat,
  And dissolution lastly close the scene;
No more shall youth your jocund acts repeat,
  Or age relate what graver years have been.   60

Yet think not death awaits the course of years,
  He comes whilst youth her shield of health supports;
In every place the potent king appears,
  To youth, to age, to every scene resorts.

But why, my heart, that palpitating beat!   65
  Can death's idea cause that pensive gloom?
Since in the world such thorny cares we meet,
  And since 'tis peace within the silent tomb.

Yet still the thought of nature's sad decay,
  And the reception in the world unknown,   70
Must cast a cloud o'er hope's celestial ray,
  If not dispell'd by conscious worth alone:

May this support me in the awful hour
  When earthly prospects fade before my view;
O! then, my friends, into my bosom pour   75
  Some soothing balsam[1] at the last adieu.

Say, in Elysium[2] we shall meet again,
  Nor there shall error hold th' enchanting rod;
But freed from earth at once we'll break the chain,
  And thus releas'd shall ne'er offend our God.   80

Then hence aversion to the body's doom,
  Nor let this scene a pensive murmur raise,
Nor let thought grieve when pondering o'er the tomb,
  Though on my grave the senseless herd should graze.

Charles Salmon, "An Elegy Written in the Abbey-Church"

Salmon (c. 1745-1779?) was a Scottish poet and friend of the noted
Scottish poet Robert Fergusson. Trained as a printer, Salmon
found his interest drawn more to politics and poetry—and to boon
companions. Salmon published a number of poems in various
newspapers and weekly magazines, but never completed his plan
to publish a volume of his works. Salmon, on an intoxicated binge,
enlisted in a regiment of the British Army (despite his opposition
to English domination of Scotland), and his regiment was posted
to India. Salmon was never heard from again.

This poem is included here not so much by virtue of its liter-
ary accomplishment, but because it may serve as a representative

1 An aromatic oily resin, extracted from various trees or shrubs, used in healing.
2 In Greek myth, that part of the underworld where the shades of the heroic or
virtuous dwelt.

example of the craze for elegiac meditations that was started by
Gray's "Elegy Written in a Country Churchyard." The success
and cultural resonance of Gray's poem led to the production of
dozens, if not hundreds, of imitations and parodies, and Salmon's
poem is among them, solid evidence of the range and influence
of Gray's most famous work and of the cultural potency of the
Graveyard School. Yet Salmon, while incorporating reflections on
the transitory nature of human life and glory, writes a much more
overtly political poem than did Gray; moral sentiment takes a back
seat to ideology here.

This poem was first published in May 1771 in *Ruddiman's Maga-
zine* in Edinburgh, for which Salmon worked as a printer at the
time; the text is taken from Joseph Robertson's *Lives of Scottish
Poets*, 3 vols. (London: Thomas Boys, 1822), vol. 2.

———

Fled from the mansions of the great and gay,
    Where idle pleasure wastes her fleeting breath,
Thro' this sad cell I'll take my lonely way,
    And view the havock made by time and death.

And, as I enter, let no swelling rage,   5
    No thought impure my pensive bosom lead,
But sweet Religion all the man engage:
    For this was once the sacred house of God.

Where oft Devotion, with her pious train,
    In silent contemplation spent her days,   10
Or wak'd to extacy the glowing strain,
    With grateful accents to her Maker's praise.

No more shall youth and beauty grace this shrine,
    Or pious sages to the portal throng;
No more the arch shall meet the voice divine,   15
    Receive the sound, or echo back the song.

The pride and glory of our country's fled,
    The great supporters of the nation's laws,

The statesmen, heroes, and the kings are dead,
  Who fought thro' fields of blood in freedom's cause.   *20*

Vast heaps of kindred here bestrew the ground,
  And skulls and coffins to my view arise;
Here's friend and foe profusely scatter'd round,
  And here a jaw, and there a thigh-bone, lies.

Perhaps this hand has in some bloody fray,   *25*
  With lofty sinews grasp'd the flaming brand,
Fought thro' the dreadful carnage of the day,
  And drove Oppression from its native land.

Yet fame and honour are but empty things,
  The fleeting sunshine of uncertain day;   *30*
For statesmen, peasants, beggars, lords and kings,
  All fall alike to cruel time a prey.

Tho' men, mere men, may unregarded rot,
  And buried in their native dust consume,
Shall Scotland's great commanders be forgot,   *35*
  And moulder unregretted in the tomb?

Will no kind bard in grateful numbers sing
  The mighty wonders of each hero's arm?
Will no kind friend protect a clay-cold king,
  Collect his bones, and keep them safe from harm?   *40*

Would some sweet muse assist me in the song,
  I'd dwell with rapture on the glowing strain,
Roll the smooth tide of harmony along,
  'Till echo undulate applause again.

When night's dark curtain hid the beams of day,   *45*
  From those sad eyes my soul should banish sleep;
Again I'd raise the sympathetic lay,
  And teach the sullen monuments to weep.

Ye sons of Scotland! tho' you cannot raise
    Your long lost monarchs from the silent bier,   50
Their deeds are worthy of your highest praise,
    And simple gratitude demands a tear.

For you they bore the faulchion[1] and the shield,
    For you each piercing winter blast they stood,
For you they struggl'd in the hostile field,   55
    For you they wither'd in their crimson blood.

Let not base slander on their mem'ry fall,
    Nor malice of their little faults complain;
They were such men, as, *take them all in all,*
    We shall not look upon their like again.[2]   60

Here lies the partner of the hero's bed,
    Whose ev'ry feature wore unequall'd grace,
Can Love's soft murmurs raise this death-struck head,
    Or take the pale complexion from the face?

Go then, ye fair! exert your utmost skill,   65
    Employ each art to keep your beauty fast;
Try each perfume, use paint, do what you will,
    Of this sad colour you must be at last.[3]

Ah me! how melancholy seem those walls,
    To earth returning with a quick decay,   70
Take heed, O Man! for as each atom falls,
    So wastes thy little spark of life away.

---

1 A curved sword.

2 Salmon is quoting, and slightly altering, Hamlet's remark to Horatio on his dead father: "He was a man, take him for all in all, / I shall not look upon his like again" (I.ii.187-188).

3 Another allusion to Hamlet in the graveyard, contemplating Yorick's skull: "Now get you to my lady's chamber and tell her, let her paint an inch thick, to this favour she must come" (V.i.192-194).

O thou, my soul! from worldly vices fly,
    And follow Innocence where'er she strays;
See with what ease an honest man can die,   75
    None but the wicked wish for length of days.

Jane Timbury, "Reflections in a Church-Yard"

Little seems to be known for certain about Timbury, not even her dates of birth and death. As a poet and novelist she was active in the late 1780s and early 1790s; her works include several moralized novels and collections of poems.

This poem clearly shows the influence of Thomas Gray's "Elegy Written in a Country Churchyard" (and the dozens of works written in imitation of Gray's poem); Timbury was riding a wave of popularity of the moralized churchyard elegy that was even in the late 1780s still surging, although the Graveyard School would soon be increasingly shaped by the less didactic and more visceral horrors of Gothic fiction.

This poem was first published in Timbury's *The History of Tobit, a Poem; and Other Poems on Various Subjects* (London, 1787); the text is taken from that first edition.

———

Awhile, opposing balmy Sleep's soft pow'r,
    By serious meditation hither led,
Here let me wander at this solemn hour,
    With no companion, save the silent dead;

While yon pale moon's mild lustre, all around,   5
    Dispels the horrors of the midnight gloom;
Lengthens the yew-trees shadow o'er the ground,
    And guides my steps between each peaceful tomb.

What awful stillness reigns in every part!
    No sound of human voice, or footsteps near: 10
A scene of terror to the guilty heart,
    For conscious guilt alone created fear.

Here shall the wicked mind from troubling cease,[1]
  And here the weary find a place of rest;
The wretch worn out with woe shall sleep in peace,   *15*
  Till call'd at last to number with the blest.

The Statesman, Hero, Patriot, great or small,
  By different paths move onward to the grave;
Inexorable Death here levels all;
  Nor youth nor beauty, wealth nor pow'r can save.   *20*

But who, alas! can think, and not repine,
  Of mould'ring into dust, in youth's full bloom;
This animated being to resign,
  And sink forgotten in the silent tomb?

His stoic firmness let the Atheist boast,   *25*
  Flatter'd with hopes of many years to come;
But, oh, how soon that fortitude is lost,
  When the grim King of Terrors seals his doom!

Philosophy alone has not the pow'r,
  Whate'er pretending Moralists have said,   *30*
To give true piece at the departing hour,
  Unless supported by Religion's aid.

That only can the drooping mind elate
  With the glad prospect of eternal bliss,
And prove the blessings of a future state,   *35*
  And ample recompence for woes in this.

It smooths the bed of sickness, want, and care,
  When every human help in vain we try;
Steals the uplifted dagger from Despair;
  Instructs us how to live, and how to die.   *40*

---

1 An allusion to Job 3, in which Job laments the fact he was born: "Why did I not perish at birth, and die as I came from the womb? . . . Or why was I not hidden in the ground like a stillborn child, like an infant who never saw the light of day? There the wicked cease from turmoil, and there the weary are at rest" (3.11, 16-17).

Inspir'd with that, my Soul can know no fear
   Amidst these gloomy mansions of the dead,
Though warn'd by all around me to prepare
   For mingling with the dust on which I tread.

What labour'd words appear on yonder stone,   45
   To tell where lie the great, the young, the gay;
Their former worth and merit to make known,
   And dignify a lump of senseless clay!

Not distant far, on the same bed of earth,
   Rest the remains of some unknown to fame: 50
No wealth or titles grac'd their humble birth,
   Nor here a single line to tell their fame.

For what avail the talents of the poor,
   When doom'd in dull obscurity to tread,
Contempt and insult fated to endure,   55
   For the small pittance of their daily bread?

But at the last account, when all shall meet,
   As summon'd by the great Arch-angel's call;
Then shall the rich and poor as equals greet—
   The Lord is judge and maker of them all.   60

Till when let humble Merit learn to bear
   The fancied ills inflicted here below:
'Tis vain to question, impious to despair,
   When fatherly correction strikes the blow.

For how can murmuring, weak, short-sighted man,   65
   Hope to exist exempt, from want or care;
And who shall dare Omnipotence to scan,
   And ask of Providence, why such things are?

Most gracious Father! till life's sands are run,
   To thy decree, oh, teach me to resign;   70
Submissive still to cry, "Thy will be done!"
   Howe'er repugnant it may seem to mine.

Hannah Cowley, "Invocation: To Horror"

Cowley (1743-1809) was an English poet and dramatist, with a number of very succesful plays, primarily comedies (although many had progressive political undertones), to her credit. This poem, influenced by William Collins's "Ode to Fear," was first published under the "Anna Matilda" pseudonym by which Cowley came to fame as a poet. "Anna Matilda" was one of the foremost poets of the "Della Cruscan" school of late-eighteenth-century English poetry, one founded on principles of sentiment and carefully cultivated rhetoric, often imitative of Milton or various Italian poetic precursors. The "Della Cruscan" poets were in fact a small group of friends and fellow poets, with the English poet Robert Merry (who published much of his poetry under the pseudonym "Della Crusca," a reference to a 16th-century Italian academy devoted to refining the Italian language) beginning the group and Hannah Cowley one of its more well-known and prolific members, along with Mary Robinson and noted diarist Hester Thrale Piozzi. Della Cruscan poetry was popular briefly in the late 1780s and early 1790s, but quickly came to be regarded as affected, artificial, and overly sentimental.

While "Invocation: To Horror" has only a limited engagement with the traditional trappings of the Graveyard School, it is notable for its use of a more intensified emotional aspect, an attempt to cultivate more powerfully and more directly the power of horror, and to do so with a carefully cultivated movement from the picturesque to the sublime to the horrific, albeit a horrific configured by its origins in and subordination to divine providence. Cowley's monstrous horror remains a potent agent of Christian justice and morality.

The text is taken from *The British Album,* London: John Bell, 1790, which is the revised version of *The Poetry of the World,* 1788, which was first book publication of the poem; it originally appeared in *The Whitehall Evening Post* of 3 January 1788.

Far be remov'd each painted scene!
What is to *me* the sapphire sky?
What is to *me* the earth's soft dye?
Or fragrant vales which sink between

Those velvet hills? yes, there I see—   5
(Why do those beauties burst on me?)
Pearl-dropping groves bow to the sun;
Seizing his beams, bright rivers run
That dart redoubled day:
Hope ye vain scenes, to catch the mind   10
To torpid sorrow all resign'd,
Or bid my heart be gay?
False are those hopes!—I turn—I fly,
Where no enchantment meets the eye,
Or soft ideas stray.   15

Horror! I call thee from the mould'ring tower,
The murky church yard, and forsaken bower,
Where 'midst unwholesome damps
The vap'ry gleamy lamps
Of *ignes fatui*,[1] shew the thick-wove night,   20
Where morbid Melancholy sits,
And weeps, and sings, and raves by fits,
And to her bosom strains the fancied sprite.

Or, if amidst the arctic gloom
Thou toilest at thy sable loom,   25
Forming the hideous phantoms of Despair—
Instant thy grisly labours leave,
With raven wing the concave cleave,
Where floats, self-borne, the dense nocturnal air.

Oh! bear me to th' impending cliffs,   30
Under whose brow the dashing skiffs
Beholds Thee seated on thy rocky throne;
There, 'midst the shrieking wild wind's roar,
Thy influence, Horror, I'll adore,
And at thy magic touch, congeal to stone.   35

---

1 "Fool's fire" (Latin), or "will o' the wisp," refers to glowing vapors sometimes
seen over marshes or bogs, attributed in folk culture to mischievous supernatural
beings or to the spirits of the dead.

Oh! hide the Moon's obtrusive orb,
The gleams of ev'ry star absorb,
And let Creation be a moment thine!
Bid billows dash; let whirlwinds roar,
And the stern, rocky-pointed shore,   40
The stranded bark, back to the waves resign!

Then, whilst from yonder turbid cloud,
Thou roll'st thy thunders long, and loud,
And light'nings flash upon the deep below,
Let the expiring Seaman's cry,   45
The Pilot's agonizing sigh
Mingle, and in the dreadful chorus flow!

Horror! far back thou dat'st thy reign;
Ere Kings th' historic page could stain
With records black, or deeds of lawless power;   50
Ere empires Alexanders curst,
Or Faction, mad'ning Cæsars nurst,
The frighted World receiv'd thy awful dower!

Whose pen Jehovah's self inspir'd;
He, who in eloquence attir'd,   55
Led Israel's squadrons o'er the earth,
Grandly terrific, paints thy birth.[1]
Th' Almighty, 'midst his fulgent seat on high,
Where glowing Seraphs round his footstool fly,
Beheld the wanton cities of the plain,   60
With acts of deadly name his laws disdain;[2]
He gave th' irrevocable sign,
Which mark'd to man the hate divine;
And sudden from the starting sky

---

1 Cowley alludes here to Moses, long held to be the author of the first five books
of the Bible (the Pentateuch).

2 See Genesis 19 for the destruction of Sodom and Gomorrah: "Then the LORD
rained upon Sodom and upon Gomorrah brimstone and fire from the LORD out
of heaven; And he overthrew those cities, and all the plain, and all the inhabitants
of the cities, and that which grew upon the ground" (19.24-25).

The Angels of his wrath bid fly!   65
Then Horror! thou presidest o'er the whole,
And fill'd, and rapt, each self-accusing soul!
Thou did'st ascend to guide the burning shower—
On Thee th' Omnipotent bestow'd the hour!

'Twas thine to scourge the sinful land,   70
'Twas thine to toss the fiery brand;
Beneath thy glance the temples fell,
And mountains crumbled at thy yell.
Once More thou'lt triumph in a fiery storm;
Once More the Earth behold thy direful form;   75
Then shalt thou seek, as holy prophets tell,
Thy native throne, amidst th' eternal shades of Hell!

Robert Southey, "The Dead Friend"

Southey (1774-1843)—it rhymes with "mouthy," according to Byron,
though in some parts of England it was and is pronounced "suthey"
—was an English poet and writer, a contemporary of Wordsworth
and Coleridge who, like them, was in his youth a political radical,
expelled from one school for challenging authority and opposing
corporal punishment, supporting abolition and the ideals of the
French Revolution, planning (but never effecting) an American
commune with Samuel Taylor Coleridge. Southey entered Oxford
University planning to become a clergyman, but his exposure to
radical political thought and the early idealism of the French Revo-
lution dissipated what was apparently only a modicum of enthu-
siasm for the clerical life. His plans to become a doctor, and then
a politician, also came to naught. He devoted himself to writing,
and by 1813 had established enough of a reputation to be appointed
Poet Laureate. By this time Southey's youthful idealistic ardor had
cooled to the point of reversing direction, and he became the target
of frequent attacks by younger poets and radicals for his turncoat
politics. Although quite popular in his time, Southey is little read
today outside of academic circles, although his cultural stock might
be higher if it were more widely known that Southey is the author

of what is now the most canonical version of "Goldilocks and the Three Bears," a tale which he adapted from an extant folktale as an amusement for his children.

The "dead friend" of this poem was Edmund Seward, whom Southey met at Oxford in 1793; the two quickly became very close friends. Seward died in 1795, an event which as late as 1818 prompted Southey to write "[Seward's] death in the year 1795 was the first severe affliction that I ever experienced—and sometimes even now I dream of him and wake myself by weeping because even in my dreams I remember that he is dead. I loved him with my whole heart, and shall remember him with gratitude and affection as one who was my moral father to the last moment of my life." The poem was written in 1799, itself a testament to the lingering depth of Southey's sense of bereavement. As such, it is very much a post-Graveyard School meditation on mortality, one which finds in the materialist facts of death not a sense of horror but a springboard to an exalted sense of friendship, its moral and even philosophical possibilities.

The text is taken from *The Poetical Works of Robert Southey: Minor Poems*, 3 vols., London: Longman, 1823. The centered layout, evident in numerous published versions of this work, is retained.

Not to the grave, not to the grave, my Soul,
Descend to contemplate
The form that once was dear!
Feed not on thoughts so loathly horrible!
The Spirit is not there
Which kindled that dead eye,
Which throbb'd in that cold heart,
Which in that motionless hand
Hath met thy friendly grasp.
The Spirit is not there!
It is but lifeless, perishable flesh
That moulders in the grave;
Earth, air, and water's ministering particles
Now to the elements
Resolved, their uses done.

Not to the grave, not to the grave, my Soul,
Follow thy friend beloved,
The Spirit is not there!

Often together have we talk'd of death;
How sweet it were to see
All doubtful things made clear;
How sweet it were with powers
Such as the Cherubim,
To view the depth of Heaven!
O Edmund! thou hast first
Begun the travel of Eternity!
I gaze amid upon the stars,
And think that thou art there,
Unfetter'd as the thought that follows thee.

And we have often said how sweet it were
With unseen ministry of angel power
To watch the friends we loved.
Edmund! we did not err!
Sure I have felt thy presence! Thou hast given
A birth to holy thought,
Hast kept me from the world unstain'd and pure.
Edmund! we did not err!
Our best affections here
They are not like the toys of infancy;
The Soul outgrows them not;
We do not cast them off;
Oh if it could be so,
It were indeed a dreadful thing to die!

Not to the grave, not to the grave, my Soul,
Follow thy friend beloved!
But in the lonely hour,
But in the evening walk,
Think that he companies thy solitude;
Think that he holds with thee
Mysterious intercourse;

And though Remembrance wake a tear,
There will be joy in grief.[1]

Robert Southey, "The Cross Roads"

It was long the practice in England and elsewhere to bury both criminals and suicides at crossroads. While this may be due to the lingering of pagan traditions, in which sacrificial victims were killed at altars located at crossroads, it was also believed by some that burials at crossroads would prevent suicides (who could not be buried in consecrated ground) from rising as vampires. While suggestive of a Wordsworthian ballad, with its old man and his moral lesson, the poem is clearly tinctured with a bit of Graveyard School sensationalism.

This poem was composed in 1798. The text is taken from *The Poetical Works of Robert Southey: Collected By Himself*, 10 vols., London: Longmans, 1838.

The tragedy related in this Ballad happened about the year 1760, in the parish of Bedminster, near Bristol. One who was present at the funeral told me the story and the circumstances of the interment, as I have versified them. [Southey's note]

I

There was an old man breaking stones
  To mend the turnpike way;
He sate him down beside a brook,
And out his bread and cheese he took,
  For now it was mid-day.

---

1 This phrase occurs several times in James Macpherson's "Ossian" poems: in "Carric-Thura" ("Pleasant is the joy of grief; it is like the shower of spring when it softens the branch of the oak, and the young leaf rears its green head") and in Book One of *Fingal*: "Send thou the night away in song, and give the joy of grief. For many heroes and maids of love have moved on Inis-fail: and lovely are the songs of woe that are heard on Albion's rocks, when the noise of the chase is past, and the streams of Cona answer to the voice of Ossian." A similar phrase occurs in Homer's *Iliad* and *Odyssey*. David Macbeth Moir's "The Child's Burial in Spring," in this volume, also employs the phrase.

2

He leant his back against a post,
　His feet the brook ran by;
And there were water-cresses growing,
And pleasant was the water's flowing,
　For he was hot and dry.

3

A soldier with his knapsack on
　Came travelling o'er the down;
The sun was strong and he was tired;
And he of the old man enquired
　"How far to Bristol town?"

4

"Half an hour's walk for a young man,
　By lanes and fields and stiles;
But you the foot-path do not know.
And if along the road you go
　Why then 'tis three good miles."

5

The soldier took his knapsack off,
　For he was hot and dry;
And out his bread and cheese he took,
And he sat down beside the brook
　To dine in company.

6

"Old friend! in faith," the soldier says,
　"I envy you almost;
My shoulders have been sorely prest,
And I should like to sit, and rest
　My back against that post.

7

"In such a sweltering day as this
   A knapsack is the devil;
And if on t'other side I sat,
It would not only spoil our chat,
   But make me seem uncivil."

8

The old man laugh'd and moved. "I wish
   It were a great-arm'd chair!
But this may help a man at need;
And yet it was a cursed deed
   That ever brought it there.

9

"There's a poor girl lies buried here,
   Beneath this very place,
The earth upon her corpse is prest,
This post was driven into her breast,
   And a stone is on her face."

10

The soldier had but just leant back,
   And now he half rose up.
"There's sure no harm in dining here,
My friend? and yet, to be sincere,
   I should not like to sup."

11

"God rest her! she is still enough
   Who sleeps beneath my feet!"
The old man cried. "No harm I trow,
She ever did herself, though now
   She lies where four roads meet.

12

"I have past by about that hour
  When men are not most brave;
It did not make my courage fail,
And I have heard the nightingale
  Sing sweetly on her grave.

13

"I have past by about that hour
  When ghosts their freedom have;
But here I saw no ghastly sight,
And quietly the glow-worm's light
  Was shining on her grave.

14

"There's one who like a Christian lies
  Beneath the church-tree's shade;
I'd rather go a long mile round
Than pass at evening through the ground
  Wherein that man is laid.

15

"A decent burial that man had,
  The bell was heard to toll,
When he was laid in holy ground,
But for all the wealth in Bristol town
  I would not be with his soul!

16

"Did'st see a house below the hill
  Which the winds and the rains destroy?
In that farm-house did that man dwell,
And I remember it full well
  When I was a growing boy.

17

"But she was a poor parish girl
  Who came up from the west:
From service hard she ran away,
And at that house in evil day
  Was taken in to rest.

18

"A man of a bad name was he,
  An evil life he led;
Passion made his dark face turn white,
And his grey eyes were large and light,
  And in anger they grew red.

19

"The man was bad, the mother worse,
  Bad fruit of evil stem;
'Twould make your hair to stand on end
If I should tell to you, my friend,
  The things that were told of them!

20

"Did'st see an out-house standing by?
  The walls alone remain;
It was a stable then, but now
Its mossy roof has fallen through
  All rotted by the rain.

21

"This poor girl she had served with them
  Some half-a-year or more,
When she was found hung up one day,
Stiff as a corpse and cold as clay,
  Behind that stable door.

22

"It is a wild and lonesome place,
  No hut or house is near;
Should one meet a murderer there alone,
'Twere vain to scream, and the dying groan
  Would never reach mortal ear.

23

"And there were strange reports about;
  But still the coroner found
That she by her own hand had died,
And should buried be by the way-side,
  And not in Christian ground.

24

"This was the very place he chose,
  Just where these four roads meet;
And I was one among the throng
That hither follow'd them along,
  I shall never the sight forget!

25

"They carried her upon a board
  In the clothes in which she died;
I saw the cap blown off her head,
Her face was of a dark dark red,
  Her eyes were starting wide:

26

"I think they could not have been closed,
  So widely did they strain.
O Lord, it was a ghastly sight,
And it often made me wake at night,
  When I saw it in dreams again.

27
"They laid her where these four roads meet,
    Here in this very place.
The earth upon her corpse was prest,
This post was driven into her breast,
    And a stone is on her face."

Robert Southey, "To Horror"

This poem was composed in 1791, when Southey was seventeen.
Not surprisingly for a work produced at such a young age, this
poem is imitative of a predecessor's work, in this case William Col-
lins's "Ode to Fear" (1746) as well as to the tradition of similar odes
and invocations, such as Hannah Cowley's "Invocation to Horror"
(1788). The poem is notable for its powerful moralized conclusion
—not, as in early Graveyard School verse, an invocation of Chris-
tian salvation, but instead a highly politicized, radical vision of
Horror's involvement in war and the slave trade, causes to which
Southey remained committed, by and large, his entire life.

The text is taken from Southey's *Poems* (Bristol: Cottle, 1797);
the poem was slightly revised for later publication.

Dark Horror! hear my call!
    Stern Genius hear from thy retreat
    On some old sepulchre's moss-canker'd seat,
Beneath the Abbey's ivied wall
    That trembles o'er its shade;   5
Where wrapt in midnight gloom, alone,
    Thou lovest to lie and hear
    The roar of waters near,
And listen to the deep dull groan
    Of some perturbed sprite   10
Borne fitful on the heavy gales of night.

Or whether o'er some wide waste hill

Thou mark'st the traveller stray,
  Bewilder'd on his lonely way,
When, loud and keen and chill,   15
The evening winds of winter blow,
Drifting deep the dismal snow.

Or if thou followest now on Greenland's shore,
  With all thy terrors, on the lonely way
Of some wreck'd mariner, where to the roar   20
  Of herded bears, the floating ice-hills round
  Return their echoing sound,
  And by the dim drear Boreal light[1]
Givest half his dangers to the wretch's sight.

Or if thy fury form,   25
  When o'er the midnight deep
  The dark-wing'd tempests sweep,
Watches from some high cliff the encreasing storm,
  Listening with strange delight,
As the black billows to the thunder rave   30
  When by the lightning's light
Thou see'st the tall ship sink beneath the wave.

Dark Horror! bear me where the field of fight
  Scatters contagion on the tainted gale,
  When to the Moon's faint beam,   35
On many a carcase shine the dews of night,
  And a dead silence stills the vale
Save when at times is heard the glutted Raven's scream.

Where some wreck'd army from the Conqueror's might
Speed their disastrous flight,   40
  With thee, fierce Genius! let me trace their way,
And hear at times the deep heart-groan
Of some poor sufferer left to die alone;
  His sore wounds smarting with the winds of night;

---

1 The Aurora Borealis.

And we will pause, where, on the wild,   45
   The mother to her breast,
On the heap'd snows reclining clasps her child
   And with him sleeps, chill'd to eternal rest!

Black Horror! speed we to the bed of Death,
   Where he whose murderous power afar   50
   Blasts with the myriad plagues of war,
Struggles with his last breath;
   Then to his wildly-starting eyes
   The phantoms of the murder'd rise;
   Then on his frenzied ear   55
Their groans for vengeance and the Demons' yell
In one heart-maddening chorus swell.
Cold on his brow convulsing stands the dew,
And night eternal darkens on his view.

Horror! I call thee yet once more!   60
Bear me to that accursed shore,[1]
Where round the stake the impaled Negro writhes.
Assume thy sacred terrors then! dispense
The blasting gales of Pestilence!
Arouse the race of Afric! holy Power,   65
Lead them to vengeance! and in that dread hour
When Ruin rages wide,
I will behold and smile by Mercy's side.

Charlotte Smith, "The Dead Beggar. An Elegy, Addressed to a Lady, who was affected at seeing the Funeral of a nameless Pauper, buried at the Expence of the Parish, in the Church-Yard at Brighthelmstone, in November 1792"

Smith (1749-1806) was an English poet and novelist and an early innovator in Romantic-era poetry. Her intensely personal and emo-

---

1 Southey may be referencing the beginning of the Haitian Revolution (1791-1804), although slavery was so endemic in the European colonies of the West Indies as to afford numerous instances of abuse, torture, and violent repression.

tionally potent sonnets strongly influenced William Wordsworth and others in the shaping of a Romantic verse practice that privileged the poetic revelation of intense emotional experience. Smith's contributions to the Graveyard School help mark the end of the traditional mode of Graveyard verse, all but abandoning the external trappings of graveyard horror and traditional forms of extended religious consolation in order to plumb emotional depths so melancholy and persistent they need no ghost come from the grave to provide the poem's emotive force. Even in her semi-Gothic early novels Smith eschewed egregious supernaturalism as the source of her works' psychological drama; it was always enough, for Smith, that the human psyche was potent, or monstrous, enough. While much of the tone of her work develops from the cult of sensibility in eighteenth-century literature, the self-revelatory nature and intensity of her verse marks her poetry as a bridge to Romanticism's introspection.

Smith's poetic self-examination, excoriated by some contemporaries as mere self-pity, derives in large part from her experiences as a woman in late-eighteenth-century culture. Married, at age 15, to a financially irresponsible man six years her senior, Smith suffered considerable financial and social hardship, briefly joining her husband in debtor's prison and giving birth, in the span of twenty years, to twelve children, only half of whom survived her. Smith turned to writing out of financial necessity, for the inheritance left to her family by her husband's wealthy father became entangled in a decades-long lawsuit, not fully resolved until well after Smith's death. While her work was respected and fairly popular during the 1790s, Smith's fame eventually faded, due in part to a combination of over-exposure and her being associated, in the public mind, with the French Revolution.

This poem was written in 1792 and published in the eighth edition of *Elegiac Sonnets and Other Poems* in 1797.

———————

I have been told that I have incurred blame for having used in this short composition, terms that have become obnoxious to certain persons.[1] Such remarks are hardly worth notice; and it is

———————
1 The terms are, of course, "the rights of Man" (line 20), associated with sup-

very little my ambition to obtain the suffrage of those who suffer party prejudice to influence their taste; or of those who desire that because they have themselves done it, every one else should be willing to sell their best birth-rights, the liberty of thought, and of expressing thought, for the *promise* of a mess of pottage.

It is surely not too much to say, that in a country like ours, where such immense sums are annually raised for the poor, there ought to be some regulation which should prevent any miserable deserted being from perishing through want, as too often happens to such objects as that on whose interment these stanzas were written.

It is somewhat remarkable that a circumstance exactly similar is the subject of a short poem called the Pauper's Funeral, in a volume lately published by Mr. Southey. [Smith's note.]

Swells then thy feeling heart, and streams thine eye
   O'er the deserted being, poor and old,
Whom cold, reluctant, Parish Charity
   Consigns to mingle with his kindred mold?

Mourn'st thou, that *here* the time-worn sufferer ends   5
   Those evil days still threatening woes to come;
Here, where the friendless feel no want of friends,
   Where even the houseless wanderer finds an home!

What tho' no kindred crowd in sable forth,
   And sigh, or seem to sigh, around his bier;   10
Tho' o'er his coffin with the humid earth
   No children drop the unavailing tear?

Rather rejoice that *here* his sorrows cease,
   Whom sickness, age, and poverty oppress'd
Where Death, the Leveller, restores to peace   15
   The wretch who living knew not where to rest.

---

porters of the French Revolution such as Thomas Paine, whose *Vindication of the Rights of Men* was a hugely popular response to Edmund Burke's conservative attack on the Revolutionaries and their rejection of tradition and inherited institutions.

Rejoice, that tho' an outcast spurn'd by Fate,
   Thro' penury's rugged path his race he ran;
In earth's cold bosom, equall'd with the great,
   Death vindicates the insulted rights of Man.   20

Rejoice, that tho' severe his earthly doom,
   And rude, and sown with thorns the way he trod,
Now, (where unfeeling Fortune cannot come)
   He rests upon the mercies of his God.

Charlotte Smith, "Sonnet LXVII: On Passing over a Dreary Tract of Country, and near the Ruins of a Deserted Chapel, during a Tempest"

This sonnet is another good example of Smith's rejection or containment of Gothic tropes, for while the setting is certainly Gothic, the agents of fear and spookiness (the owl and fox) avoid the foul weather and gloomy ruins which for the speaker are not the site of psychological disruption but of connection and sympathy. Her interior gloom is more than a match for external gloom.

    The text is taken from *Elegiac Sonnets* (London: Cadell and Davies, 1800).

Swift fleet the billowy clouds along the sky,
   Earth seems to shudder at the storm aghast;
While only beings as forlorn as I,
   Court the chill horrors of the howling blast.
Even round yon crumbling walls, in search of food,   5
   The ravenous Owl foregoes his evening flight,
And in his cave, within the deepest wood,
   The Fox eludes the tempest of the night.
But to *my* heart congenial is the gloom
   Which hides me from a World I wish to shun;   10
That scene where Ruin saps the mouldering tomb,
   Suits with the sadness of a wretch undone.

Nor is the deepest shade, the keenest air,
Black as my fate, or cold as my despair.

Charlotte Smith, "Sonnet XLIV: Written in the Churchyard at Middleton in Sussex"

Smith's revision of the graveyard poem here is an excellent example of her poetic practice: to remove the external trappings of graveyard gloom and horror, distilling the funeral landscape to the simple yet powerful images of damaged graves and of bones mingling with shells and seaweed. From that compelling sight the speaker is driven not to moralizing or to trembling horror, but to an introspective declaration, compressed into the final couplet, of personal despair.

The text is taken from *Elegiac Sonnets* (London: Cadell and Davies, 1800).

Press'd by the Moon, mute arbitress of tides,
    While the loud equinox its power combines,
    The sea no more its swelling surge confines,
But o'er the shrinking land sublimely rides.
The wild blast, rising from the Western cave,   5
    Drives the huge billows from their heaving bed;
    Tears from their grassy tombs the village dead,[1]
And breaks the silent sabbath of the grave!
With shells and sea-weed mingled, on the shore
    Lo! their bones whiten in the frequent wave;   10
    But vain to them the winds and waters rave;
They hear the warring elements no more:
While I am doom'd—by life's long storm opprest,
To gaze with envy on their gloomy rest.

---

1 "Middleton is a village on the margin of the sea, in Sussex, containing only two or three houses. There were formerly several acres of ground between its small church and the sea, which now, by its continual encroachments, approaches within a few feet of this half-ruined and humble edifice. The wall, which once surrounded the church-yard, is entirely swept away, many of the graves broken up, and the remains of bodies interred washed into the sea; whence human bones are found among the sand and shingles on the shore." [Smith's note.]

William Parr Greswell, "Stanzas on a Decayed Yew-Tree in a Country Church-Yard"

Greswell (1765-1854) was an English cleric, poet, bibliographer, and schoolteacher whose literary career met with little popular or critical success in his lifetime. Greswell and his wife raised a large family, with most of their children achieving substantial scholarly success, a fact all the more remarkable given that Greswell's clerical post paid so little; Greswell was eulogized, in the popular *Gentleman's Magazine*, as "an example of how much persevering energy can achieve upon means so small at one time that we wonder how they could be of service" (April 1854, 427).

This poem is another Graveyard School work testifying to the long-running influence of Gray's "Elegy Written in a Country Churchyard," although Greswell does not use Gray's quatrains and sees the decayed yew as the token not of human mortality but the waning of religious fervor. The church referenced in the headnote, Denton Chapel, was Greswell's clerical homeground for sixty-three years.

The text of this poem, first published c. 1795, is taken from an 1823 edition of Greswell's poems privately published in Manchester.

————

Concerning this Yew-tree (which continued to shew some remains of vegetation till nearly the end of the last century) the reader is presented with the following *literal extract* from the Parochial Register of Denton Chapel:—

"A.D. 1714-5.—On Tuesday Feb. 1st, about noon, there happen'd a violent and terrible storm of wind which shattered and blew down ye highest and greatest part of ye yew-tree in ye chapl-yard; which before was supposed to be one of ye noblest and largest in the kingdom, being a very great ornament as well as shelter to the Chappel." [Greswell's note.]

> While silent ages glide away,
> And turrets tremble with decay,
> Let not the pensive Muse disdain
> The tribute of one humble strain,

To mourn in plaints of pity due   5
The fate of yonder blasted YEW.

Long blotted from the rolls of time
The day that mark'd thy early prime,
No hoary sage remains to say
Who kindly rear'd thy tender spray;   10
Who taught its slow-maturing form
From age to age to brave the storm.

Beneath thy widely branching shade
Perchance his weary limbs were laid,
Content, without a stone, to share   15
The umbrage of thy grateful care;
His utmost wish for thee to shed
Oblivion's dews around his head.

And long thy darkling foliage gave
A hallowed stillness to his grave;   20
For there—if legends rightly tell,
No vagrant reptile dar'd to dwell:
Even sprights, by moonlight wont to stray,
Scar'd at thy presence fled away.

As thus, in contemplative mood   25
The venerable trunk I view'd,
Forth issuing from the sapless rind
A hoarse voice trembled on the wind.
Amaz'd I stood: and wing'd with fear
These accents caught my wondering ear.   30

"ME to the precincts of the place,
That antique hallowed Pile to grace,
From native woods, in days of yore,
The fathers of the hamlet bore:
Foster'd by Superstition's hand,   35
A late memorial now I stand.

My spreading shade extending wide,
The village wonder, and its pride,
I mark'd as years revolv'd, the blow
That laid thy hardiest grandsires low.   40
Now, worn with all-consuming age,
I yield to Time's relentless rage.

Nor fondly blame, with strain severe,
The simple zeal that plac'd me here;
Nor dare thy fathers to despise,   45
And deem their upstart sons more wise:
Let self-conviction check thy pride
To error both too near allied.

Of zeal's unletter'd warmth possest,
Yet still, Religion fir'd their breast;   50
Frequent the hallowed court to tread,
Where Mercy hears Repentance plead;
Constant the grateful hymn to raise.
Our Zion echoed with their praise.

Their sons superior knowledge boast!   55
Knowledge how vain! since zeal is lost.
Now gradual, as my branches pine,
I see Devotion's flame decline.
And while, like me, RELIGION wanes,
Alas! her vestige scarce remains."   60

Thomas Dermody, "Written in a Burial Place"

Dermody (1775-1802) was an Irish-born poet and writer, something
of a child prodigy in languages and literature but undisciplined in
his habits (which included heavy drinking). By the time he was ten
Dermody had experienced the loss of both a beloved brother and his
mother, and with his father's alcoholism driving the family into pov-
erty, Dermody left home before his eleventh birthday, supporting
himself by tutoring other boys in Greek and Latin. His profligacy

and sometimes volatile temper combined with Dermody's pride to
keep him close to poverty and homelessness despite repeated en-
counters with would-be benefactors. One such benefactor, Gilbert
Austin, arranged, when Dermody was only thirteen, for the private
publication of a collection of his poems, an event which brought
Dermody to the attention of a number of noble, cultivated patrons
and which brought him, as well, some much-needed financial sup-
port. But Dermody proved unable to take advantage of his good
luck; in a fit of pique he wrote verses insulting Austin and his family
and when those verses found their way to his benefactor (passed
along by Dermody's landlord, who resented Dermody's refusal to
convert to Methodism), Dermody was banished, and his reputation
and character so impugned that he soon found himself struggling.
He eventually found support from the Countess of Moira, and for
several years pursued his studies and his writing while keeping out
of serious trouble. Yet Dermody's "almost insatiable desire for ale
and good fellowship"[1] and his unwillingness to subject himself to
the niceties of decorum (despite his insistent pursuit of upper-
class patronage) soon caused Dermody and the Countess to part
ways, and Dermody fell into poverty again. Introductions to subse-
quent benefactors ended the same way: in estrangement and with
Dermody returning to poverty and homelessness. He was nearly
impressed into military service twice, both times rescued by ac-
quaintances, but later voluntarily joined the army out of desper-
ation. He served honorably, and was wounded several times, but
his stint in the army failed to create a lasting sense of responsibility
and self-discipline. Upon his discharge Dermody went to London
and his old patterns of behavior quickly returned; money earned
from the publication of a volume of poems was quickly spent and
subsequent benefactors repeatedly found themselves disappointed
by Dermody's return to debauchery. As James Grant Raymond,
his biographer and literary executor, noted, "Few indeed have ex-
perienced so liberal and exalted a patronage as Dermody, and it is
infinitely to be regretted that none ever made so unwise a use of
it."[2] Dermody's dissipations and alcoholism weakened his health,

---

1 James Grant Raymond, *The Life of Thomas Dermody*. London: Miller, 1806, vol.
I, p. 224.
2 Raymond, II: 220.

already complicated by asthma (or possibly tuberculosis), and he died, penniless, at the age of twenty-seven.

Dermody remained much more an Augustan than a Romantic in his poetic sensibilities; as he himself wrote, "My professed aversion to the arbitrary and ill-founded innovations of some modern reformers, has induced me to aim at the manly style of our poetical fathers, and to attempt the revival of spirited sentiment, relieved by the chaste and graceful simplicity of forcible diction."[1] Though Dermody's work was known to many of the signficant literary figures of his day, few thought it worth their while to mention it; by the time Dermody was dead, the poetic revolution inaugurated by Wordsworth and Coleridge's *Lyrical Ballads* had changed the literary landscape and Dermody's work was largely anachronistic.

A slightly revised version of lines from this poem were used as the epitaph on Dermody's tomb.

Text: From *The Harp of Erin, Containing the Poetical Works of the Late Thomas Dermody.* 2 vols, edited by James Grant Raymond, London: Richard Phillips, 1807, II: 252-253.

> Ah me! and must I, like the tenant lie
> Of this dark cell, all hush'd the witching song,
> And will not Feeling bend his streaming eye
> On my green sod, as slow he wends along,
> And, smiting his rapt bosom, softly sigh,   5
> "His genius soar'd above the vulgar throng!"
>
> Will he not fence my weedless turf around,
> Sacred from dull-ey'd Folly's vagrant feet,
> And there, soft-swelling in aerial sound,
> Will he not list, at eve, to voices sweet,   10
> Strew with the spring's first flow'rs the little mound,
> And often muse within the lone retreat!
>
> Yes;—though I not affect th' immortal bay,[2]
> Nor bold effusions of the learned quill,

1 Raymond, II: 316.

2 Crowns of bay (or laurel) leaves were often awarded to victors in athletic and poetic competitions in ancient Greece and Rome.

Nor often have I wound my tedious way   15
Up the steep summit of the Muse's hill,
Yet sometimes have I pour'd th' incondite lay,[1]
And sometimes have I felt the rapt'rous thrill;

Him therefore, whom ev'n once, the sacred Muse
Has blest, shall be to feeling ever dear,   20
And soft as sweet sad April's gleamy dews,
On my cold clay shall fall the genial tear,
While pensive as the springing herb he views,
He cries, "Though mute, there is a poet here!"

Henry Kirke White, "Lines Supposed to be Spoken by a Lover at the Grave of his Mistress. Occasioned by a Situation in a Romance"

White (1785-1806) was an English poet and essayist who published his first poem (a translation of Horace) when he was 15; by 18 he published his first volume of poems, by which he hoped to raise enough money to begin study for the priesthood. The volume was not well received, although the poet Robert Southey was supportive and encouraging. White, through his friendship with an evangelical educator at Cambridge, was able to begin studies there in 1805, but died the next year (at the age of 21) of tuberculosis ("consumption" as it was then called). His early death and poetic promise led many of his contemporaries, including Byron and Southey (who served as executor of White's literary remains) to regard White as another example of poetic genius tragically cut short. The collection of White's poetry which Southey edited (1807) went through ten editions in eleven years, but despite this popularity in the Romantic period White is virtually unknown now, even in the world of Romantic studies.

This poem, an evocative work that contributes to the shifting of the original Graveyard School emphasis on morality to the realm of private feeling, evincing an almost Keatsian sensibility toward

---

1 Unpolished or "rude" song.

the commingling of death and love and the half-sought approach
of death (a common theme in White), appeared in White's first
collection, *Clifton Grove, a Sketch in Verse, with other Poems*, published
in 1803. The text is taken from the sixth edition of Southey's *The
Remains of Henry Kirke White* (London: Longmans, 1813).

———

Mary, the moon is sleeping on thy grave,
And on the turf thy lover sad is kneeling,
The big tear in his eye.—Mary, awake,
From thy dark house arise, and bless his sight
On the pale moonbeam gliding. Soft, and low,   5
Pour on the silver ear of night thy tale,
Thy whispered tale of comfort and of love,
To soothe thy Edward's lorn, distracted soul,
And cheer his breaking heart.—Come, as thou didst,
When o'er the barren moors the night wind howled,   10
And the deep thunders shook the ebon throne
Of the startled night!—Oh! then, as lone reclining,
I listened sadly to the dismal storm,
Thou, on the lambent lightnings wild careering
Didst strike my moody eye;—dead pale thou wert,   15
Yet passing lovely.—Thou didst smile upon me,
And oh! thy voice it rose so musical,
Betwixt the hollow pauses of the storm,
That at the sound the winds forgot to rave,
And the stern demon of the tempest, charmed,   20
Sunk on his rocking throne to still repose,
Locked in the arms of silence.
                              Spirit of her!
My only love! Oh! now again arise,
And let once more thine aëry accents fall
Soft on my listening ear. The night is calm,   25
The gloomy willows wave in sinking cadence
With the stream that sweeps below. Divinely swelling
On the still air, the distant waterfall
Mingles its melody;—and, high above,
The pensive empress of the solemn night,   30

Fitful, emerging from the rapid clouds,
Shows her chaste face in the meridian sky.
No wicked elves upon the *Warlock-knoll*
Dare now assemble at their mystic revels.
It is a night when, from their primrose beds,   35
The gentle ghosts of injured innocents
Are known to rise, and wander on the breeze,
Or take their stand by the oppressor's couch,
And strike grim terror to his guilty soul.
The spirit of my love might now awake,   40
And hold its customed converse.
                                    Mary, lo!
Thy Edward kneels upon thy verdant grave,
And calls upon thy name.—The breeze that blows
On his wan cheek, will soon sweep over him
In solemn music, a funereal dirge,   45
Wild and most sorrowful.—His cheek is pale,
The worm that preyed upon thy youthful bloom
It canker'd green on his.—Now lost he stands,
The ghost of what he was, and the cold dew,
Which bathes his aching temples, gives sure omen   50
Of speedy dissolution.——Mary, soon,
Thy love will lay his pallid cheek to thine,
And sweetly will he sleep with thee in death.

Henry Kirke White, "Lines Written in Wilford Churchyard, on Recovery from Sickness"

Wilford is in the shire of Nottingham, in central England; White spent several weeks there in 1804 recovering from illness, and it is likely the poem was written at this time. While much of White's later verse reflects his increasing sense of religious fervor, this graveyard poem's very personal reflection—almost an anticipation—of death is only lightly touched by White's piety.

Here would I wish to sleep.—This is the spot
Which I have long mark'd out to lay my bones in;[1]
Tir'd out and wearied with the riotous world,
Beneath this yew I would be sepulchred.
It is a lovely spot! The sultry sun,   5
From his meridian height, endeavours vainly
To pierce the shadowy foliage, while the zephyr[2]
Comes wafting gently o'er the rippling Trent,[3]
And plays about my wan cheek. 'Tis a nook
Most pleasant. Such a one perchance, did Gray[4]   10
Frequent, as with a vagrant muse he wanton'd.

Come, I will sit me down and meditate,
For I am wearied with my summer's walk;
And here I may repose in silent ease;
And thus, perchance, when life's sad journey's o'er,   15
My harass'd soul, in this same spot, may find
The haven of its rest—beneath this sod
Perchance may sleep it sweetly, sound as death.

I would not have my corpse cemented down
With brick and stone, defrauding the poor earth-worm   20
Of its predestin'd dues; no, I would lie
Beneath a little hillock, grass o'ergrown,
Swath'd down with osiers, just as sleep the cotters.[5]
Yet may not *undistinguish'd* be my grave;
But there at eve may some congenial soul   25
Duly resort, and shed a pious tear,
The good man's benison—no more I ask.
And, oh! (if heavenly beings may look down
From where, with cherubim, inspir'd they sit,
Upon this little dim-discovered spot,   30

---

1 Despite this expressed wish, White, who died while attending Cambridge University, was buried in All Souls' Churchyard in Cambridge.
2 The gentle west wind.
3 The river which runs through Wilford.
4 Thomas Gray, author of "Elegy Written in a Country Churchyard" (1751).
5 Peasant cottagers.

The earth,) then will I cast a glance *below*
On him who thus my ashes shall embalm;
And I will weep too, and will bless the wanderer,
Wishing he may not long be doom'd to pine
In this low-thoughted world of darkling woe,   35
But that, ere long, he reach his kindred skies.

Yet 'twas a silly thought, as if the body,
Mouldering beneath the surface of the earth,
Could taste the sweets of summer scenery,
And feel the freshness of the balmy breeze!   40
Yet nature speaks within the human bosom,
And, spite of reason, bids it look beyond
His narrow verge of being, and provide
A decent residence for its clayey shell,
Endear'd to it by time. And who would lay   45
His body in the city burial-place,
To be thrown up again by some rude sexton,
And yield its narrow house another tenant,
Ere the moist flesh had mingled with the dust,
Ere the tenacious hair had left the scalp,   50
Expos'd to insult lewd, and wantonness?
No, I will lay me in the *village* ground;
There are the dead respected. The poor hind,
Unlettered as he is, would scorn to invade
The silent resting-place of death. I've seen   55
The labourer, returning from his toil,
Here stay his steps, and call his children round,
And slowly spell the rudely sculptur'd rhymes,[1]
And, in his rustic manner, moralize.
I've mark'd with what a silent awe he'd spoken,   60
With head uncover'd, his respectful manner,
And all the honours which he paid the grave,
And thought on cities, where ev'n cemeteries,[2]

---

1 Roughly carved epitaphs.
2 A cemetery is distinct from a churchyard: the former is municipal property,
located within a city's bounds, and not connected to or affiliated with a particular
church building; a "churchyard," although technically any property belonging to

Bestrew'd with all the emblems of mortality,
Are not protected from the drunken insolence   65
Of wassailers[1] profane, and wanton havock.
Grant, Heav'n, that here my pilgrimage may close!
Yet, if this be deny'd, where'er my bones
May lie—or in the city's crowded bounds,
Or scatter'd wide o'er the huge sweep of waters,   70
Or left a prey on some deserted shore
To the rapacious cormorant,[2]—yet still,
(For why should sober reason cast away
A thought which soothes the soul?) yet still my spirit
Shall wing its way to these my native regions,[3]   75
And hover o'er this spot. Oh, then I'll think
Of times when I was seated 'neath this yew
In solemn rumination; and will smile
With joy that I have got my long'd release.

George Townsend, "Elegy, Supposed to be Written in Barnet Church-Yard"

Townsend (1788-1856) was, like so many eighteenth-century Grave-yard School poets, a Cambridge-educated clergyman who earned his M.A. in 1816, two years after having been ordained a priest. Most of Townsend's writings were related to religious matters.

This poem features many of the standard elements of Grave-yard School poetry, following the model established by Blair and Parnell of beginning with Gothic horrors and spectral visions, then shifting to didactic episodes, in this case illustrating the conventional Graveyard pieties of eschewing ambition, forswearing suicide, and recognizing the inescapable power of Death, the Great Leveller. Perhaps because of his vocation, Townsend's Graveyard

---

a church, is used to denote a graveyard that is on church property, usually adjacent to a church.

1 Drunks.

2 A large sea-bird, noted for a voracious appetite; thus, any greedy or consuming animal or person.

3 White was born in, and spent much of his early life in, Nottinghamshire.

School poem is much closer in intent, if not in style, to those of his Augustan predecessors.

The text of this poem is taken from Townsend's earliest work, *Poems* (London: Longman, Hurst, Reese and Orme; Cambridge: Deighton, 1810).

The last long echo of the midnight bell
  Sweeps with dull roar across the barren heath:
Enwrapt in thought, I bid the world farewell,
  And seek with trembling step th' abode of Death.

On iron hinge the door grates harsh; the wind   5
  Pours through the trees a melancholy sound;
While Fancy, rousing with strange awe the mind,
  Calls Contemplation terror-wing'd around.

Say, whence this secret fear of things unknown,
  This sudden horror and resistless dread,   10
That chills my bosom as I trace alone
  The grave's dull monuments, the silent dead?

Why should I fear to tread this thick'ning gloom?
  Or why this wild emotion seize my frame?
A solemn myst'ry hovers round the tomb,   15
  The consciousness of things I dare not name.

Beyond that yew-tree shade, still seem to glide
  The grisly tenants of the darksome tomb,
Their shadowy forms flit past in silent pride,
  And blame the steps that visit their dull home.   20

See, how on high their meagre arms they wave!
  See, how their eyeless sockets seem to glare!
They wave my trembling footsteps from the grave,
  And tread sublime upon the viewless air.

And we are spirits, though on earth confin'd,   25
  Imprison'd in this tenement of clay:

The body drops; then soars th' immortal mind
  'Mid other spirits of celestial ray.

We are surrounded by the world of souls;
  Attendant spirits fly around unseen;   30
Our mortal state alone the mind controuls,
  And hides the beings of immortal mien.

Enthron'd in certain mystery of fate
  Death sits, and summons to his court mankind;
Subjects and kings, in melancholy state,   35
  Hear the stern call, and leave the world behind.

Sceptres and mitres, coronets and crowns,
  The conqueror's laurel, and the poet's wreath,
Alike the monarch's and the peasant's bones,
  Strew the long road, and mark the way to death.   40

Propp'd by this marble tomb around I see
  Confus'dly scatter'd near, without a plan,
The mould'ring relics of mortality,
  The liveliest monitors to thoughtless man.

There lies a youth, whose disappointed pride   45
  Urg'd to tremendous deeds the daring soul,
Ambition's potent laws his only guide,
  His only aim ambition's luring goal.

Visions of grandeur, and immortal fame,
  Strew'd with delusive flow'rs life's blissful way,   50
But, lightning-wing'd, stern Disappointment came,
  And rang'd her adverse ills in long array.

Contempt exulted, and with iron frown
  Abash'd the youth, o'erwhelm'd with conscious grief;
Reason's loud calls Despair and Pride disown,   55
  And urge the sullen soul to base relief.

If life begin in misery and woe,
  "How sad must life conclude!" the suff'rer cried;
Rous'd to the desp'rate deed, the fatal blow
  He struck, and with remorseless anguish died!   60

Teach me, Almighty Power, to bear the woes,
  Which wait on life, and rise at thy command;
Ne'er let me seek within the grave repose,
  Nor check Death's long delay with impious hand.

There, in the distant shade so deep and dull,   65
  Close by the side of his domestic tomb,
Is thrown with careless scorn a parent's skull,
  To give the remnant of his offspring room.

There, through the branches of yon cheerless yew,
  In sov'reign majesty the Queen of Night,   70
With lustre back reflected by the dew,
  Pours on these sod-clad graves her pensive light.

And those, who sleep below, in life's gay bloom,
  At summer eve, or in the pride of spring,
Heedless of cares that cloth'd their age in gloom,   75
  Around this tree have form'd the festive ring.

And still in spring the village children come
  With lightsome steps at evening's tranquil hour,
Unconscious sport upon a parent's tomb,
  There join the dance, or pluck the radiant flow'r.   80

But these, when smiling infancy is past,
  And manhood claims the tenants of the soil,
Must bear alike misfortune's varied blast,
  Labour, and want, and poverty, and toil.

Let not presumption say, the poor alone,   85
  Alone the rich, have joy or sorrow here;

The checquer'd scenes of life to each are known,
  Howe'er diversified its active sphere.

There slowly crawling o'er the flesh-fed soil,
  To seek yon new-turn'd earth the graves among,   90
Wreathing his length in many a twining coil,
  The tardy earthworm drags his form along.

Child of corruption, truly dost thou seek
  With mortal appetite thy destin'd prey;
There thou shalt fatten on a lovely cheek,   95
  And glut thy noisome length with virgin clay.

In yonder new-made grave, consumption-worn
  The gay, the great, the lov'd Eliza lies:
Foul reptile, gorge upon the proud high-born,
  Nor spare the beauty of thy youthful prize.   100

There penetrate, there sweetly feed, dig deep,
  Pierce the sunk eyes, and revel on the breast;
The fair one at thy banquet will not weep,
  Nor rival lovers claim thy nauseous feast.

Attend ye gay, ye proud, who love to tread   105
  The paths of joy, by pleasure's train ador'd:
Ye too must bow, and mingle with the dead,
  The grave your home, the reptile worm your lord.

And when, soft streaming on the dewy air,
  The song of pleasure lifts your courage high,   110
With bliss eternal earthly joys compare,
  But think on Death's dread hour, and learn to die.

William Wordsworth, "We Are Seven"

Wordsworth (1770-1850) is one of the major figures of the British Romantic period. His exploration of a new style of poetry—written in ordinary language (for his time) and on ordinary subjects, avoiding the rhetorical techniques and classical topics of mainstream Augustan poetry—is one of his most important innovations, one that has shaped poetry to this day. His other is his major contribution to the development of a "nature poetry" that explored, in a new way, the relationship between humanity and the natural world, including its philosophical and spiritual implications.

Wordsworth was little interested in literary supernaturalism; his condemnation of the Gothic craze of his own moment is well known and often quoted. Referring to a general sense of an intellectual malaise afflicting his countrymen, Wordsworth, after pointing a finger at traumatic political events and the explosion of urban populations, remarks specifically on a literary decline in which Gothic fictions figure prominently: "The invaluable works of our elder writers, I had almost said the works of Shakespeare and Milton, are driven into neglect by frantic novels, sickly and stupid German tragedies, and deluges of idle and extravagant stories in verse. When I think upon this degrading thirst after outrageous stimulation I am almost ashamed to have spoken of the feeble effort with which I have endeavored to counteract it . . ." (Preface to *Lyrical Ballads*).

Yet in some of his earlier works Wordsworth himself flirted with Gothic elements, as in the ghostly figure of "The Danish Boy" or the Gothic mood of "Guilt and Sorrow." He left such subjects behind quickly, although some traces of the Gothic and its predecessors may still be discerned in his work. His *Essays on Epitaphs* and the "Churchyard Among the Mountains" section of the *The Excursion* demonstrate that Wordsworth's acquaintance with Graveyard School verse was considerable, and that while his own revolutionary revisions of poetic practice distanced him from the forms and style of conventional Graveyard poetry, he also, like other Romantics, recognized both a poetic and moral power in graveyard tropes, and sought to recast them in forms consistent with his own poetics.

One of his better-known short poems, "We Are Seven" would seem to have little in common with Augustan graveyard poetry other than the setting. That is true—in fact, that's precisely the point, for while this graveyard remains a site of contention, it is not one of moral or spiritual struggle or aspiration. Indeed, Wordsworth has recast the gravesite encounter that is so common in the more horrific examples of Graveyard verse. Here there is no spectre, no looming figure of Death whose role in the didactic drama is to redirect our life's attention to spiritual endeavor. The encounter here is, however, with something almost as Other, to the adult figure in the poem, as any ghost. As the voice of a strict empiricism, the adult speaker of "We Are Seven" is almost a counter for the Augustan rationalism that Wordsworth rejected in his poetic practice. The little girl, in her emotionally charged graveyard setting, is the Romantic voice—and she has the last word—not of spiritual correction, but of emotional and psychological engagement, the advocate of a richer realm than the neoclassical speaker can comprehend.

This poem was composed in spring of 1798 and first published in *Lyrical Ballads* later that year. Wordsworth explained that "the little girl who is the heroine I met within the area of Goodrich Castle in the year 1793." He returned to the area in 1841 hoping to find the girl, but as he never knew her name, he had no luck. Goodrich Castle is in Hertfordshire, in west-central England, and was an abandoned and partly ruined castle in Wordsworth's time, as it is today.

> ——— A simple Child,
> That lightly draws its breath,
> And feels its life in every limb,
> What should it know of death?
>
> I met a little cottage Girl: 5
> She was eight years old, she said;
> Her hair was thick with many a curl
> That clustered round her head.
>
> She had a rustic, woodland air,
> And she was wildly clad: 10

Her eyes were fair, and very fair;
—Her beauty made me glad.

"Sisters and brothers, little Maid,
How many may you be?"
"How many? Seven in all," she said   15
And wondering looked at me.

"And where are they? I pray you tell."
She answered, "Seven are we;
And two of us at Conway¹ dwell,
And two are gone to sea.   20

"Two of us in the church-yard lie,
My sister and my brother;
And, in the church-yard cottage, I
Dwell near them with my mother."

"You say that two at Conway dwell,   25
And two are gone to sea,
Yet ye are seven!—I pray you tell,
Sweet Maid, how this may be."

Then did the little Maid reply,
"Seven boys and girls are we;   30
Two of us in the church-yard lie,
Beneath the church-yard tree."

"You run about, my little Maid,
Your limbs they are alive;
If two are in the church-yard laid,   35
Then ye are only five."

"Their graves are green, they may be seen,"
The little Maid replied,
"Twelve steps or more from my mother's door,
And they are side by side.   40

---

1 A seaport in Wales.

"My stockings there I often knit,
My kerchief there I hem;
And there upon the ground I sit,
And sing a song to them.

"And often after sunset, Sir,   45
When it is light and fair,
I take my little porringer,
And eat my supper there.

"The first that died was sister Jane;
In bed she moaning lay,   50
Till God released her of her pain;
And then she went away.

"So in the church-yard she was laid;
And, when the grass was dry,
Together round her grave we played,   55
My brother John and I.

"And when the ground was white with snow,
And I could run and slide,
My brother John was forced to go,
And he lies by her side."   60

"How many are you, then," said I,
"If they two are in heaven?"
Quick was the little Maid's reply,
"O Master! we are seven."

"But they are dead; those two are dead!   65
Their spirits are in heaven!"
'Twas throwing words away; for still
The little Maid would have her will,
And said, "Nay, we are seven!"

Washington Irving, "The Widow and Her Son"

Irving (1783-1859) is one of the best-known American writers of the early nineteenth century, best remembered now for "The Legend of Sleepy Hollow" and "Rip Van Winkle" (both of which appeared in the same collection from which the present essay is taken). Deeply interested in the character and origins of the young American nation, Irving explored both America's future promise in his frontier writing and its past in his reworkings of European folklore and his explorations of America's cultural debts to the Old World.

In "The Widow and Her Son" Irving shifts the sentimental register of the conventional Graveyard School away from melancholy, with its focus on interiority, and onto compassion and sympathy, feelings that bind us to our fellow beings. Not, in his graveyard observation of a grieving mother, does Irving's persona of Geoffrey Crayon find the raw material for meditation on matters spiritual. While clearly siting the experience in a Christian context, both literally and figuratively, Irving tropes the churchyard as a place where tears and sorrow for another are the primary emotional responses, those responses are expressed in pragmatic terms—offers of financial assistance, rendered unnecessary because of the prompt compassion of the mother's neighbors—and in social and moral terms —the press-ganging of the young man precipitates the death of his father and the decline into poverty of his mother, and is responsible for his own ill health and untimely death. The church provides the background against which we see the mother, first alone and then bereft, but Irving's concern is with the hearts of living more than with the souls of the dead.

This essay is chapter twelve of *The Sketch-Book of Geoffrey Crayon* (1819-20); the text is taken from *The Sketch-Book of Geoffrey Crayon, Esq.*, Author's Revised Edition, New York: Putnam, 1848.

> Pittie olde age, within whose silver haires
> Honour and reverence evermore have rain'd.
>
> Marlowe's *Tamburlaine*

Those who are in the habit of remarking such matters must have noticed the passive quiet of an English landscape on Sunday.

The clacking of the mill, the regularly recurring stroke of the flail, the din of the blacksmith's hammer, the whistling of the plough-man, the rattling of the cart, and all other sounds of rural labor are suspended. The very farm-dogs bark less frequently, being less disturbed by passing travellers. At such times I have almost fancied the winds sunk into quiet, and that the sunny landscape, with its fresh green tints melting into blue haze, enjoyed the hallowed calm.

> Sweet day, so pure, so calm, so bright,
> The bridal of the earth and sky.[1]

Well was it ordained that the day of devotion should be a day of rest. The holy repose which reigns over the face of nature, has its moral influence; every restless passion is charmed down, and we feel the natural religion of the soul gently springing up within us. For my part, there are feelings that visit me, in a country church, amid the beautiful serenity of nature, which I experience nowhere else; and if not a more religious, I think I am a better man on Sunday than on any other day of the seven.

During my recent residence in the country, I used frequently to attend at the old village church. Its shadowy aisles; its mouldering monuments; its dark oaken panelling, all reverend with the gloom of departed years, seemed to fit it for the haunt of solemn medita-tion; but being in a wealthy aristocratic neighborhood, the glitter of fashion penetrated even into the sanctuary; and I felt myself continually thrown back upon the world by the frigidity and pomp of the poor worms around me. The only being in the whole congre-gation who appeared thoroughly to feel the humble and prostrate piety of a true Christian was a poor decrepit old woman, bending under the weight of years and infirmities. She bore the traces of something better than abject poverty. The lingerings of decent pride were visible in her appearance. Her dress, though humble in the extreme, was scrupulously clean. Some trivial respect, too, had been awarded her, for she did not take her seat among the village poor, but sat alone on the steps of the altar. She seemed to have

---

1 The opening lines of a hymn, entitled "Vertue," by the Welsh poet and clergy-man George Herbert (1593-1633).

survived all love, all friendship, all society; and to have nothing left her but the hopes of heaven. When I saw her feebly rising and bending her aged form in prayer; habitually conning her prayer-book, which her palsied hand and failing eyes would not permit her to read, but which she evidently knew by heart; I felt persuaded that the faltering voice of that poor woman arose to heaven far before the responses of the clerk, the swell of the organ, or the chanting of the choir.

I am fond of loitering about country churches, and this was so delightfully situated, that it frequently attracted me. It stood on a knoll, round which a small stream made a beautiful bend, and then wound its way through a long reach of soft meadow scenery. The church was surrounded by yew-trees which seemed almost coeval with itself. Its tall Gothic spire shot up lightly from among them, with rooks and crows generally wheeling about it. I was seated there one still sunny morning, watching two laborers who were digging a grave. They had chosen one of the most remote and neglected corners of the church-yard; where, from the number of nameless graves around, it would appear that the indigent and friendless were huddled into the earth. I was told that the new-made grave was for the only son of a poor widow. While I was meditating on the distinctions of worldly rank, which extend thus down into the very dust, the toll of the bell announced the approach of the funeral. They were the obsequies of poverty, with which pride had nothing to do. A coffin of the plainest materials, without pall or other covering, was borne by some of the villagers. The sexton walked before with an air of cold indifference. There were no mock mourners in the trappings of affected woe; but there was one real mourner who feebly tottered after the corpse. It was the aged mother of the deceased—the poor old woman whom I had seen seated on the steps of the altar. She was supported by a humble friend, who was endeavoring to comfort her. A few of the neighboring poor had joined the train, and some children of the village were running hand in hand, now shouting with unthinking mirth, and now pausing to gaze, with childish curiosity, on the grief of the mourner.

As the funeral train approached the grave, the parson issued from the church porch, arrayed in the surplice, with prayer-book in hand, and attended by the clerk. The service, however, was a mere act of charity. The deceased had been destitute, and the survivor was penniless. It was shuffled through, therefore, in form, but coldly and unfeelingly. The well-fed priest moved but a few steps from the church door; his voice could scarcely be heard at the grave; and never did I hear the funeral service, that sublime and touching ceremony, turned into such a frigid mummery of words.

I approached the grave. The coffin was placed on the ground. On it were inscribed the name and age of the deceased—"George Somers, aged 26 years." The poor mother had been assisted to kneel down at the head of it. Her withered hands were clasped, as if in prayer, but I could perceive by a feeble rocking of the body, and a convulsive motion of her lips, that she was gazing on the last relics of her son, with the yearnings of a mother's heart.

Preparations were made to deposit the coffin in the earth. There was that bustling stir which breaks so harshly on the feelings of grief and affection; directions given in the cold tones of business: the striking of spades into sand and gravel; which, at the grave of those we love, is, of all sounds, the most withering. The bustle around seemed to waken the mother from a wretched reverie. She raised her glazed eyes, and looked about with a faint wildness. As the men approached with cords to lower the coffin into the grave, she wrung her hands, and broke into an agony of grief. The poor woman who attended her took her by the arm, endeavoring to raise her from the earth, and to whisper something like consolation—"Nay, now—nay, now—don't take it so sorely to heart." She could only shake her head and wring her hands, as one not to be comforted.

As they lowered the body into the earth, the creaking of the cords seemed to agonize her; but when, on some accidental obstruction, there was a justling of the coffin, all the tenderness of the mother burst forth; as if any harm could come to him who was far beyond the reach of worldly suffering.

I could see no more—my heart swelled into my throat—my eyes filled with tears—I felt as if I were acting a barbarous part in standing by, and gazing idly on this scene of maternal anguish. I wandered to another part of the church-yard, where I remained until the funeral train had dispersed.

When I saw the mother slowly and painfully quitting the grave, leaving behind her the remains of all that was dear to her on earth, and returning to silence and destitution, my heart ached for her. What, thought I, are the distresses of the rich! they have friends to soothe—pleasures to beguile—a world to divert and dissipate their griefs. What are the sorrows of the young! Their growing minds soon close above the wound—their elastic spirits soon rise beneath the pressure—their green and ductile affections soon twine round new objects. But the sorrows of the poor, who have no outward appliances to soothe—the sorrows of the aged, with whom life at best is but a wintry day, and who can look for no after-growth of joy—the sorrows of a widow, aged, solitary, destitute, mourning over an only son, the last solace of her years; these are indeed sorrows which make us feel the impotency of consolation.

It was some time before I left the church-yard. On my way homeward I met with the woman who had acted as comforter: she was just returning from accompanying the mother to her lonely habitation, and I drew from her some particulars connected with the affecting scene I had witnessed.

The parents of the deceased had resided in the village from childhood. They had inhabited one of the neatest cottages, and by various rural occupations, and the assistance of a small garden, had supported themselves creditably and comfortably, and led a happy and a blameless life. They had one son, who had grown up to be the staff and pride of their age.—"Oh, sir!" said the good woman, "he was such a comely lad, so sweet-tempered, so kind to every one around him, so dutiful to his parents! It did one's heart good to see him of a Sunday, dressed out in his best, so tall, so straight, so cheery, supporting his old mother to church—for she was always fonder of leaning on George's arm, than on her good man's; and, poor soul, she might well be proud of him, for a finer lad there was not in the country round."

Unfortunately, the son was tempted, during a year of scarcity and agricultural hardship, to enter into the service of one of the small craft that plied on a neighboring river. He had not been long in this employ when he was entrapped by a press-gang, and carried off to sea.[1] His parents received tidings of his seizure, but beyond

---

1 The British Navy long relied on the practice of "impressing" young men into service, a crude and sometimes quite physical form of conscripting or "drafting"

that they could learn nothing. It was the loss of their main prop. The father, who was already infirm, grew heartless and melancholy, and sunk into his grave. The widow, left lonely in her age and feebleness, could no longer support herself, and came upon the parish.[1] Still there was a kind feeling toward her throughout the village, and a certain respect as being one of the oldest inhabitants. As no one applied for the cottage, in which she had passed so many happy days, she was permitted to remain in it, where she lived solitary and almost helpless. The few wants of nature were chiefly supplied from the scanty productions of her little garden, which the neighbors would now and then cultivate for her. It was but a few days before the time at which these circumstances were told me, that she was gathering some vegetables for her repast, when she heard the cottage door which faced the garden suddenly opened. A stranger came out, and seemed to be looking eagerly and wildly around. He was dressed in seaman's clothes, was emaciated and ghastly pale, and bore the air of one broken by sickness and hardships. He saw her, and hastened towards her, but his steps were faint and faltering; he sank on his knees before her, and sobbed like a child. The poor woman gazed upon him with a vacant and wandering eye—"Oh, my dear, dear mother! don't you know your son? your poor boy, George?" It was indeed the wreck of her once noble lad, who, shattered by wounds, by sickness and foreign imprisonment, had, at length, dragged his wasted limbs homeward, to repose among the scenes of his childhood.

I will not attempt to detail the particulars of such a meeting, where joy and sorrow were so completely blended: still he was alive! he was come home! he might yet live to comfort and cherish her old age! Nature, however, was exhausted in him; and if any thing had been wanting to finish the work of fate, the desolation of his native cottage would have been sufficient. He stretched himself on the pallet on which his widowed mother had passed many a sleepless night, and he never rose from it again.

---

sailors that was practiced from the later 17th century into the early 19th century. Merchant sailors, such as the young man of this story, were the most frequent targets since they already had knowledge of shipcraft.

1 To "come upon the parish" is to become reliant upon publicly supplied financial support and, often, housing; an early version of "welfare."

The villagers, when they heard that George Somers had returned, crowded to see him, offering every comfort and assistance that their humble means afforded. He was too weak, however, to talk—he could only look his thanks. His mother was his constant attendant; and he seemed unwilling to be helped by any other hand.

There is something in sickness that breaks down the pride of manhood; that softens the heart, and brings it back to the feelings of infancy. Who that has languished, even in advanced life, in sickness and despondency; who that has pined on a weary bed in the neglect and loneliness of a foreign land; but has thought on the mother "that looked on his childhood," that smoothed his pillow, and administered to his helplessness? Oh! there is an enduring tenderness in the love of a mother to her son that transcends all other affections of the heart. It is neither to be chilled by selfishness, nor daunted by danger, nor weakened by worthlessness, nor stifled by ingratitude. She will sacrifice every comfort to his convenience; she will surrender every pleasure to his enjoyment; she will glory in his fame, and exult in his prosperity:—and, if misfortune overtake him, he will be the dearer to her from misfortune; and if disgrace settle upon his name, she will still love and cherish him in spite of his disgrace; and if all the world beside cast him off, she will be all the world to him.

Poor George Somers had known what it was to be in sickness, and none to soothe—lonely and in prison, and none to visit him. He could not endure his mother from his sight; if she moved away, his eye would follow her. She would sit for hours by his bed, watching him as he slept. Sometimes he would start from a feverish dream, and look anxiously up until he saw her bending over him; when he would take her hand, lay it on his bosom, and fall asleep, with the tranquillity of a child. In this way he died.

My first impulse on hearing this humble tale of affliction was to visit the cottage of the mourner, and administer pecuniary assistance, and, if possible, comfort. I found, however, on inquiry, that the good feelings of the villagers had prompted them to do every thing that the case admitted: and as the poor know best how to console each other's sorrows, I did not venture to intrude.

The next Sunday I was at the village church; when, to my surprise, I saw the poor old woman tottering down the aisle to her accustomed seat on the steps of the altar.

She had made an effort to put on something like mourning for her son; and nothing could be more touching than this struggle between pious affection and utter poverty: a black ribbon or so—a faded black handkerchief, and one or two more such humble attempts to express by outward signs that grief which passes show. When I looked round upon the storied monuments, the stately hatchments, the cold marble pomp, with which grandeur mourned magnificently over departed pride, and turned to this poor widow, bowed down by age and sorrow, at the altar of her God, and offering up the prayers and praises of a pious, though a broken heart, I felt that this living monument of real grief was worth them all.

I related her story to some of the wealthy members of the congregation, and they were moved by it. They exerted themselves to render her situation more comfortable, and to lighten her afflictions. It was, however, but smoothing a few steps to the grave. In the course of a Sunday or two after, she was missed from her usual seat at church, and before I left the neighborhood, I heard, with a feeling of satisfaction, that she had quietly breathed her last, and had gone to rejoin those she loved, in that world where sorrow is never known, and friends are never parted.

David Macbeth Moir, "The Child's Burial in Spring"

Moir (1798-1851) was a Scottish physician and poet—becoming both, formally, at the age of eighteen, when he earned his medical degree and published his first volume of poems. A prolific poet, Moir was closely allied with the Blackwood's circle, publishing many of his works in *Blackwood's Edinburgh Magazine* and doing editorial work for the publishing house; indeed, Moir even named two of his sons after William Blackwood and John Wilson.

Moir's literary output covered a range of themes and topics, including a number of works readily locatable within the late Graveyard School tradition and others which extend Gothic tropes into the mid-nineteenth century in a way that seems redolent of Poe. Like most practitioners of late Graveyard verse, Moir generally rejects the troping of potent horrors in favor of a milder emotional tone; a softened melancholy evokes feelings that prepare the reader for a moral or philosophical observation without the hectoring, sermonizing energy often characteristic of earlier Graveyard School work.

All of the texts of Moir's poems are taken from *The Poetical Works*, 2 vols., edited by Thomas Aird, Edinburgh: Blackwood's, 1852.

I

Where Ocean's waves to the hollow caves murmur a low wild hymn,
    In pleasant musing I pursued my solitary way;
Then upwards wending from the shore, amid the woodlands dim,
    From the gentle height, like a map in sight, the downward country lay.

II

'Twas in the smile of "green Aprile,"[1] a cloudless noontide clear;   5
    In ecstasy the birds sang forth from many a leafing tree;
Both bud and bloom, with fresh perfume, proclaim'd the awaken'd year;
    And Earth, array'd in beauty's robes, seem'd Heaven itself to be.

III

So cheerfully the sun shone out, so smilingly the sky
    O'erarch'd green earth, so pleasantly the stream meander'd on,   10
So joyous was the murmur of the honey-bee and fly,
    That of our fall, which ruin'd all, seem'd traces few or none.

IV

Then hopes, whose gilded pageantry wore all the hues of truth—
    Elysian thoughts—Arcadian dreams—the poet's fabling strain—

---

1 "Grene Aprile," the favourite appellation of the month by Chaucer, Spenser, Browne, and the older poets. A prose character, equally impregnated with emerald, is given to its personification, in a curious duodecimo of 1681, entitled "The Queen-like Closet or Rich Cabinet," quoted in Hone's "Every-Day Book," (vol. ii. 517,) by Charles Lamb, in which the fair author, Anne Wooley, thus describes him:—"Aprile—A young man in green, with a garland of myrtle, and hawthorn buds; Winged; in one hand Primroses and Violets, in the other the sign Taurus." [Moir's note.]

Again seem'd shedding o'er our world an amaranthine¹ youth,   15
    And left no vestiges behind of death, decay, or pain.

V

At length I reach'd a churchyard gate—a churchyard? Yes! but there
    Breathed out such calm serenity o'er every thing around,
That "the joy of grief" (as Ossian sings) o'erbalm'd the very air,
    And the place was less a mournful place than consecrated ground. 20

VI

Beneath the joyous noontide sun, beneath the cloudless sky,
    'Mid bees that humm'd, and birds that sang, and flowers that gemm'd
        the wild,
The sound of measured steps was heard—a grave stood yawning by—
    And lo! in sad procession slow, the funeral of a child!

VII

I saw the little coffin borne unto its final rest;   25
    The dark mould shovell'd o'er it, and replaced the daisied sod;
I mark'd the deep convulsive throes that heaved the father's breast,
    As he return'd (too briefly given!) that loan of love to God!

VIII

Then rose in my rebellious heart unhallow'd thoughts and wild,
    Daring the inscrutable decrees of Providence to scan —   30
How death should be allotted to a pure, a sinless child,
    And length of days the destiny of sinful, guilty man!

IX

The laws of the material world seem'd beautiful and clear;
    The day and night, the bloom and blight, and seasons as they roll
In regular vicissitude to form a circling year,   35
    Made up of parts dissimilar, and yet a perfect whole.

---

1 Everlasting, immortal.

X

But darkness lay o'er the moral way which man is told to tread;
   A shadow veil'd the beam divine by Revelation lent:
"How awfully mysterious are thy ways, O Heaven!" I said;
    "We see not whence, nor know for what fate's arrows oft are sent!   *40*

XI

Under the shroud of the sullen cloud, when the hills are capp'd with snow,
   When the moaning breeze, through leafless trees, bears tempest on
     its wing —
In the Winter's wrath, we think of death; but not when lilies blow,
   And, Lazarus-like, from March's tomb walks forth triumphant Spring.

XII

As in distress o'er this wilderness I mused of stir and strife,   *45*
   Where, 'mid the dark, seem'd scarce a mark our tangled path to scan,
A shadow o'er the season fell; a cloud o'er human life —
   A veil to be by Eternity but ne'er by time withdrawn!

David Macbeth Moir, "The Graves of the Dead. A Dirge"

> A pickaxe, and a spade, a spade,
>   But and a shrouding sheet;
> O, a pit of clay for to be made
>   For such a guest is meet!
>   Lord de Vaux[1]

I

Oh, when should we visit the graves of the dead,
To hallow the memory of days that are fled?

At Morning,—when the dewdrops glisten
  On the bladed grass and the whispering leaves,

---

1 Moir is quoting Thomas, Lord Vaux (1509 -1556), from whose poem "The Aged Lover Renounceth Love" the epigraph is taken. Several stanzas from this poem are sung by the gravediggers in *Hamlet* (V.i).

When the heart-struck silence delights to listen   5
    As the solitary blackbird grieves;
Then the glorious orient sun, adorning
    The landscape, asks us, where are they,
Who, like larks, with us in life's sweet morning,
    Carelessly sung all blithe and gay?   10
We listen in vain for their gentle voices,
    We look in vain for their pleasant smiles;
Yet Nature still in her youth rejoices,
    And almost the bosom to joy beguiles.
We find them not within the wildwood,   15
    Up in the mountain, down in the plain,
As erst of yore, when the skies of childhood
    Gleam'd bluely o'er us without a stain.
              Alas! and alas!
              Green grows the grass—   20
    Like the waves we come, like the winds we pass!

II
Oh, when should we visit the graves of the dead,
To hallow the memory of days that are fled?

At Noontide,—when the wide world round us
    Busily hums with tumultuous strife,   25
And Fate with her viewless chain hath bound us
    Within the enchanted ring of life;
'Tis then that the startled soul, recoiling,
    Turns, sickening turns, from the noisy crowd,
And feels how empty is all our toiling,   30
    When the certain finish is in the shroud.
Lone, lone—by the living all forsaken—
    Bud the wild-flowers, and bloom around;
The fierce-eyed sunbeams no more awaken
    From that dreamless slumber, sad and sound;   35
Then in the green fields flocks are bleating,
    And neighs the proud steed beneath his palm,
To whose covert boughs the birds retreating,

In coolness chant their choral psalm.
  But alas! and alas!   *40*
  Green grows the grass—
Like the waves we come, like the winds we pass!

III

Oh, when should we visit the graves of the dead,
To hallow the memory of days that are fled?

At Evening,—when the flowery meadows   *45*
 With the haze of twilight begin to fill,
And darkly afar the eastward shadows
 Stretch from the peaks of the sunless hill;
When the laggard oxen from fields of clover
 Low mournfully as on they roam;   *50*
And, with sooty wing, sails slowly over
 The night-o'ertaken crow to its home:
Oh, then the forms of the dear departed
 Float, spectre-like, in Fancy's eye—
They come—the pale—the broken-hearted— *55*
 They come—the mirthful—flitting by;
We scan their features, we list[1] their voices,
 The sights, the sounds of remembered years—
This in its buoyant tone rejoices,
 That softly thrills on the brink of tears.   *60*
  Oh, alas! and alas!
  Green grows the grass—
Like the waves we come, like the winds we pass!

IV

Oh, when should we visit the graves of the dead,
To hallow the memory of days that are fled?   *65*

At Midnight,—when the skies are clouded,
 The stars seal'd up, and the winds abroad;

---

1 Listen to.

When earth in a dreary pall is shrouded,
  And sere leaves strew the uncertain road;
When desolate tones are around us moaning,   *70*
  O'er gravestone grey, and through ruined aisle;
When startled ravens croak, and the groaning
  Tempest uptosses forests the while—
Then let us pause by ourselves, and listen
  To nature's dirge over human life;   *75*
And the heart will throb, the eye will glisten,
  When Memory glances to prospects rife
With pleasures, which Time's rude whirlwind banish'd,
  With meteor visions that flamed and fled,
With friends that smiled, and smiling vanish'd   *80*
  To make their lone homes with the dead.
         For alas! and alas!
         Green grows the grass—
Like the waves we come, like the winds we pass.

V

Oh, when should we visit the graves of the dead,   *85*
To hallow the memory of days that are fled?

In Grief,—for then reflection gleaneth
  A lesson deep from unstable fate;
And Wisdom's small voice the spirit weaneth
  From earth's forlorn and low estate:—   *90*
In Mirth,—because 'tis mockery surely
  Of what we feel, and perceive around;
And the chasten'd bosom beats more purely,
  When press our footsteps on hallowed ground:—
At all times,—for 'tis wisely loosing   *95*
  The soul from ties that bind it down;
And a godlike strength is gained from musing
  On the fate which soon must prove our own:
For here Sorrow's reign is short, if bitter;
  And Pleasure's sunshine, though bright, is brief;   *100*
And pass our days o'er in gloom or glitter,

Death comes at length, like a silent thief!
　　　　Then alas, and alas!
　　　　Like the dews from grass—
Like the clouds from heaven, away we pass!　　　　　　*105*

David Macbeth Moir, "The Unknown Grave"

In this poem is evident Moir's debt to more conventional Grave-
yard School verse, particularly Thomas Gray's "Elegy Written in
a Country Churchyard." Moir's contemplation of an anonymous
grave leads him to a survey of human possibilities that touches
on issues of class, glory, social status, and moral accomplishment,
ending with a gesture of Christian piety and faith.

———

　　Man comes into the world like morning mushrooms, soon thrusting
up their heads into the air, and conversing with their kindred of the same
production, and as soon they turn into dust and forgetfulness.
　　　　　　　　　　　　　　　　　　　　Jeremy Taylor.[1]

I

Who sleeps below? who sleeps below?—
　　It is a question idle all!
Ask of the breezes as they blow,
　　Say, do they heed, or hear thy call?
They murmur in the trees around,　　　　　　*5*
And mock thy voice, an empty sound!

II

A hundred summer suns have shower'd
　　Their fostering warmth, and radiance bright;
A hundred winter storms have lower'd
　　With piercing floods, and hues of night,　　　　*10*

———

1 Slightly adapted from Jeremy Taylor's *Holy Living and Dying: With Prayers Con-
taining the Whole Duty of a Christian* (1650-1651). Taylor was an Anglican divine
and author who was imprisoned, as a Royalist sympathizer, during the Protector-
ate of Oliver Cromwell.

Since first this remnant of his race
Did tenant his lone dwelling-place.

III

Say, did he come from East, from West?
    From Southern climes, or where the Pole,
With frosty sceptre, doth arrest   15
    The howling billows as they roll?
Within what realm of peace or strife
Did he first draw the breath of life?

IV

Was he of high or low degree?
    Did grandeur smile upon his lot?   20
Or, born to dark obscurity,
    Dwelt he within some lowly cot,
And, from his youth to labour wed,
From toil-strung limbs wrung daily bread?

V

Say, died he ripe, and full of years,   25
    Bow'd down, and bent by hoary eld,[1]
When sound was silence to his ears,
    And the dim eyeball sight withheld;
Like a ripe apple falling down,
Unshaken, 'mid the orchard brown;   30

VI

When all the friends that bless'd his prime,
    Were vanish'd like a morning dream;
Pluck'd one by one by spareless Time,
    And scatter'd in oblivion's stream;
Passing away all silently,   35
Like snow-flakes melting in the sea:

---

1 Age.

VII

Or, 'mid the summer of his years,
  When round him throng'd his children young,
When bright eyes gush'd with burning tears,
  And anguish dwelt on every tongue,   40
Was he cut off, and left behind
A widow'd wife, scarce half resign'd?

VIII

Or, 'mid the sunshine of his spring,
  Came the swift bolt that dash'd him down;
When she, his chosen, blossoming   45
  In beauty, deem'd him all her own,
And forward look'd to happier years
Than ever bless'd this vale of tears?

IX

By day, by night, through calm and storm,
  O'er distant oceans did he roam,   50
Far from his land, a lonely form,
  The deck his walk, the sea his home:
Toss'd he on wild Biscayan[1] wave,
Or where smooth tides Panama lave?

X

Slept he within the tented field,   55
  With pillowing daisies for his bed?
Captived in battle, did he yield?
  Or plunge to victory o'er the dead?
Oft, 'mid destruction, hath he broke
Through reeking blades and rolling smoke?   60

---

1 The Bay of Biscay is a gulf of the Atlantic Ocean north of Spain and west of France.

XI

Perhaps he perish'd for the faith—
  One of that persecuted band,
Who suffer'd tortures, bonds, and death,
  To free from mental thrall the land,
And, toiling for the martyr's fame,   65
Espoused his fate, nor found a name!

XII

Say, was he one to science blind,
  A groper in Earth's dungeon dark?
Or one who with aspiring mind
  Did, in the fair creation, mark   70
The Maker's hand, and kept his soul
Free from this grovelling world's control?

XIII

Hush! wild surmise!—'tis vain—'tis vain—
  The summer flowers in beauty blow,
And sighs the wind, and floods the rain,   75
  O'er some old bones that rot below;
No other record can we trace
Of fame or fortune, rank or race!

XIV

Then, what is life, when thus we see
  No trace remains of life's career?—   80
Mortal! whoe'er thou art, for thee
  A moral lesson gloweth here;
Putt'st thou in aught of earth thy trust?
'Tis doom'd that dust shall mix with dust.

XV

What doth it matter, then, if thus,   85
  Without a stone, without a name,

To impotently herald us,
   We float not on the breath of fame;
But, like the dewdrop from the flower.
Pass, after glittering for an hour?   90

XVI

The soul decays not, freed from earth,
   And earthly coils, it bursts away;—
Receiving a celestial birth,
   And spurning off its bonds of clay,
It soars, and seeks another sphere,   95
And blooms through Heaven's eternal year!

XVII

Do good; shun evil; live not thou,
   As if at death thy being died;
Nor Error's syren voice allow
   To draw thy steps from truth aside;   100
Look to thy journey's end—the grave!
And trust in Him whose arm can save.

David Macbeth Moir, "The Dream"

This poem, which evokes—indeed, almost revels in—some of the grisly graphic horror of Gothicism, was published in the *Edinburgh Magazine and Literary Miscellany* in January 1825.

Methought I died, and to the silent grave
My friends did bear me. Still and motionless
I lay, yet not without the power to have
Full knowledge of my utter helplessness,
In that my dreadful grim hour of distress;   5
My thought remain'd, and feeling, actively
As they were wont, nor was sensation less
Active; but my pulse was not, and mine eye
Seem'd death-like fix'd, and glaz'd, to those standing by.

They wrapt me in my white funereal shroud,   10
And clos'd my useless eyes, then gently drew
The death-robes o'er them, like a fleecy cloud;
My mother kiss'd me, and my sisters too,
Then my thoughts like the wind-swept ocean grew,
And horror was my own: a fire flash'd red,   15
And gleam'd, as through my scorched brain it flew,
And wildly o'er mine eyes its lightning sped,
When my dream changed, and darkness came instead.

I heard them talk, and heard my mother's wail,
I heard the sobbings of my father's breast,   20
And struggled—but in vain; and nail by nail
Was driven; then my tortur'd head was prest,
As with a crushing weight, which straightway pass'd,
And then I felt them carry me away
From all my kindred, weeping and distrest.   25
Oh how I inward shudder'd at decay,
And pray'd in anguish for the blessed light of day!

I heard the measured march, and sullen tread,
And, now and then, a murmur pass along,
Hollow and deep, as best befits the dead   30
To be spoke of, although men say no wrong:
They went the graves and sepulchres among,
And all, in still and solemn silence, stood
To let the coffin down; and earth they flung
Upon me, and I heard them beat the sod—   35
I rav'd, and in my madness did blaspheme my God!

But that too pass'd away, and I could think,
And feel, and know my dismal, helpless state;
My body knew corruption; I did shrink
To feel the icy worm—my only mate,   40
For thousands crawl'd upon me, all elate
At their new prey, and o'er my rotting face
They blindly crept and revell'd, after that

They did their noisome, vile, dark passage trace,
To make my burning brain their loathsome resting-place.   *45*

Then, eager to renew their feast, would press
My skull and eyeless sockets, passing through,
And intertwining, till they grew a mass
Within my mouth, when my soul froze anew,
And shudder'd,—'twas in vain: alas! I knew   *50*
I was a victim to corruption's power.
My horrid dream was o'er—but the cold dew
Was on my forehead, like the glistering show'r
That falls from church-yard cypress at the midnight hour.

Caroline Bowles Southey, "Chapters on Churchyards: 1"

Southey (1786-1854) was an English poet and writer—and a fairly accomplished painter who, as a child, received instruction from her local vicar, who just happened to be William Gilpin. Her early mentor and supporter Robert Southey, the noted poet, became her husband shortly after the death of his first wife (Bowles was by this time 52; he was 65, and would soon become seriously troubled by senile dementia). Much of her work was, despite her political conservatism, progressive for its time, often lamenting the restricted opportunities available to women and siding with oppressed factory workers.

"Chapters on Churchyards" was a series of essays, first published serially in *Blackwood's* from April 1824 to May 1829, then published in book form (two volumes) in 1829. The book was reissued (in one volume) in 1841 in an attempt to capitalize upon Caroline Bowles's recent marriage to Robert Southey, by then the Poet Laureate. The work was, according to one recent scholar, "very popular,"[1] and in an age when Young's *Night Thoughts* and Hervey's *Meditations Among the Tombs* still enjoyed some currency, it is not difficult to see why. The "chapters" are, typically, loco-descriptive moralistic

---

1 Virginia Bain, *Caroline Bowles Southey, 1786-1854: The Making of a Woman Writer* (Aldershot, England: Ashgate, 1998), 120.

essays that move from a consideration of a church or churchyard to some moralized tale or reflection, although some of the "chapters on churchyards" in fact have nothing to do with churchyards whatsoever. Most of the chapters (fifteen of the twenty-six) essentially constitute one short tale ("Broad Summerford") and two novellas ("Andrew Cleaves" plus the introductory "The Haunted Churchyard"—which is haunted only by a dead man's horse—and "The Grave of the Broken Heart"), the main concern of these works also being the depiction of moral rectitude and moral failure. In that, they constitute a largely secularized continuation of standard Graveyard School practice.

The chapter below is the first of the "Chapters on Churchyards," published April 1824; the text is taken from the first book publication, *Chapters on Churchyards*, 2 vols. (Edinburgh: William Blackwood, 1829) 1-11.

―――――――

Many are the idle tourists who have babbled of country churchyards—many are the able pens which have been employed on the same subjects. One in particular, in the delightful olio[1] of the "Sketch-book,"[2] has traced a picture so true to nature, so beautifully simple and pathetic, that succeeding essayists might well despair of success in attempting similar descriptions, were not the theme, in fact, inexhaustible, a source of endless variety, a volume of instructive records, whereof those marked with least incident are yet replete with interest for that human being who stands alone amongst the quiet graves, musing on the mystery of his own existence, and on the past and present state of those poor relics of mortality which everywhere surround him, mouldering beneath his feet—mingling with the common soil—feeding the rank churchyard vegetation—once sentient like himself with vigorous life, subject to all the tumultuous passions that agitate his own heart, pregnant with a thousand busy schemes, elevated and depressed by alternate hopes and fears—liable, in a word, to all the

―――――――

1 Any volume containing a mixture of diverse literary pieces.

2 Southey refers to "The Widow and Her Son," a chapter in Washington Irving's *The Sketch-Book of Geoffrey Crayon* (1819-20). This chapter, included above, is a moving description of a pauper's funeral and a telling of the grieving mother's tale.

pains, the pleasures, and "the ills, that flesh is heir to."[1]

The leisurely traveller arriving at a country inn, with the intention of tarrying a day, an hour, or a yet shorter period, in the town or village, generally finds time to saunter towards the church, and even to loiter about its surrounding graves, as if his nature (solitary in the midst of the living crowd) claimed affinity, and sought communion, with the populous dust beneath his feet.

Such, at least, are the feelings with which I have often lingered in the churchyard of a strange place, and about the church itself—to which, indeed, in all places, and in all countries, the heart of the Christian pilgrim feels itself attracted as towards his very home, for there at least, though alone amongst a strange people, he is no stranger: It is his Father's house.

I am not sure that I heartily approve the custom—rare in this country, but frequent in many others—of planting flowers and flowering shrubs about the graves.[2] I am *quite* sure that I hate all the sentimental mummery with which the far-famed burying-place of Pere La Chaise is garnished out.[3] It is faithfully in keeping with Parisian taste, and perfectly in unison with French feeling; but I should wonder at the profound sympathy with which numbers of my own countrymen expatiate on that pleasure-ground of Death, if it were still possible to feel surprise at any instance of degenerate taste and perverted feeling in our travelled islanders—if it were not, too, the vulgarest thing in the world to wonder at anything. The custom, so general in Switzerland, and so common in our own principality of Wales, of strewing flowers over the graves of departed friends, either on the anniversaries of their deaths, or on other memorable days, is touching and beautiful. Those frail blossoms scattered over

---

1 From *Hamlet*'s "'To be or not to be" soliloquy: "To die: to sleep; / No more; and by a sleep to say we end / The heart-ache and the thousand natural shocks / That flesh is heir to, 'tis a consummation / Devoutly to be wish'd" (III.i).

2 See William Mason's "Elegy VI: Written in a Church-yard in South Wales, 1787," in the present volume, for a sympathetic treatment of this practice.

3 Père Lachaise, the largest cemetery in the city of Paris, was established in 1804 and became extremely popular by 1820, in part because of high-profile burials (and reburials) orchestrated by the French government. It is this high profile, and the fact Père Lachaise became the final resting place of many French notables, often buried with elaborate ceremony and with grand monuments, to which Southey is here referring disdainfully.

the green sod, in their morning freshness, but for a little space retain their balmy odours, and their glowing tints, till the sun goes down, and the breeze of evening sighs over them, and the dews of night fall on their pale beauty, and the withered and fading wreath becomes a yet more appropriate tribute to the silent dust beneath. But rose-trees in full bloom, and tall staring lilies, and flaunting lilacs, and pert priggish spirafrutexes,[1] are, methinks, ill in harmony with that holiness of perfect repose which should pervade the last resting-place of mortality. Even in our own unsentimental England, I have seen two or three of these flower-plot graves. One, in particular, I remember, had been planned and planted by a young disconsolate widow, to the memory of her deceased partner. The tomb itself was a common square erection of freestone,[2] covered over with a slab of black marble, on which, under the name, age, &c. of the defunct, was engraven an elaborate epitaph, commemorating his many virtues, and pathetically intimating, that, at no distant period, the vacant space remaining on the same marble would receive the name of "his inconsolable Eugenia."[3] The tomb was hedged about by a basket-work of honeysuckles. A Persian lilac drooped over its foot, and, at the head, (substituted for the elegant cypress, coy denizen of our ungenial clime,) a young poplar perked up its pyramidical form. Divers other shrubs and flowering plants completed the ring-fence, plentifully interspersed with "the fragrant weed, the Frenchman's darling,"[4] whose perfume, when I visited the spot, was wafted over the whole churchyard. It was then the full flush of summer. The garden had been planted but a month; but the lady had tended, and propped, and watered those gay strangers with her own delicate hands, evermore in the dusk of evening returning to her tender task, so that they had taken their removal kindly, and grew and flourished as carelessly round that cold marble, and in

---

1 Members of the *Spirea* family of flowering shrubs (most likely S. tomentosa and S. crenata), known for their spiky flower clusters.

2 "Any fine-grained sandstone or limestone that can be cut or sawn easily" (*OED*).

3 Eugenia is a generic Greek name, Southey's imitation of 18th-century poetic practice.

4 The phrase is from William Cowper's *The Task*, "Book IV: The Winter's Evening" (764-765). It refers to mignonette, a genus of flowering plants noted for their fragrance.

that field of graves, as they had done heretofore in their own shel-
tered nursery.

A year afterwards—a year almost to a day—I stood once more
on that same spot, in the same month—"the leafy month of June."[1]
But—it was leafless there. The young poplar still stood sentinel in
its former station, but dry, withered, and sticky, like an old broom
at the mast-head of a vessel on sale. The parson's cow, and his
half-score fatting wethers,[2] had violated the sacred enclosure, and
trodden down its flowery basket-work into the very soil. The plants
and shrubs were nibbled down to miserable stumps, and from the
sole survivor, the poor straggling lilac, a fat old waddling ewe had
just cropped the last sickly flower-branch, and stood staring at me
with a pathetic vacancy of countenance, the half-munched conse-
crated blossom dangling from her sacrilegious jaws. "And is it even
so?" I half-articulated, with a sudden thrill of irrepressible emo-
tion. "Poor widowed mourner! lovely Eugenia! Art thou already
re-united to the object of thy faithful affection? And so lately! Not
yet on that awaiting space on the cold marble have they inscribed
thy gentle name. And those fragile memorials! were there none to
tend them for thy sake?" Such was my sentimental apostrophe and
the unwonted impulse so far incited me, that I actually pelted away
the sheep from that last resting-place of faithful love, and reared
against its side the trailing branches of the neglected lilac. Well
satisfied with myself for the performance this pious act, I turned
from the spot in a mood of calm, pleasing melancholy, that, by
degrees, (while I yet lingered about the churchyard,) resolved itself
into a train of poetic reverie, and I was already advanced in a sort
of elegiac tribute to the memory of that fair being, whose tender
nature had sunk under the stroke "that reft her mutual heart,"[3]
when the horrid interruption of a loud shrill whistle startled me
from my poetic vision, cruelly disarranging the beautiful com-
bination of high-wrought, tender, pathetic feelings, which were
flowing naturally into verse, as from the very fount of Helicon.[4]

---

1 From Coleridge's "The Rime of the Ancient Mariner" (370).
2 A wether is a castrated ram.
3 An alteration of a phrase from Thomas Campbell's *Gertrude of Wyoming*:
"When fate had reft his mutual heart" (I:X,8).
4 Helicon was, in Greek myth, a mountain sacred to the Muses.

Lifting my eyes towards the vulgar cause of this vulgar distur-
bance, the cow-boy (for it was he, "who whistled as he went, for
want of thought")[1] nodded to me his rustic apology for a bow, and
passed on towards the very tomb I had just quitted, near which his
milky charge, the old brindled cow, still munched on, avaricious
of the last mouthful. If the clown's obstreperous mirth had before
broken in on my mood of inspiration, its last delicate glow was
utterly dispelled by the uncouth vociferation, and rude expletives,
with which he proceeded to dislodge the persevering animal from
her rich pasture-ground. Insensible alike to his remonstrances, his
threats, or his tender persuasion—to his "Whoy! whoy! old girl!
Whoy, Blossom! whoy, my lady!—I say, come up, do; come up ye
plaguey baste!" Blossom continued to munch and ruminate with
the most imperturbable calmness—backing and sideling away,
however, as her pursuer made nearer advances, and ever and anon
looking up at him with most provoking assurance, as if to calcu-
late how many tufts she might venture to pull before he got fairly
within reach of her. And so, retrograding and manoeuvring, she
at last intrenched herself behind the identical tombstone beside
which I had stood so lately in solemn contemplation. Here—the
cow-boy's patience being completely exhausted—with the inten-
tion of switching old Blossom from her last stronghold, he caught
up, and began tearing from the earth, that one long straggling stem
of lilac which I had endeavoured to replace in somewhat of its
former position. "Hold! hold!" I cried, springing forward with the
vehement gesture of impassioned feeling—"Have you no respect
for the ashes of the dead? Dare you thus violate with sacrilegious
hands the last sad sanctuary of faithful love?" The boy stood like
one petrified, stared at me for a moment, with a look of indescrib-
able perplexity, then screwing one corner of his mouth almost into
contact with the corresponding corner of one crinkled-up eye—at
the same time shoving up his old ragged hat, and scratching his
curly pate; and having, as I suppose, by the help of that operation,
construed my vehement address into the language of inquiry, he
set himself very methodically about satisfying my curiosity on
every point wherever he conceived it possible I might have inter-

---

1 From *Cymon and Iphigenia* (84) by John Dryden (1631-1700).

rogated him—taking his cue, with some ingenuity, from the one word of my oration, which was familiar to his ear—"Dead! Ees, Squoire been dead twelve months last Whitsuntide;[1] and thick be his'n moniment, an' madam was married last week to our measter, an' thick be our cow—"

Oh, Reader! Is it to be wondered at, that, since that adventure, I have ever been disposed to look with an unglistening, and even cynical eye, on those same flower-pot graves? Nay, that, at sight of them, I feel an extraordinary degree of hard-heartedness stealing over me? I cannot quit the subject without offering a word or two of well-meant advice to all disconsolate survivors—widows more especially—as to the expediency or non-expediency of indulging this flowery grief. Possibly, were I to obey the dictates of my own tastes and feelings, I should say, "Be content with a simple record—perhaps a scriptural sentence, on a plain headstone. Suffer not the inscription to become defaced and illegible, nor rank weeds to wave over it; and smooth be the turf of the green hillock." But if—to use a French phrase—*Il faut afficher ses regrets*[2]—if there *must* be *effect*, sentimentalities, prettinesses, urns, flowers—not only a few scattered blossoms, but a regular planted border, like the garnish of a plateau;—then, let me beseech you, fair inconsolables! be cautious in your proceedings—Temper with discreet foresight (if that be possible) the first agonizing burst of sensibility—Take the counsels of sage experience—Temporize with the as yet unascertained nature of your own feelings —Proclaim not those vegetable vows of eternal fidelity—Refrain, at least, from the trowel and the spade—Dig not—plant not—For one year only—for the *first* year, at least—For one year only, I beseech you—sow annuals.

---

1 The week following the seventh Sunday after Easter, a Christian tradition honoring the Holy Spirit's descent to the Apostles.
2 "If you must make a show of your grief," a French phrase that allows Southey to return to her disparagement of French funerary practice.

Caroline Bowles Southey, "The Churchyard"

This poem is constructed very much along the standard Grave-yard School pattern that was developed by Parnell, with an opening descent into gloom and melancholy that is redeemed by the soaring movement toward light and heaven of the closing stanzas. Although Virginia Blain has remarked that Southey's relationship to nature was more eighteenth century than Romantic,[1] this poem is strongly reminiscent of John Keats's "Ode to a Nightingale," with its use of a bird as a symbol of transcendent desire and its speaker being "half in love with easeful Death" (published 1819) and Percy Bysshe Shelley's "To A Skylark," with the bird as its "blithe Spirit" (published August 1820).

Text: The text for this poem is taken from *The Anniversary, or Poetry and Prose for 1829*, edited by Allan Cunningham (London: John Sharpe, 1829).

> The thought of early death was in my heart;
>   Of the dark grave, and "dumb forgetfulness;"[2]
>   And with a weight like lead,
>   And overwhelming dread,
>   Mysteriously my spirit did oppress.   5
>
> And forth I roamed in that distressful mood
>   Abroad into the sultry, sunless day;
>   All hung with one dark cloud,
>   That like a sable shroud
>   On Nature's deep sepulchral stillness lay.   10
>
> Black fell the shadows of the churchyard elms—
>   Unconsciously my feet had wandered there—
>   And through that awful gloom—
>   Head-stone and altar tomb
>   Among the green heaps gleamed with ghastlier glare.   15

---

1 *Caroline Bowles Southey, 1786-1854: The Making of a Woman Writer* (Aldershot, England: Ashgate, 1998), 131.

2 From Thomas Gray's "Elegy Written in a Country Churchyard," line 85.

Death—death was in my heart, as there I stood,
  Mine eyes fast fixed upon a grass-grown mound;
    As though they would descry
    The loathsome mystery
  Consummating beneath that charnel ground.   20

Death—death was in my heart. Methought I felt
  A heavy hand, that pressed me down below;
    And some resistless power
    Made me, in that dark hour,
  Half long to be, where I abhorred to go.   25

Then suddenly, albeit no breeze was felt,
  Through the tall tree-tops ran a shivering sound—
    Forth from the western heaven
    Flashed out the flaming levin,[1]
  And one long thunder-peal rolled echoing round.   30

One long, long echoing peal, and all was peace;
  Cool rain-drops gemmed the herbage—large and few;
    And that dull vault of lead,
    Disparting over head,
  Down beamed an eye of soft celestial blue.   35

And up toward the heavenly portal sprang
  A skylark, scattering off the feathery rain—
    Up from my very feet;—
    And oh! how clear and sweet
  Rang through the fields of air his mounting strain.   40

Blithe, blessed creature! take me there with thee—
  I cried in spirit—passionately cried—
    But higher still and higher
    Rang out that living Lyre,
  As if the Bird disdained me in his pride.   45

---

1 Lightning.

And I was left below, but now no more
  Plunged in the doleful realms of Death and Night—
    Up with the skylark's lay,
    My soul had winged her way
  To the supernal[1] source of Life and Light.   50

---

1 Belonging to a "higher" world.

CPSIA information can be obtained
at www.ICGtesting.com
Printed in the USA
BVOW08s0905220317
479152BV00001B/80/P